CONFLICT, COMMERCE AND FRANCO-SCOTTISH RELATIONS, 1560–1713

PERSPECTIVES IN ECONOMIC AND SOCIAL HISTORY

Series Editors: Andrew August
Jari Eloranta

TITLES IN THIS SERIES

CONFLICT, COMMERCE AND FRANCO-SCOTTISH RELATIONS, 1560–1713

BY

Siobhan Talbott

Routledge
Taylor & Francis Group

LONDON AND NEW YORK

First published 2014 by Pickering & Chatto (Publishers) Limited

Published 2016 by Routledge
2 Park Square, Milton Park, Abingdon, Oxfordshire OX14 4RN
711 Third Avenue, New York, NY 10017, USA

First issued in paperback 2015

Routledge is an imprint of the Taylor & Francis Group, an informa business

© Taylor & Francis 2014
© Siobhan Talbott 2014

To the best of the Publisher's knowledge every effort has been made to contact relevant copyright holders and to clear any relevant copyright issues.
Any omissions that come to their attention will be remedied in future editions.

Notice:
Product or corporate names may be trademarks or registered trademarks, and are used only for identification and explanation without intent to infringe.

BRITISH LIBRARY CATALOGUING IN PUBLICATION DATA

Talbott, Siobhan, author.
Conflict, commerce and Franco-Scottish relations, 1560–1713. – (Perspectives in economic and social history)
1. Scotland – Foreign relations – France. 2. France – Foreign relations – Scotland. 3. Scotland – Commerce – France – History – 17th century. 4. France – Commerce – Scotland – History – 17th century. 5. Great Britain – Foreign relations – 16th century. 6. Great Britain – Foreign relations – 1702–1714. 7. France – Foreign relations – 1589–1789.
I. Title II. Series
382'.09411044-dc23

ISBN-13: 978-1-138-66225-4 (pbk)
ISBN-13: 978-1-8489-3407-8 (hbk)

Typeset by Pickering & Chatto (Publishers) Limited

CONTENTS

ACKNOWLEDGEMENTS

Early modern merchants operated within communities and networks of people they relied upon and trusted, assisted by financial support and gracious letters of recommendation. The same might be said of historians in the twenty-first century. I owe a great debt to many people who have selflessly assisted me in various capacities over a number of years.

It is a lamentable fact that money remains the ultimate champion of scholarship, and inevitably this book would not exist without the generous financial support of a number of institutions. The Arts and Humanities Research Council, the Burnwynd Local History Foundation, the Russell Trust and the Faculty of Arts at the University of St Andrews funded the doctoral research on which much of this book is based, affording me the privilege of three years of uninterrupted study within an extremely supportive environment. I have since been fortunate enough to enjoy postdoctoral research fellowships funded by the Economic History Society at the Institute of Historical Research (University of London) and the Hallsworth Fund at the University of Manchester, providing me the time and security to revise my doctoral thesis as well as enabling me to undertake additional research that has improved the quality and expanded the reach of the final product.

As anyone who has undertaken prolonged periods of research can attest, it can be both daunting and lonely. I wholeheartedly thank the following people for providing accommodation, advice or fun-filled distractions: Lesley Graham (Bordeaux), Zoë Frayne, Graeme Kemp, Joanna Milstein, Marianne Stewart and Malcolm Walsby (Paris), Sophie Casays (Rouen), Kathrin Zickermann (Edinburgh), Henry and Adrienne Sullivan (Glasgow), Louise Taggart (London) and Allan Macinnes (Huntington Library, California). During these research trips I was fortunate to work within a range of archives, and I would like to thank all of the staff in these repositories who assisted me, both remotely and in person. Especial thanks are due to the staff at the National Archives of Scotland (now National Records of Scotland), the Archives départementales de la Gironde, the Archives municipales de Bordeaux, the Archives départementales de la

Charente-Maritime and the Archives départementales de la Loire-Atlantique, all of which were a pleasure to work in.

Many colleagues have contributed, in both large and small ways, to my academic career to date, and the following in particular deserve my thanks for various kindnesses. Steve Murdoch, my doctoral supervisor, was a paragon of patience during both my undergraduate and graduate studies, and has since been extremely generous in providing innumerable references. Keith Brown and Allan Macinnes have also provided too many references to count, as well as offering indispensable advice, both intellectual and practical. For additional scholarly and emotional sustenance, I thank Sheryllynne Haggerty, Alan MacDonald, Adam Marks, Roger Mason, Claire McLoughlin, Gordon Pentland, Guy Rowlands, Katie Stevenson, Daniel Szechi and Isla Woodman.

On a personal note, I count myself extremely fortunate to have the friendship and support of a range of people, particularly when a reminder is needed that there is more to life than early modern commerce. The excellent food, wine and chat provided by Eilidh, Anthony and Sophie Cumbor, Sarah and Ian Chesworth and Debbie and Jeremy Bristow have enlivened many a weekend, while holidays with the St Andrews shinty girls continue to be both relaxing and surprising. Kenneth and Jane Boyd were a constant source of comfort and cake while I was completing my PhD, and remain great friends despite my defection to England. I treasure the friendship of Louise Taggart, who has always been there (often with a G&T) through the good times and the bad.

Predictably, those we love the most tend to bear the brunt of emotions when research trips are unsuccessful, we suffer from writers' block, or 3a.m. seems a suitable time to debate our future career path. My parents, Lynda and Rob, have always provided unwavering support and belief in me. There are no words suitable to express sufficiently my gratitude to Mark, my fellow intrepid castler, for his everlasting love, support, encouragement and cooking. In reading and rereading countless drafts of this book, he has returned my favour with interest.

For Filbert and G
who helped and hindered the writing of this book in almost equal measure

LIST OF FIGURES AND TABLES

INTRODUCTION

In 1634 a Scot, John Clerk, travelled to France as the apprentice of an Edinburgh merchant named John Smith. In 1646 Clerk returned to Scotland where eight years later he purchased the barony of Penicuik with the fortune he had made on the Continent. Living in Paris, Clerk operated within a wide network of merchants, factors, manufacturers and skippers. Some of his business associates he knew personally, others he did not, and the people he dealt with hailed from throughout Britain and Europe. This network traded in a wide variety of goods: bulk commodities including salt and wine but also diamonds, luxury cloths and furs, brushes made of agate and tortoiseshell, atlases and book-bindings.[1] John Clerk is just one of a host of individuals who pursued Franco-Scottish commerce in this period, but his activities remain relatively unknown despite the high-profile descendants who benefited from his success.[2] Throughout the early modern period mercantile networks and communities such as those in which Clerk operated were at the forefront of international exchanges, functioning for their own financial gain but simultaneously influencing commercial and economic development throughout Europe.

The success of these communities is more striking when the environment within which they were active is considered. The long seventeenth century was riven by conflict, creating a context ostensibly hostile to trade. The numerous wars that erupted have contributed to descriptions of the period by generations of historians as one of 'general crisis'.[3] In a century dominated by developments in military technology, tactics and organization under a 'military revolution',[4] warfare has remained the focus of many studies of this period. Indeed, both France and Scotland, along with many of their European counterparts, had to contend with both internal and external conflict during the long seventeenth century. Domestically the Wars of Religion and the Fronde disrupted France while the British Civil Wars and Interregnum had serious implications for Scottish trade, politics and society. Internationally, the Franco-Stuart Wars of 1627–9 and 1666–7, the Nine Years' War (1688–97) and the War of the Spanish Succession (1702–13) governed European concerns for large parts of this period, pitting France and Britain directly against each other. Each of these conflicts generated legislation and policies that would seem to have damaged international commerce and domestic economic development. Declarations of war, higher taxes, increased customs duties, and prohibitions and restrictions on trade have been taken as indicative of deteriorating commercial links between the two nations. War against France as part of the Nine Years' War, for example, allegedly fostered a period when Scotland's continental trade was 'declining or stagnant'.[5] The claim that war necessarily hindered commerce continues to be repeated, with the accepted notion remaining that 'war disrupted trade and communications' in whatever context it raged.[6]

These two notions – of successful commercial activity and a context hostile to international exchange – seem at odds with one another. Conversely, this volume demonstrates that successful commercial activity was neither confined to periods of peace nor dictated by national, governmental, political or diplomatic concerns. Though the school of thought supporting the notion of a 'general crisis' does not agree on its primary causes or catalysts, most do agree that the crisis was all-encompassing – 'a crisis which was not only political or economic but social and intellectual, and which was not confined to one country but felt throughout Europe'.[7] Even scholarship recognizing that the pattern of crisis was 'different in each society: the relationship between state and society varied' nevertheless supports the notion that disorder was present in 'the whole of Europe'.[8] As this volume will demonstrate, however, the repercussions of the upheaval of this period were not felt across all sectors. Further, a modern understanding of warfare has contributed to anachronistic assumptions regarding the nature of, and therefore the impact of, historical conflict. As emphasized by Peter Wilson, 'historians have defined total war by looking back from twentieth-century experience', but in the early modern period war was not 'total'; it did not 'entail the complete mobilization of a belligerent's society and economy'.[9] Early modern nations did not seek to cripple established international trade links; national economies were interdependent and whatever was occurring politically, nations needed economic relationships to survive. Instead of warfare bringing a total halt to any form of economic exchange (no matter the wording of official sanctions), alterations in the political context caused gradual adjustments rather than immediate and dramatic change.[10] In addition, though the progress of mercantilism and the rise of protectionist policies did have an impact on international trade, it is contended here that domestic concerns were foremost in shaping economic policy and commercial activity; such policies were not 'first and foremost a weapon in the struggle against the foreigner, a tool of war'.[11] The almost continuous warfare of the period, coupled with shifts in approaches to economic policy, has contributed to the idea of a 'general crisis', but in fact ubiquitous conflict meant that all those involved in commercial exchanges were prepared for it. Commercial agents were used to conflict, and when economic sanctions were imposed 'elaborate and effective evasion schemes kicked into place almost naturally'.[12]

As well as reconsidering the impact of conflict on Franco-Scottish commerce in a broad sense, this volume gives greater attention to the individuals who implemented these evasion schemes and thus underpinned European trade. Close analysis of their activities provides a picture that differs from general interpretations of the early modern European framework. Though the conflicts listed above did, of course, affect the conduct of trade, networks such as the one within which John Clerk operated continued to facilitate commerce along routes that were officially closed due to war or economic policy. By placing these mercantile networks at the core of a deeper exploration of commerce, a century emerges that was not hostile to but in many ways conducive to trade. Commercial networks continued to operate with the same people and in the same areas as they did in times of peace, making huge contributions to the flourishing of trade and skillfully circumventing obstacles present during times of conflict.

This is not, crucially, to categorize all trade that continued under prohibition as 'smuggling'. As will be seen, there were merchants who employed evasive methods and participated in illegal trade, but many others applied for and were granted permission to continue their business, raising questions about the extent to which prohibitive legislation was enforced. Merchant groups and individuals influenced governmental strategy during some of the most inclement moments of the long seventeenth century, proving that they were not passive receptors of policy but played a significant role in the shaping of international commercial relations. As Junko Takeda notes of commercial development in Marseille in this period, 'commercial aggrandizement did not involve the mere imposition of policies unilaterally decided on by the Crown ... individuals involved in commerce and debates about market society altered social relationships and triggered political developments in ways that often interrupted the Crown's authority'.[13] Indeed, as Ball pointed out many years ago, 'if commerce had to accommodate itself to war, it is equally true that in certain circumstances war had to accommodate itself to commerce'.[14]

I.

In order to establish the role of mercantile agents involved in trade, and to assess the impact of their actions, a specific methodology has been adopted. The realization that communities and informal networks were essential to the maintenance and development of trade has precipitated a shift in the way in which commercial histories have been written in recent years.[15] Several scholars working on a range of periods and locations have adopted micro-level methodologies alongside the traditional macro-economic approach, prioritizing the communities and individuals that effected trade at ground level. Their research has yielded important new perspectives on international commerce in several spheres, most notably enhancing our understanding of the trade links between Nantes and Rotterdam in the seventeenth century, between Liverpool and Philadelphia in the years either side of the Revolutionary War in North America, and within the Spanish Atlantic world throughout the eighteenth century.[16] Application of social methodologies to traditionally economic topics has enhanced, and in places fundamentally altered, our understanding of key historical trading relationships. By applying these methodologies to the Franco-Scottish association, this volume demonstrates that at times when the political context suggests that certain routes stagnated, commercial agents were in fact able to adapt their trading methods to allow them to continue to flourish.

Traditionally, commercial histories have consisted of two core elements. The first has placed bi-lateral exchanges within broad political contexts, viewing commercial relationships through the lenses of official legislation and the actions of governments. In considering the impact of conflict on commerce, this includes focus on declarations of war and commercial embargoes. The second invokes focus on quantitative analyses of sources produced by official agencies and institutions, including port books and customs records, often with the primary goal of assessing the extent of overseas commerce through calculating volumes of trade or quantifying economic status.[17] While providing an overview of commercial exchange, both of these elements have given rise to misinterpretations of international trade. The first set of problems lies in interpreting government legislation and policy. Prohibitions on commerce implemented during periods of conflict have been taken as indicative of a desire to damage fundamentally an enemy's trade, not to mention the assumption that such legislation was successful whenever it was implemented. As Chapter 3 discusses at length, neither of these conclusions are accurate. Motivations for implementing economic legislation were complex and destroying trade with a political enemy was counter-productive – as indicated above early modern economies were fundamentally linked, and whatever the state of political relationships commercial ties were necessary for continued economic health. Further, that legislation was formally enacted does not necessarily mean that it was upheld to its full extent, or that the promise of damage to trade was realized. Certainly in the conflicts examined here, such assumptions do not hold true.

The second set of problems with this conventional approach lies in the statistical source material employed to gauge where trade routes were situated, what the volume of goods exchanged along them was, and which commodities comprised these exchanges. In her reassessment of the wine and brandy trade between France and the Dutch Republic in the first half of the seventeenth century, Henriette de Bruyn Kops notes that 'the scarcity of reliable statistics on wine and brandy imports into the Dutch Republic and the exports from France make the macro-economic implications of the trade the most difficult ones to assess'.[18] The same might be said of the Franco-Scottish relationship. Quantifiable records survive, many of which have informed areas of the present study, but reliance on these records alone does not allow for a comprehensive picture of any trading relationship to be formed. Statistical sources are rarely complete, and when a run of material does exist entries are not uniform, with the information given differing from year to year, month to month, or even entry to entry. Though some broad trends are identifiable, accurate calculations are virtually impossible. As will be seen in the Franco-Scottish context, conclusions drawn from statistical analyses are frequently contradicted by those drawn from qualitative material.

Problems with data reconstruction aside, official records exclude many incidences of exchange that were vital to commercial relationships, as well as providing skewed interpretations of the strength of particular trade routes. Using records that identify the presence of ships and commodities only at the point of entry or departure is problematic, as it encourages a linear approach to economic exchange. Goods that were later re-shipped, sold on by those who imported them or carried over land to alternative destinations cannot always be identified.[19] A customs book of Aberdeen dated from 15 April to 31 May 1614 includes quantities of imports of French and Italian silks, taffeta, grograne, napkening, cambrics, tapestries, velvets and satins, among many other goods.[20] As Louise Taylor argues, Aberdeen could not have provided a market for all of these items. Some must have been redistributed, either domestically or internationally, but this information is not included in these accounts.[21] Likewise, if goods en route to France were shipped through the Scottish trading staple in the Netherlands and then transported by Scots to a Scottish community in Dieppe these figures would appear in official port records as trade between Scotland and the Netherlands, rather than between Scotland and France.[22] Merchants did not operate solely along linear lines, or between only two nations. The Watson family of Kirkcaldy, for example, fostered trade relations with a range of European ports simultaneously, on one round trip in 1668 calling at Bordeaux, Rotterdam, London and an unspecified port in Norway.[23]

Much of the activity that contributed to the development of international commerce was conducted beyond the gaze of port officials, making calculating volumes of trade or identifying the goods that were traded problematic. Official records encourage an emphasis on commodities that were exchanged in bulk, but many smaller, valuable items were sent via alternative routes, for example with business associates or with friends or family as explored in Chapter 2. These exchanges were not covert, but were recorded only in the private records of the individuals involved. The range of commodities exchanged within John Clerk's network included items that originated elsewhere in the world, such as those made of jade, ivory, agate and tortoiseshell. Thus the activities of networks involved in Franco-Scottish trade take on a global dimension, demonstrating the necessity of appreciating a range of influences and participants.[24] Most pertinently for the issues discussed in this volume, brought to the fore in Chapter 7, a bi-lateral approach based on national trends does not allow for local or regional comparisons that dramatically alter our perception of international commercial activity. Patterns of trade differed markedly between different ports, in many cases – certainly those examined here – directed not by decentralized government but dictated by the social contexts within which merchant networks operated.

The approach advocated here prioritizes private records, including merchants' correspondence, account books and letter-books, in order to identify elements of exchange that are missing from official records. Where possible, direct comparison is provided between conclusions drawn from this qualitative material and those suggested by a combination of government and quantitative sources. A qualitative source base, of course, has its own problems, and criticizing quantitative material for being incomplete is somewhat hypocritical. While a lone account indicates the presence of the Scottish merchant Samuel Hamilton in Rouen, for example, without further information it is impossible to know whether his purchase of glass in 1675 is indicative of wider trends, or whether the incident is significant to broader assessments of Franco-Scottish commerce.[25] Surviving correspondence, whether letters received or records of letters sent, is often one-sided; only on very rare occasions is it possible to marry the two. It is also inevitable that a great deal of surviving material is weighted unevenly towards the upper echelons of both the merchant class and of society itself – much of the evidence relating to John Clerk highlights commercial exchanges with figures such as the Earl of Lothian, Lady Pittendrum and Lady Newliston. Insights into the exchange of goods among the lower strata of society are less common, though as will be seen throughout this volume they are available on occasion.

Though focusing on the specific Franco-Scottish relationship, this volume contributes more broadly to an emergent debate regarding the categorization of historical studies.[26] Conventional statistical sources remain significant, but are of greatest use when they are used in conjunction with the qualitative evidence prioritized here. The theoretical framework employed in this volume is neither entirely economic nor solely social, but uses a combination of approaches aimed at providing a far more cohesive picture of Franco-Scottish commerce in the early modern period than is currently available. Fundamental to the arguments presented is the notion that conclusions regarding the economic history of any nation are more accurate when they do justice to the social framework within which mercantile agents operated. The evidence presented here is intended to nuance, rather than replace, quantitative analyses of early modern commercial exchange, but its application to the Franco-Scottish relationship provides a more accurate assessment of what will be argued was one of the most pivotal international associations in early modern Europe.

II.

Historically the Franco-Scottish relationship is seen as a medieval phenom-enon, and its sustained role in early modern European politics and commerce has not been afforded the attention it deserves. This neglect is symptomatic of a historiographical tradition holding that the Auld Alliance, a reciprocal, defen-sive, military treaty against England and the cornerstone of the Franco-Scottish relationship, ended in 1560. Studies of the Franco-Scottish relationship have tended to span the period 1295–1560, or to skip forward altogether to the Jacobite period or to the 'British' relationship with France in the eighteenth cen-tury.[27] Precipitated by the Scottish Reformation and the Treaty of Edinburgh, a closer Anglo-Scottish association from 1560 apparently precluded the need for a defensive Franco-Scottish alliance. The retrospective knowledge that Scotland was to be united with England in the Union of Crowns in 1603 and the Union of Parliaments in 1707 has encouraged progressive, Whiggish analyses holding that Scotland's primary international relationship shifted seamlessly from close ties with her auld ally to domination by her auld enemy. This shift has been seen as an inherent part of the European Reformation, as a political alliance between Scotland and France 'could not survive the chill blast of Protestantism and, later, of the union with England'.[28]

An examination of the Auld Alliance uncoloured by established notions of the wider political context or future events reveals a different story, one in which this association survived the events of 1560 and persisted through the rest of the sixteenth, seventeenth and into the eighteenth centuries. Recent research into continued military and intellectual ties between France and Scotland has sug-gested that not all elements of this relationship ended in 1560.[29] Significantly, the continuation of this historic alliance supported persistent commercial connections between Scotland and France. Conventionally, the importance of Scotland's trade with France in the early modern period has been margin-alized in favour of focus on more obvious outlets for commercial ambition. Scotland's historic links with the Low Countries, for example, have received detailed historical attention, and for good reason.[30] The importance of the Low Countries to Scotland's commerce is confirmed by the presence of the Scottish trading staple at Veere (and briefly at Dordrecht), by the presence of the office of Conservator, and by institutional support offered to merchant Scots in this location (see Chapter 2). The staple was, in theory, the only place that Scottish merchants could land 'staple commodities' – defined in 1602 as any goods that paid customs in Scotland.[31] The actions of the Convention of Royal Burghs, the representative assembly of Scotland's premier trading towns, seem to confirm the significance of this relationship, as they pursued a highly organized trade with the Low Countries. In contrast, the activities of the Convention have been seen as confirming that Scotland's trade with France was more opportunistic and less regulated: 'if further organization had been required, the Convention would have undertaken it, but the scope of the trade with England, France etc. was probably too insignificant to necessitate further organization'. Scottish trade through the staple, it is agreed, was more organized, and implicitly more important, than trade elsewhere.[32]

However, the Convention paid much attention to Scotland's trade with France, commissioning individuals such as Henry Nisbett, Thomas Fischer, Ninian Cockburn, Gilbert Logan and James Maxwell to negotiate the renewal of Scotland's historic privileges with her auld ally.[33] Further, though the only official Scottish Conservator was in the Low Countries, James VI made a concerted effort to establish a similar office in France, of the same name, when concluding a commercial treaty with Henri IV in 1606.[34] Although trade with France may not have been organized through official institutions or through a staple port in the same manner, it does not necessarily follow that it was therefore less organized, less lucrative or any less beneficial to the Scottish nation. The significance of Scotland's trade with France can be seen clearly through the actions of individuals involved in it, and the impact they had on Scotland's overseas relationships more broadly in the long seventeenth century.

An investigation into the significance of Scotland's continued commerce with France in the early modern period necessitates consideration of a number of aspects of Scotland's history, including her own domestic economic position and her overseas migration. Our knowledge of Scotland's early modern economy and trade has improved dramatically in the last half-century. The pioneering studies of Edgar Lythe and Christopher Smout in particular have had stunning results in enhancing – even initiating – our understanding of Scotland's economic position in early modern Europe, inspiring a proliferation of subsequent works considering Scotland's overseas trade and economic development.[35] Throughout such assessments, though, the notion that Scotland's economy was inherently weak, particularly when compared to England's, abounds.[36] If the health of nations' trade or economy is equated with the wealth of the Treasury or the profile of governmentally controlled commercial institutions, this view of Scotland is supported. England was populous, wealthy and with significant manufacturing capability; Scotland saw low returns to her Treasury from trade and her attempt to emulate England's successful trading companies ended infamously in the collapse of the Darien scheme and the sale of the Company of Scotland to the East India Company through Article XV of the 1707 Treaty of Union.[37] An alternative analysis based on the methodologies outlined above allows different conclusions to be drawn. Non-governmentally controlled commercial networks have been shown in other contexts to have been more effective than ventures tied to companies or monopolies,[38] qualifying the apparent disadvantage of Scotland's lack of formal trading companies. When emphasis is placed on the actions of individuals and informal networks, rather than on national companies or wealth, Scotland's alleged backwardness is far less obvious. Rather than being 'almost mediaeval in her organization of trade and industry',[39] Scotland's merchants and their networks adopted a range of sophisticated tactics to allow them to profit from commercial ventures.

The vehicle through which Scotland's overseas links were established – migration – was essential to these processes. The burgeoning field examining the presence of Scots abroad, their roles in overseas communities, and the importance of the links they maintained with their homeland has enhanced our understanding of Scotland's complex international relations, as well as providing insights into how Scotland and the Scots perceived, and were perceived by, a wider European world. In the European context scholarship has to date been focused primarily on northern, Protestant states, including Scandinavia, the Baltic and the Netherlands.[40] Our understanding of Scottish activity in and trade with these nations has been explored against a backdrop of Protestant co-operation and mutual interests in Europe,[41] although some scholarship has started to appear on Catholic encounters.[42]

Excepting work on the continuation of Franco-Scottish links in military and intellectual spheres, as noted above, Scottish ties to France in the early modern period have been dominated by discussions of Jacobitism. The exiled Stuart court formed an essential part of Scotland's relationship with France, but this focus has precluded detailed examination of Scots in France who were not tied to St Germain, or to other intellectual institutions such as the Scots Colleges.[43] A more balanced understanding of the range of people involved in Scotland's migration to France, particularly in the commercial sphere, is needed, especially as the broader political or religious context was seldom of primary importance to mercantile agents seeking profitable business ventures, as explored in Chapter 7. As David Allan cautions, however,

> it is not unknown for Scottish historians to be accused (in fact, to accuse one another, only half in jest) of 'jock-spotting' – meaning the arid pursuit of individuals with more or less tenuous Scottish affiliations whose historical significance in almost any field of human endeavour can then be proudly proclaimed.[44]

In firmly linking the presence of Scots in France to wider political, economic and commercial agendas, it is hoped that the present study will successfully avoid criticism, at least on these grounds.

III.

It is impossible to provide an accurate picture of Scotland's interactions overseas without considering the impact of this activity on relations closer to home. Consideration of Scotland's relationship with England, and particularly comparison of the economic activities of the three kingdoms of Great Britain, is imperative in a period during which Britain underwent significant domestic changes. This is particularly pertinent in light of the continued interest in a New British History.[45] As argued convincingly by Nicholas Canny, this approach has 'proved constricting for the study of Irish and Scottish history because its sponsors, coming mostly from backgrounds in English political history, privilege political over social and economic history'. Further, Canny argues, by accentuating the insular dimension of 'British' history, continental influences have been downplayed.[46] As Éamon Ó Ciosáin suggests, 'enquiry will benefit from an historical approach that takes account of the differing circumstances affecting the various nations of the three kingdoms'.[47] It is essential that there is clear delineation in historical studies between the activities of Scotland, Ireland and England. The unions of 1603 or 1707 – or indeed 1801 – did not produce a new nation overnight with a single identity and consolidated aims. Pertinently for our purposes, it is clear that French authorities and merchants alike continued to treat Scotland and England as independent, autonomous nations, despite the unions. They were held to different legislation, particularly during periods of conflict, and as a result their merchants had markedly different experiences of trading with France during the long seventeenth century.

That Scotland has been seen as economically weaker than England has already been discussed, but another accepted historiographical tradition has seen Scotland being increasingly dominated politically by her more powerful southern neighbour as the early modern period progressed. Scotland's ostensibly closer relationship with England following 1560, coupled with an emphasis on the significance of both the 1603 and 1707 unions, has created a situation in which Scotland has been considered unable to pursue independent trading links.[48] Scotland 'paid for a Union of the Crowns which deprived them of an independent foreign policy and obliged them to participate in English quarrels with their best friends and customers'.[49] Scotland was 'handicapped' from 1603, sharing a monarchy with England and thereafter having an 'anomalous' political position within the United Kingdom.[50] In the post-1688 period, Scottish concerns were allegedly ignored as the desires of England were prioritized, the net result being damage to Scotland's commercial affairs.[51] Moreover, beyond the scholarly community in Scotland, the kingdom is not always viewed as a nation in her own right, with 'Great Britain' being used as a veritable pseudonym for 'England', and vice-versa.[52] As we will see, however, in reality Scotland was not subordinate to England in all respects, and continued to pursue her own agendas in both commercial and political spheres.

This study considers not only the specific Franco-Scottish relationship, but highlights problems with the conventional narrative of Britain's international commerce in a period dominated by domestic political changes. While Robert Burns's charge that Scotland was 'bought and sold for English gold' at the time of the 1707 union is no longer upheld in all academic quarters, the notions that association with England after this date 'opened the door' to Empire, that Scotland needed free trade with England and access to England's overseas markets to survive economically after the union continue to proliferate.[53] Ostensibly, Scotland's merchants did benefit from some aspects of incorporating union, including the freedom of trade granted in Article IV that granted legal access to all English colonies. This allowed them to import commodities such as tobacco and thus enabled them to open up the tobacco trade with France and boost their trade with the Netherlands.[54] Such benefits, though, were not the lifeline of Scottish overseas trade. Scottish merchants pursued trade with the colonies during the seventeenth century regardless of the Navigation Acts, and although unrestricted access after 1707 may have allowed Glasgow to secure dominance in the tobacco trade, Scottish merchants were present in many colonial communities before this date.[55] As Allan Macinnes demonstrates, there was an 'unswerving conviction in the Scottish capacity to continue circumventing the English Navigation Acts'.[56] In her relationship with France, Scotland maintained commercial independence throughout the seventeenth century and after the 1707 union; far from increasing her commercial potential, Scotland's closer political relationship with England significantly hindered trade with France in both political and practical terms. Instead of relying on or being bullied by her more powerful neighbour, Scotland drew on her continuing commercial privileges in France and on the abilities of her informal merchant networks to maintain lucrative trade with an apparent enemy. Through an assessment of the Franco-Scottish relationship, therefore, much can be learned about wider British international and internal affairs.

IV.

This study is by no means comprehensive. The need for coherency imposes some boundaries, and geographically it is France's west coast ports that receive primary attention. Bordeaux, Nantes and La Rochelle feature most prominently, though examples from the smaller ports of Dieppe, Le Havre and Rouen both complement the analysis and allow for consideration of the transient nature of Scottish merchant activity in France in this period. Paris, though not strictly an Atlantic port, had access to the sea through the fluvial system and housed a number of Scottish merchants and bankers such as John Clerk and James Mowat who were central to the networks discussed. Focus on the west coast Atlantic ports of France is governed partly by the notable presence of Scottish mercantile agents in these ports and thus their centrality to Franco-Scottish exchanges, but such focus provides scope for the regional and local comparison crucial to understanding fully the development of patterns of Scottish and British trade in this region of Europe.

Some previous assertions relating to Scotland's commercial interests in France in geographic terms are easy to challenge. Suggestions that '[Rouen] did very little trade with Scotland' do not reflect the sources held in this port.[57] The presence of prominent Scottish merchants and bankers in Rouen speaks for itself; the Scots Andrew Russell and Robert Arbuthnot, both of whom were successful merchants with connections throughout Europe, had commercial interests here, and for Arbuthnot Rouen was his primary operating ground.[58] The province of Normandy was central to Scottish commercial concerns in France, and the *parlement* of Rouen played a crucial role in confirming Scotland's trading privileges; it was this *parlement* to whom the Convention of the Royal Burghs of Scotland turned in 1690 when seeking to have the 'exemptions and privileges in favour of Scottish merchants in the kingdome of France' confirmed.[59] In Scotland, it is the east coast ports that have been hailed as central to Scottish economic development and her overseas exchanges. Isobel Guy attests that 80 per cent of all customs revenue between 1460 and 1599 was generated by the major eastern burghs – Edinburgh, Aberdeen, Dundee and Perth.[60] Leith, in particular, has been seen as central to Scotland's commerce. In the 1520s it was arguably 'the major player in Scotland's limited overseas trade', importing large quantities of wine and salt from France.[61] Studies of the eighteenth century suggest that this trend continued, and Henry Hamilton cites the eastern ports of Kirkcaldy, East and West Anstruther, Burntisland, Crail and Dysart as the most important.[62] Scotland's west coast ports, though, should not be neglected. Christopher Smout demonstrates, as have others, that the ports of Glasgow saw a significant amount of Scotland's overseas trade in the later seventeenth century, and the west coast ports of Scotland feature prominently in this study.[63]

This book comprises two parts. Part I is largely thematic, providing a reassessment of the Franco-Scottish relationship in both political and commercial terms. Chapter 1 specifically analyses the Auld Alliance, questioning the tradition that sees this alliance end in 1560 and providing evidence that speaks to its formal and informal continuation throughout the rest of the early modern period. In seeking to establish the nature of continuing Scottish 'privileges' in

France, this chapter provides the background against which the rest of the book is situated. In Chapter 2 attention shifts to the practicalities of Franco-Scottish trade in the long seventeenth century, considering both the commodities exchanged and the individuals who made these exchanges possible. This analysis emphasizes new perspectives on this relationship gleaned from an approach that is predominantly micro- rather than macro-economic. Central to this chapter is the contention that the people involved in international trade were central to commercial development. This segues into Chapter 3, which questions existing interpretations of early modern legislation, focusing on regulations that sought to control commerce. It considers the types of legislation implemented, the complex motivations behind this legislation, and how effectively regulations were upheld, particularly during periods of conflict. Crucially, the role played by mercantile agents in influencing and altering legislation is examined.

Part I thus provides the broad framework within which Part II analyses the impact of specific conflicts on experiences of commerce, prioritizing those in which France and Scotland/Britain were pitted directly against each other. Chapter 4 evaluates the impact of domestic conflict and internal changes on both political and commercial aspects of the Franco-Scottish relationship. Civil war in France, including the Wars of Religion and the Fronde, are considered, but it is the British Civil Wars and Interregnum that are prioritized, in preparation for later discussion of the relationship between the British kingdoms and their relative contributions to Britain's overseas trade. In addition to war, less obvious 'conflict' is considered, including the implementation of economic policies in each country – such as Colbert's protectionism – and the impact of these policies on the specific Franco-Scottish association. Chapters 5 and 6 concern themselves more directly with international warfare. Chapter 5 considers wars fought between the houses of Bourbon and Stuart – the Anglo-French War of 1627–9 and the Anglo-French conflict as part of the Second Anglo-Dutch War, 1666–7. Chapter 6 moves on, both chronologically and in widening geographic focus, to the major European conflicts of the period, the Nine Years' War, 1688–97, and the War of the Spanish Succession, 1702–13. The ways in which these conflicts may have adversely affected Franco-Scottish commerce are considered, before alternative analyses are presented, drawing on the issues raised throughout Part I. In all three of these chapters interpretation of official documentation is questioned, private sources are brought to light and emphasis is placed on the ways in which merchants operated to pursue trade in the face of adversity, often with the assistance of the institutions officially charged with preventing this activity.

Throughout Part II, the importance of the British dimension to this relationship becomes increasingly apparent. Chapters 4–6 consider whether Scotland was dragged into 'England's' wars, subjugated by a dominant partner, or whether she maintained her autonomy and participated on her own terms. In Chapter 6 it is suggested that despite the ostensibly closer relationship enjoyed by Scotland and England after 1603 and 1707, the three kingdoms of the British Isles had very different experiences of trading with France during the conflicts of the seventeenth century. Chapter 7 explores these disparities in more detail, offering explanations that go beyond broad political contexts. In particular, this final chapter highlights the importance of exploring regional and local variations, emphasizing again the drawbacks of a political, linear approach to commercial relationships in this period. Patterns of trade can only be fully understood, it is argued, by considering economic exchange as shaped by the specific social environments within which merchants operated. On the French Atlantic coast, patterns of trade were mirrored in patterns of migration, settlement and integration.

The primary aim of this volume is to propose a new analysis of the Franco-Scottish relationship in early modern Europe, but the net result of the arguments presented here goes much further. This study informs debates on relations between the British nations, having great significance for our understanding of 'British' overseas trade in the post-1603 and 1707 periods. In developing a picture of Franco-Scottish trade that is contrary to the accepted broad political context, understandings of the European framework in this period are probed, as is our interpretation of the nature and impact of early modern warfare and legislation. Perhaps most pertinently, this volume fully advocates an approach to commercial history that utilizes social methodologies. Government initiatives and trading figures do not produce a clear understanding of the state of Franco-Scottish trade; instead, this should be based on the sum of all of the commercial endeavours of the nation, whether governmental, corporate or individual. Before these conclusions can be drawn, however, the nature of the continuing relationship between France and Scotland in this period must be explored, and it is to the Auld Alliance that we turn first.

1 BEYOND 1560: THE AULD ALLIANCE

On 5 July 1560 the commissioners of Elizabeth I of England and the Scottish Lords of the Congregation, along with French representatives in Scotland, drew up the Treaty of Edinburgh. This treaty formally concluded the Siege of Leith, the twelve-year occupation by French troops of that port. It was agreed that 'all the military forces pertaining to either party [England and France] shall depart out of Scotland' and that 'all manner of warlike preparations ... in France against the English ... shall hereafter cease'.[1] Shortly after the signing of this treaty the Reformation Parliament met, approving the Scots Confession and confirming Scotland's conversion to Protestantism. Both of these events have contributed to a tradition of scholarship that sees the year 1560 as marking the end of the historic Auld Alliance between France and Scotland: a mutual, defensive, military alliance against the might of England that had been in force since 1295.[2] This chapter tests such claims, highlighting certain facets of the Auld Alliance that remained in place after 1560. In the process, a fundamental contention of this book will be established: that the Auld Alliance contributed to the ongoing development of the Franco-Scottish relationship throughout the early modern period. This perspective not only alters our view of this specific association, but changes how we should view the development of Great Britain domestically, her overseas relationships and the broader political dynamic within Europe.

I.

On 23 October 1295, prompted by the ambitions of Edward I, France and Scotland agreed a mutually defensive alliance against England in the Treaty of Paris.[3] The alliance was conceived as a military one, intended to guarantee both parties support from the other in the case of an English invasion. The Treaty was ratified at Dunfermline on 23 February 1296, cementing Scotland's 'inward love and affection' for France 'on an ever more solid basis'.[4] Throughout the fourteenth and fifteenth centuries, the Auld Alliance – and specifically its military nature – was confirmed through numerous renewals and specific references to assistance in conflict.[5] The terms of the Treaty of Edinburgh in 1560, then, with the French agreeing to withdraw 'all military forces' from Scotland and to 'cease warlike preparations' against the English, seems to undermine fundamentally the central component of this alliance.

Crucially, however, the Treaty of Edinburgh did not provide for the formal conclusion of the Auld Alliance. Not all military ties were severed, and

> a certain number of French soldiers excepted, as shall be condescended upon by the commissioners of France, and the lords of Scotland ... remain in the castle of Dunbar, and fort of Inch-keith ... untill the Estates should find means to maintain the said forts upon their own charges.[6]

Though retrospectively the Treaty of Edinburgh seems to mark a shift from a Franco- to an Anglo-Scottish accord, English as well as French forces were asked to leave Scotland, and France still held the advantage in Scottish relations in the form of the French dowager queen, Mary Stuart – indeed, her marriage to Francis II in 1558 has been heralded as the apogee of the Auld Alliance.[7] Further, the Treaty of Edinburgh was wholly concerned with the military aspects of the Franco-Scottish relationship, making no mention of other benefits and privileges that had, by 1560, become central to this association. As Elizabeth Bonner recognizes, by 1560 the Auld Alliance 'had long ceased to be just a military alliance. It had developed many other social, cultural, architectural, commercial, artistic, literary and educational links which certainly did not cease in 1560'.[8] Though Bonner, focusing on the medieval context, does not elaborate further on her claim, it is clear that by 1560 the Auld Alliance had grown into far more than simply a military agreement. Though the Treaty of Edinburgh certainly shaped and altered the historic Franco-Scottish relationship, it did not formally conclude the Auld Alliance, nor did it put an end to many established aspects of it.

The Scottish Reformation, confirmed a few days later in the Reformation Parliament, appeared to indicate further a shift in allegiance, with France remaining Catholic and England having already asserted her Protestant faith. If we accept the notion that a common religion was a crucial force in early modern political relationships,[9] this shift seems both inevitable and obvious. The Scottish Reformation has been seen as fundamental in breaking the Auld Alliance, fostering the belief that 'a significant element [of the Reformation of 1560] was rejection of the long-established association with France'.[10] Recent work has repeated past assertions without question, perpetuating the notion that 'the onset of the Protestant Reformation shattered Scotland's close relationship with France (enshrined in the "Auld Alliance")'.[11] These contentions build too on a tradition of scholarship believing Scotland's change in religion to have been fundamentally linked to a move towards England, as 'confessional realignment was accompanied by a radical shift away from the traditional political axis of the Auld Alliance between Scotland and France ... England became a focus of Scottish diplomatic attention as the two converged through the Protestantism of both nations'.[12] As with the Treaty of Edinburgh, however, the Reformation Parliament made no formal provision for formally concluding the Franco-Scottish relationship. While Scotland's religious conversion would of course have some impact on its overseas associations, a formal break with France was neither provided for nor, as we shall see, desired by either party.

The events of 1560, as well as being seen as a move away from France, have been heralded as a move towards Protestant England, as 'the progress of Protestantism, meat to the Scottish Anglophile party, was poison to the French alliance'.[13] Retrospective knowledge that Scotland and England were to be formally united in 1603 and 1707 has fuelled acceptance of this notion. In reality, however, the remaining bonds between France and Scotland 'were much stronger than the fairly fragile peace with England'[14] directly following the events of 1560. Further, as the remainder of this volume will demonstrate, this in some aspects remained the case throughout the long seventeenth century, with Scotland and England being far from fully united in 'British' relations with France after the Union of Crowns or of Parliaments.

II.

Thomas Moncrieff's *Memoirs Concerning the Ancient Alliance between the French and the Scots*, published in the mid-eighteenth century, states that 'it is unquestionable, that, to begin from Philip the Fair [r. 1285–1314], there runs an uninterrupted train of alliances between the Kings of France and Scotland, down to Henry IV and James VI'.[15] More recent research confirms that the Auld Alliance was indeed renewed by every Scottish and French monarch up to the mid-sixteenth century – except Louis XI (r. 1461–83).[16]

The obvious question, then, requires an answer. If the Auld Alliance was not brought to an end in 1560, when did it cease to exist? It is true that by 1560 the military defence on which the alliance was originally based had become anachronistic, but as Bonner points out, military concerns were no longer its crux. Throughout the seventeenth and into the eighteenth century there were persistent overtures from both France and Scotland seeking to confirm the continued existence of the alliance and the 'privileges' it granted to both parties. French and Scottish representatives, monarchs and governments consistently referred to the 'ancient friendship' or 'ancient alliance' when it was politically or economically expedient to do so – but this was not simply rhetoric. Both Scotland and France strongly asserted their desire to have at least some of the terms of the Auld Alliance confirmed in their pre-Reformation form. The trading privileges enjoyed by both parties took centre stage, though military concerns were not absent, despite the implementation of the Treaty of Edinburgh.

The first formal overtures came in 1561, and came from France. The senator of Bordeaux, Noalins, came as an ambassador to Scotland, 'craving that the league betwixt Scotland and England might be brokin, the ancient league betweene Scotland and France might be renued'.[17] The events of the previous year did lead, it would seem, to concerns that Scotland's allegiance would shift from France to England, but Noalins's advance indicates an immediate desire that the historic, 'ancient league' remain unchanged. It is all the more interesting that the first overtures to secure the continuation of the Franco-Scottish alliance were instigated by France. Auld Alliance scholarship has not seen the relationship as an equal one but one in which Scotland was the weaker partner, needing the alliance more than France and gaining more from it than she contributed.[18] Some have gone so far as to say that between 1550 and 1560 'Scotland was in some danger of becoming a French province'.[19] Indeed, it has been suggested that attempts at renewal came solely from Scotland after 1560, as 'it was only by constant embassies and agitation by the Convention of Royal Burghs that ... exemptions [and privileges] were maintained'.[20]

From 1561, though, the desire to rekindle the Auld Alliance lay with the French as much as with the Scots, with the 'gude freindschip and amytie standing betuix the realmis of France and Scotland' reported in 1577 being felt on the French as much as on the Scottish side.[21] Scotland's reaction to French overtures tells a story that belies her apparently inferior status in the relationship, for rather than bending to France's desire she used the opportunity to strengthen her political position within the British Isles.

> On the 14th [May 1583] there arrived an embassy from Scotland ... [Colonel Stuart] is to request this Queen [Elizabeth, of England] to give a firm assignment for £12,000 to pay the pensions and the guard that holds the King, and to lend him a sum of money to repair the fortresses, some of which are in ruins. It is even said that if she will not agree to it they will be obliged to renew the alliance with France, and accept the subsidy and pensions from that country, which are again being offered by the French.[22]

Reports such as this suggest that Scotland was fully capable of maintaining diplomacy with both France and England on her own terms, rather than being the inferior partner in either relationship. Five years later, while acting as ambassador to France, the Bishop of Glasgow suggested to the Queen Mother that 'it would be detrimental to France if you should fall into other hands in default of the friendship and continued alliance of the French crown'.[23] Into the mid-seventeenth century, France continued to demonstrate desire to renew the ancient terms of her alliance with Scotland. In 1644 French diplomats, concerned with the visit of Sir Thomas Dishington of Ardross, reported that the first thing to be done is to re-establish promptly and efficiently the privileges of his nation and its ancient alliance with France. That without this re-establishment nothing can be done in the present state of things ... It is necessary that those of his country be satisfied with the treatment they receive here.[24]

When Charles I authorized the Privy Council of Scotland in 1644 to appoint an ambassador to the French court to ask that Scotland 'micht be restored to the former priviledges and enjoy the samene in tyme cuming without diminutione',[25] Scotland would not officially commit to any French alliance but instead obtained all she could from France without offending England.[26]

Despite her political candidness, Scotland did seek to re-enforce her trading privileges in France after 1560. In 1570 the Privy Council of Scotland voiced concern that a proclamation that no-one may 'repair in the pairtis of France in their accustumat traid of merchandice without a testimonial frome the Queen' was being

> sinisterlie purchest be the malice of wickit persounes to steir up occasioune of trubill and unquyetnes betuix our Soverane Lord and his darrest brother, the maist Christian King of France, their realms, dominions, and subjectis, in hurt and prejudice of the ancient league and constant amitie that so lang hes continewit betuix the nationis.[27]

In 1597 James VI opened formal negotiations for 'observing the old liberties and privileges granted to Scottish merchants trading with France, and for obtaining discharge of customs and imposts raised on goods imported into that realm or transported furth thereof', prioritizing the maintenance of specific commercial links.[28]

It is unsurprising that either nation pushed for the continuation of this relationship, or that Scotland sought to strengthen her own position by maintaining diplomacy with both her auld ally and auld enemy, and there were wider motivations at play. Though James sought to maintain the 'old liberties and privileges', his assertion that 'benefits redounding to the merchants of this country from the discharge of the said customs and exactions to be annexed to the crown' suggests financial motivation.[29] In 1561 France's overtures were governed by the wider European political climate: a fractured Britain was more attractive than a united front. Further, it was a relationship that could be used to strengthen France's position with England – in 1570, 'the French ambassador continues his audiences with the object of frightening the queen of England into the idea that his master will not forsake the cause of the queen of Scotland, but little has come of it hitherto'.[30] Henri III was more diplomatic, stating in 1584 that he did not wish to affect Scotland's relationship with England, merely to preserve his country's league with Scotland.[31] Despite the Treaty of Edinburgh apparently bringing the military aspect of the alliance to an end, the historic military benefits both nations enjoyed were drawn upon; French ambassadors in the 1640s consistently reported that maintenance of the relationship with Scotland would be a means of facilitating levies.[32] The desire to prolong the Auld Alliance was not always borne out of a sense of loyalty, but prioritized political expediency. In 1646, no doubt influenced by events at home, Charles I actively encouraged the continuation of the Auld Alliance, although this compromised his 'anglocentric' policies. The French diplomat Jean de Montereul wrote that the Scots 'had little care to perform what they promised', but that Charles

> found it necessary for me not to break with the Scots, as much because he judges it would induce them further to try, even more eagerly than they do at present, to come to terms, at his expense, with the English Parliament, if they thought that France wished to give them up.

He stated that the Scottish Parliament would always try to retain the friendship of the English Parliament, 'even when they may be assured of the assistance of France', speaking to the care that continued to be taken by Scotland not to offend her southern neighbour.[33] Whatever the motivations, 1560 did not see a clean break for Scotland with France, nor the end of the Auld Alliance for any of the three protagonists.

Yet 1560 is not the only date that has been seen as a turning point in the Franco-Scottish relationship. While recognizing that the Auld Alliance continued past 1560, in more than a military guise, Elizabeth Bonner describes the Alliance as 'slowly declining' after the union of monarchies in 1603, 'the decline becoming more rapid following the parliamentary union of those two kingdoms in 1707'.[34] Christopher Smout is more emphatic, asserting that 'the Auld Alliance in a political sense was killed by the Union of Crowns'.[35] Contemporary concerns regarding potential impact of the union on the Franco-Scottish relationship were evident. When a list of articles to be discussed at the union conference of 1604 was drawn up, the Convention of Royal Burghs added an item emphasizing that 'the ancient preweledgeis, honouris, officeis, dignities, imwnities, and exeptiouns fra customeis, grantit to Scottis men be the Kingis of France, be na wayis tuichit or prejudgeit be the said Treatie'.[36] Despite the union, a clear distinction was maintained in France between the country's relationships with Scotland and with England. When an English proclamation in 1614 prohibited any goods being imported into England except in English ships, the French issued an edict to the same effect in retaliation. The Convention of Royal Burghs voiced concern that this was also 'to the great prejudice of the merchant estait of the Kingdome of Scotland',[37] but when Scottish factors appealed to the *parlement* of Paris they were assured that this edict 'did no ways extend towards the subjects of the Kingdome of Scotland, their ancient friends and allayes'.[38] Post-1603, Scotland continued to value her relationship with France. In 1638 Alexander Guthrie, common clerk for the Convention of Royal Burghs, compiled an 'Inventory of Writs concerning the Privileges of Scotland in France', as part of 'Ane Inventar of

the Whole Wreats belonging to the City of Edinburgh'. These included notes on
the privileges granted in 1510, 1520 and 1554, and were used as the basis on which
embassies were sent to France to have these privileges renewed.[39]

Other scholarship has seen wider European events as crucial in bringing an
end to the Auld Alliance. In addition to citing the effect of the 1603 union,
Edgar Lythe holds the impact of the 1627–9 war with France responsible, as
does Ian Whyte.[40] The year 1663 is cited as a key date in the breakdown of the
historic Franco-Scottish relationship by a number of scholars. Gordon Donaldson recognizes that Louis XIV reconfirmed Scottish trading privileges, but
maintains that these were abolished in 1663.[41] Christopher Smout, too, asserts
that French protectionist policy in the mid-seventeenth century 'deprived the
Scots of the last of their ancient privileges in France', a claim supported by Lythe
and John Butt who note that 'after 1663 no amount of protest would induce
Louis XIV to exempt the Scots from a special levy on foreign ships in French
harbours'.[42] At the same time as the 'practical exclusion' of Scottish commodities
from England by the renewal of the Navigation Acts, which arguably disposed
Scottish merchants to attach greater importance to their trading privileges with
France, Colbert's mercantilist policies caused a shift in French attitudes towards
Scottish traders (for more on this see Chapter 3). The French impost of 50 sous
per tun of cargo exported in foreign bottoms implemented in 1659 was extended
to include Scots in 1663, who claimed they were 'in hazard to be reduced to
the common condition of strangers and losse the benefit of these antient priviledges which for many ages they have enjoyed'.[43] Yet despite the apparent apathy
of the state towards their historic alliance, French merchants continued to seek a
renewal of alliance terms.[44] In respect of this, in 1664 the Privy Council forbade
the farmers of the customs

> to exact any more customes or other deuty for goods imported and exported in
> French bottomes then is payed be the natives of this kingdome, and that in regard
> of the priviledges and immunities that the natives of this kingdome doe enjoy in the
> kingdom of France for their vessells and goods.[45]

That these privileges and immunities were specifically granted on a reciprocal
basis suggests the continuation of Scottish trading privileges in France notwithstanding the implementation of the 1663 impost.

Though the political context may seem to have been inhibitive to continued
Franco-Scottish accord, attempts to renew the formal Auld Alliance continued
throughout the later seventeenth century. In 1684 the Privy Council informed
the king that 'the subjects of this his Majesties antient kingdome have right to
the priviledges of succeeding in France as natives, and [are] free from all impositions due by strangers'.[46] Though this apparently annulled the 1663 levy, later
that year the Provost and Magistrates of Edinburgh asked Charles II to instruct

his ambassador at the Court of France to negotiate with the French king 'that the Scotts merchants and all other his Majesties subjects in this kingdom may be restored to ther ancient priviledges in France, and particularly that the Scotts merchants may be free of the fifty souse upon the tunn'.[47] The Convention of Royal Burghs was still attempting to get this imposition lifted in March 1698.[48] French concerns continued to be influenced by the broader political climate, and in the wake of the 1697 Treaty of Ryswick which ended the Nine Years' War, French diplomats considered Scottish antipathy to the English as potentially beneficial to Louis XIV. As such it is perhaps no surprise that in 1701 the French accorded the Scots 'favoured-nation status' in the War of the Spanish Succession.[49]

If the Auld Alliance survived the 'chill blast of Protestantism',[50] the union of 1603 and Colbert's protectionism, the final nail in its coffin would surely be the 1707 union. Contemporaries were convinced that this would be the case, including the Duke of Atholl who stated that incorporating union had only become necessary because of

> the evident decay of our trade since the union of our Crowns, the hardships put on us by the Act of Navigation, the seising of our ships and seamen, the hindering of our planting of colonies, as latly at Darien, the high duties on linen cloath etc.[51]

In 1700, George Ridpath cited his fears that incorporating union would result in

> The loss of our Ancient Alliance with that Famous and Great Kingdom [France], and of the Honourable and Advantagious Priviledges we enjoyed there; is one of the great Dammages we sustained by the Union of the Crowns ... There's no way of retrieving this, but by our Parliaments asserting our Independency and Freedom against all those Invasions and Neglects, and by making it appear to the World, that we are still a Sovereign Nation, and have as much Right to consult our own Interest, without any regard to that of *England*, as they have to do so by us.[52]

For several years following the event, London newspapers dissected the effect of the union on the Franco-Scottish trading relationship. Six years after parliamentary union came into force the *Mercator* articulated concerns regarding the 'present miserable condition of the trade from Scotland to France', stating that 'those Scots gentlemen who appear warm against the said Treaty, either deserve very ill of their Country, or shew that they understand very little of the Trade of it'. This publication referred to 'the ill share' Scotland would henceforth have in French trade and talked of the November 1706 union negotiations at which a group of individuals led by John Hamilton, Lord Belhaven, stated that 'the French trade was much more to the advantage of Scotland than the trade to England could be, or than England could any way make us amends for'.[53]

Whether London publications provided an impartial view of the situation is debatable in itself, but as later chapters will demonstrate distinct Franco-Scottish trade survived parliamentary union. In terms of formal alliance, overtures from France to preserve their relationship with Scotland continued up to and including 1707. During an audience with Louis XIV in 1703 the Jacobite Simon Fraser, Lord Lovat, 'enlarged upon the antient alliance between France and Scotland', Louis responding that 'himself and the whole French nation had their hearts unfeignedly Scottish; and that ... he desired to be understood as from that moment renewing all antient alliances between the two nations'. A year later, Colonel Nathaniel Hooke was sent to Scotland in secrecy to report on the prospects for a resurrection of 'l'ancienne alliance'. Louis XIV was afterwards thanked 'for the hopes he had given us by Colonel Hooke, of haveing our priveleges restored in France, and of seeing our king and this nation included in the future peace'.[54] As union between England and Scotland approached, the French became increasingly concerned with re-establishing the precise terms of the Franco-Scottish alliance. A letter from Lewis Innes to Colonel Hooke in January 1707 stated that the Marquis de Torcy had 'asked about the French league'. Hooke stated that Torcy was 'very impatient to have the treaties', to which Innes replied that

> I have sent him the treaties and priviledges confirmed by Louis 12th, which are the most ample, and the confirmation of all by Henry the 4th and Louis the 13th, which are the latest ... the said priviledges [are] still in vigour.[55]

While Scotland's favoured-nation status in the War of the Spanish Succession was terminated by parliamentary union, 1707 – like 1560, 1603 and 1663 before it – did not see the historic relationship between France and Scotland formally concluded. Four weeks after the Act of Union took effect, a letter to the French King from the Earl of Errol talked of 'the renewal of ancient and happy alliances that your Majesty and your predecessors had with the Scottish nation, as also for the conservation of freedom and independence of the kingdom'.[56]

Hence, 147 years after its alleged demise, despite the apparent confirmation of Scotland's move towards an alliance with England in 1707, the privileges that had been historically granted continued to be valued by both Scotland and France, and attempts to have the alliance formally renewed came at consistent junctures throughout the period, though not necessarily at the most obvious times. As later chapters will address, for example, though Jacobites prioritized political overtures to the French, royalism did not underpin all of these advances. Further, subsequent chapters would reassure George Ridpath that despite incorporating union, Scotland continued to assert her 'independency and freedom', indeed making it appear to the world that she continued to 'consult [her] own interest'.[57] The 'ancient and happy alliance' between France and Scotland continued to be felt across all sectors of society, underpinning the commercial activity that endured.

III.

It is clear that both France and Scotland, for a variety of reasons, sought to ensure that the Auld Alliance remained a formally established relationship following 1560 and into the eighteenth century. As a result of such overtures, certain benefits and privileges remained in force. Though 1560 did, in some respects, bring the mutual defensive military alliance by which the Franco-Scottish relationship was originally conceived to an end, this did not herald the immediate cessation of martial links. Historically, Scottish soldiers had played a prominent role in the French military; by the sixteenth century the Scottish soldier abroad was found primarily in France,[58] before their prominence in Scandinavia grew during the wars of the seventeenth century.[59] The position of Scots in the French military, as well as the close relationship between Scotland and France, was confirmed in 1418 when Charles II of France founded the *Garde Écossaise*, a regiment acting as the French King's personal bodyguard. Between 1419 and 1424 there were an estimated 15,000 Scots in French military service.[60] The privileges enjoyed by members of the Scots Guard included the captain of the Scots Guard having the title 'First Captain'; being able to stand nearest to the body of the King; receiving the keys of the towns they entered; always taking precedence over other troops; having preference in choice of lodgings; and crucially, 'as a sign of distinction and in remembrance of the old league between France and Scotland, have the prerogative to bear on their weapons the fringed lace of silver and white silk and the royal coat of arms.'[61]

In 1560 the Treaty of Edinburgh apparently ended this military allegiance, and it has been alleged that following this date the position of the *Garde Écossaise* became 'ambiguous to both Kingdoms'.[62] Neither the flow of Scots to the French military, however, or the privileges granted to Scots in French service ceased. Fifteen years following the Treaty of Edinburgh,

> the captain of the King's guard in like manner to be given to a Scotsman ... The yearly pension of money or munition contained in the old league shall be yearly paid and sent into Scotland. All these offers shall be performed sua your grace with the rest of the nobility will observe and keep the old and ancient league betweixt the two realms.[63]

In 1584 troops were levied in France for service in Scotland, and less than a decade later this was reciprocated.[64] As Henri IV was engaged in trying to win back Paris from the hands of the Catholic League in 1590, James VI offered his support, writing to the Viscount of Turenne that

> since the present danger of France ... your master may count upon the whole of our forces, means or credit for the advancement of this most just and holy war, which manifestly also touches us closely, by reason of the ancient alliance between our crowns.[65]

James wrote to the German Princes in this year in an attempt to expedite the sending of succour to Henri IV, promising to send 3,000 Scots to serve in France if it became necessary.[66] In addition to military assistance, James prohibited 'the carriage of wine to Newhaven, St. Valirie [Saint-Valery-sur-Somme], and other Catholic places disobedient to the present authority of the King of France', compromising his nation's commerce in order to offer political support to Henri.[67]

Following their Reformation, Scottish emigration to France continued to be motivated by military service. On 21 August 1574 Charles Crawfurde was noted as 'Archear of the Corps in France'; William Baillie of Cormistoun was acknowledged as 'archer of the Cross to the King of France' in 1583; James Colville of Easter Weymis was acknowledged and favoured in a financial dispute for passing a 'grite parte of his yowth in the service of his Majesties darrest brother and confederat the King of France' in 1599.[68] While Henry II's promise that 'he shall not allow any person to enter [the *Garde Écossaise*] who is not a gentleman of the said nation of Scotland' was not fully realized under his successors – by 1599 only 75 per cent of the guards were Scots – Scotsmen continued to hold prominent roles within the French military with specific privileges appertaining to Scots serving in France being reconfirmed in the middle of the seventeenth century. In 1642 Scots in French service were 'restored to thair said privileges, and injoy the same without anie diminutioun in all time coming',[69] and six years later the Committee of Estates of the Parliament of Scotland wrote to Mazarin regarding the privileges of the *Garde Écossaise*, stating their desire to 'perpetuate the old friendship between Scotland and France'.[70]

While the alliance may have been conceived as a military one, intellectual links were almost as historic with the Scots College at Paris being established in 1326. Scots registered at French institutions during the fourteenth and fifteenth centuries at a steady pace, arguably as a result of the lack of adequate intellectual provision for them at home. As with military links, focus on intellectual links between Scotland and France has prioritized the medieval period, or skipped forward altogether to Franco-Scottish intellectual exchanges during the Enlightenment.[71] Throughout the early modern period, however, Scots remained familiar figures at universities in almost every part of the continent, including France, as recent work – notably that of Marie-Claude Tucker – has confirmed.[72] In addition to exploring the continuation of Franco-Scottish intellectual links, Tucker's work has lent an important religious balance to existing scholarship. It has been suggested that in 1574, on the accession of Henri III and following the conclusion of the Marian Civil War, 'Scottish Catholics were crowding into France in quest of a new fatherland' as a result of the Reformation.[73] Further, during religious crisis in Europe Protestants and Catholics apparently became entrenched within their respective creeds, leading to a decline in registrations almost everywhere.[74] Indeed, studies on post-Reformation education in Europe

have placed great emphasis on the Catholic/Protestant 'divide' which is perceived to have affected the destinations of Scots studying in France post-1560,
as French institutions arguably served political and religious purposes as well as
merely academic.[75] The Reformation has been seen as 'shatter[ing] ... the pattern of student mobility ... changing the confessional character of universities,
profoundly affecting choice of universities'.[76] Thus Scots exiled as a result of their
Catholicism might be expected to favour the universities at Paris, Tournon,
Pont-à-Mousson and Toulouse, with their Protestant counterparts choosing
instead to study at the academies of Sedan, Saumur, Orange and Montaubon.

In practice, however, two things are evident. One, both Catholic and Protestant Scots continued to make use of French educational institutions after the
Scottish Reformation, and two, that few notable allowances were made for religion on an individual basis. Scottish Protestants enjoyed access to universities
throughout France, even before the Edict of Nantes was enacted in 1598.[77] Sir
Thomas Craig, a lawyer from Edinburgh, chose to leave St Andrews to pursue his
studies at the Catholic University of Paris despite his Reformist sympathies, bas-
ing his decision on the superior education available rather than prioritizing his
chosen institution's religious affiliation.[78] James Bassantin, a steadfast Protestant,
settled in Lyon and later taught mathematics in Paris.[79] David Cunningham,
who accepted Protestantism and became minister of Lanark in Scotland in
1562, studied at both Catholic Paris and Protestant Bourges, apparently placing little import on religious affiliation.[80] The converse is also true, with those
who adhered to Catholicism finding their educative home at Protestant institutions even before the Scottish Reformation had been confirmed – they were
not Catholic exiles but chose France based on intellectual considerations. Henry
Scrimgeour, a diplomat and book collector from Dundee, studied in Paris and
retained his Catholicism. Nevertheless, he also studied at the Protestant institution of Bourges, and his *Exemplum memorabile desperationis in Francisco Apera,
propter abiuratam fidei confessionem*, published at Geneva in 1550, incorporated
a preface by John Calvin.[81]

For these Scots, religious tendencies did not preclude study at top French
institutions. France remained one of the preferred destinations for Scottish
graduates, owing to its exclusive academies and superior teaching in certain dis-
ciplines. The importance of religion in determining successful or unsuccessful
integration and business is an issue prevalent throughout much of this volume,
and similar themes will be seen among commercial networks and communities
as merchants chose to do business with those who could offer them lucrative
opportunities rather than dealing exclusively with – or even prioritizing – those
who shared their religion. Assertions that the overthrow of the Catholic Church
in Scotland led to several 'waves' of confessional exiles between 1560 and the
eighteenth century, and that the majority of Catholics went to strongly sympa-

thetic countries such as France has led to far too great an emphasis being placed on 'religious migrations'. There may have been ripples of confessional exiles, but there were many migrants who were wholly concerned with other issues such as employment, education and profit.

IV.

The Auld Alliance may have been implemented initially on military grounds, but the broadening of the association to incorporate commercial concerns began relatively early. On 11 December 1482 a complaint was made to the Scottish Parliament that the goods of Scottish merchants were being requisitioned in France, contrary to the Auld Alliance:

> The complaint made by diverse merchants of this realm, that their goods are arrested and kept from them in France by command of the king, as is alleged, without cause or form of justice, and that they are not treated as friends, rather their goods are forcibly stolen and kept from them in contradiction to the alliance and bond between the realms.[82]

Though in this case Scottish merchants felt that they were not receiving the privileges to which they were entitled, nevertheless it is demonstrated that by the end of the fifteenth century the Auld Alliance embodied economic, as well as military, links. The events of 1560 allegedly removed this commercial cooperation, and it has been asserted that 'as a first economic result [of the Reformation], the trading privileges enjoyed by Scotsmen in France became less secure'.[83] Just as military and intellectual links survived 1560, however, Franco-Scottish trade remained healthy and lucrative. In the post-1560 period, it was in commerce where the Auld Alliance was perhaps the most apparent, and tangible practical benefits can be discerned.

Specific commercial privileges had been granted under the auspices of the pre-1560 Auld Alliance. On 5 October 1518, the French Court of Accounts exempted Scottish merchants from a 'new impost of twelve French deniers per livre, raised in the city of Dieppe upon foreign merchandise', the Scots being obliged to pay only four deniers per livre, which 'hath been anciently collected'.[84] In 1554 Scottish merchants were granted a further exemption that 'the subjects of the said country of Scotland shall not be bound to pay for the commodities which they shall take and carry out of our country and duchy of Normandy, whatsoever they be, if designed for the said country of Scotland', a privilege re-confirmed in 1599.[85] These pre-1560 privileges speak to the changing nature of the Alliance, that it had moved away from the purely military agreement that had characterized the formal establishment of Franco-Scottish accord in the middle ages.

After 1560, specific commercial privileges continued to be confirmed. In 1584 Henri III wrote to the diplomat Monsieur de Castelnau: 'my intention was, that the Scottish merchants might exercise their trade in my kingdom, in all freedom and surety, with no harassment or extortion'.[86] Four years later the Archbishop of Glasgow, the King's ambassador in France, secured from Henri IV a customs reduction of one half for goods exported to Scotland.[87] We have already seen that in 1597 James VI opened 'negotiations for observing the old liberties and privileges granted to Scottish merchants trading with France'.[88] Not only did this commercial activity remain significant enough that James believed potential revenue to be lucrative, but the 'old liberties and privileges' persisted more than three decades after the Scottish Reformation. Henri IV's 1599 'confirmation of the privileges' spoke of 'the same franchises, privileges and immunities for foreign customs and imposts, and after the same sort and manner that they enjoyed them in the days of the kings Francis and Henry'.[89]

In 1606, James VI and I concluded a formal commercial treaty with France. This treaty, 'for the more commodious entercourse in traffique betweene their subjects', reasserted the 'amitie and intelligence between the two princes'. The treaty encompassed 'Great Britain ... and all her ports', though reference to 'conservators' makes it is clear that the specific Franco-Scottish relationship was the primary concern.[90] England had no conservators – in the 1660s there remained confusion in England over what a conservator was – but Scotland had precedent of filling this office at their trading staple in the Dutch Republic.[91] It may have been James's intention to equate Scotland's trade with France to that with the Netherlands, enhancing the notion raised in the Introduction that Scotland's French trade was just as important as her trade through the Dutch staple. Whether this was his motivation or not, this treaty served to reconfirm the Auld Alliance, in essence if not in name, despite the 1603 Union of Crowns which ostensibly brought Scotland and England closer together.

In March 1607 in Dieppe, the 1518 exemption was reconfirmed. This document describes 'the previledges which the Scottish nation injoy in France' as being 'two fould'. First, Scots paid 'only the ancient dutie, called domaine foraine' on goods transported out of France, Normandy and Picardy, a privilege 'peculiar to the Scottish alone, above the French themselves, and above all other strangers'. The second privilege,

> general through France, but reciprocal with the French, who injoy the like in Scotland ... upon pretence of gratification for ancient services performed by the Scottish nation, against the Inglish, in favour of the French, the said Scottish are received as naturall regnicoles, and originall French in every respect.

The document describes in detail the exemptions and privileges Scots continued to enjoy in France in purchasing land or property, holding office, naturalization, postal costs and importation of goods. Most pertinently, it states several times that these were privileges 'the Inglish cannot atteine', speaking to the strength of the Franco-Scottish alliance despite Anglo-Scottish union.[92] The maintenance of these privileges manifested itself in practical benefits for Scottish merchants in France. When the Governor of Guyenne seized the fleet of English and Scottish vessels bringing in wine from Bordeaux in 1626 the Scottish vessels, but not the English, were released 'in respecte of the ancient league',[93] and in 1635 the Scottish merchant John Trotter succeeded in securing a reduction in import duties on Scottish wool and hides.[94] In 1647 Montereul wrote to Mazarin that he had informed the members of the Edinburgh Town Council that 'you had kindly granted their request on their first application, to prevent the Scots who are in France from being obliged to pay their tax',[95] and though four years later Scots were encompassed under Colbert's legislation as 'strangers', they were initially exempted from his 1659 duty of 50 sous per ton on foreign vessels trading to France.[96]

An eighteenth-century copy of several of the privileges granted to Scots trading with France sheds some further light on their terms. This document suggests the disparity in the ways in which Scottish and English mercantile agents were treated in France even following the 1603 and 1707 unions, as is explored in detail throughout Part II. In the mid-1620s Scots continued to receive equality of treatment with French subjects in terms of inheritance, and Scottish merchants paid only a quarter of the duties charged to other foreign nations. Further, reciprocal commercial privileges remained in force despite the 1603 union of crowns: 'this privilege they have always enjoyed and continue to enjoy at present, even when there was a break between the crowns of France and England because of the union of the kingdom of England to that of Scotland'. Of further significance is that the Scots were able to take advantage of these privileges 'without taking any letter of naturalization'.[97] This explains why letters of naturalization for Scots in France are relatively few and far between in surviving records. Peter Sahlins calculates that between 1660 and 1789, 978 Britons were naturalized in France, with 69 per cent being of Irish origin, 28 per cent English and only 3 per cent Scottish. That Scots did not need formal letters of naturalization suggests that these figures skew our perception of the Scottish presence in France, and the significance of this is discussed further in Chapter 7.[98]

Aspects of the privileges that were not specifically commercial, including naturalization, benefited the Scottish merchant classes in facilitating their presence and therefore their business in France. Louis XII granted 'general letters of naturalization for all of the nation of Scotland' in September 1513.[99] Naturalization privileges were formally re-confirmed throughout the rest of the sixteenth and seventeenth centuries. In 1598 Henri IV granted a patent of nobility to David Kinloch, a doctor of medicine and a native Scot who had studied and worked in France for more than twenty years, and his wife, Grisel Hay, granting them the same rights and privileges as the nobles of France 'in consideration of the friendship and confederation we have long held with the Scots and which continues today ... and whom [our Kings] have favoured as if they were the natural subjects of our Kingdom'.[100] A year later, Henri declared that

> we desiring to treat well and favourably the subjects of the King of Scotland ... in consideration of the ancient confederation and alliance so long kept and observed between the two crowns ... the said privilege ... we grant and confirm to them.[101]

Scottish naturalization privileges were reconfirmed by Louis XIV at Fontainebleau in September 1646. In the same year Louis issued a decree stating that 'there has never been any difference in this Kingdom between his Majesty's subjects and those of Scotland'.[102] As we will see later in this volume, automatic naturalization and the integration of Scottish merchants into French society played a direct role in the ongoing development of Franco-Scottish commerce during the early modern period.

Despite these obvious benefits, and the clear desire to maintain the economic aspects of the Auld Alliance, the comprehensive terms of the 'privileges' are almost impossible to ascertain by modern scholars, mirroring the difficulties faced by contemporaries in establishing conclusively their reciprocal rights.[103] In 1562 the French ambassador 'sent for all the treaties in force between France and England and Scotland in order to provide against any injury being done to his masters' interests',[104] desiring to be in possession of the exact terms of any agreement as the French sought to confirm the continuation of their alliance with Scotland. Production of such documents was not always possible. In 1597 James VI and I noted that

> we find no letters patent of this privilege earlier than the time of the said King Francis, whether because there was no occasion to demand them, or whether because our people have been too careless about preserving our muniments, yet it is to be presumed that the nation enjoyed this privilege before that date.[105]

While mid-negotiation with Louis XIV in 1684 in respect of the 50 sous impost the Privy Council of Scotland reported the existence of

> severall ancient papers and records that wer in the touns charter house which are absolutly necessary to have for clearing the Scotts priviledges in France ... bot these papers are all now abstracted and withdrawen, and, albeit the Lord Provest and magistrates hes made all the dilligent search that could be for getting of them, yit they cannot be found; and, seing Sir James Rochhead certainly had these papers when the inventar was made ... they crave that Sir James Rochheade may be ordered to exhibit and deliver to the lord provest these records and papers concerning the Scots privileges in France, so that the principals or authentic copies may be sent to France now when the matter is being considered by the French King.[106]

While it was stated six years later that the Convention had 'not only obtained extracts [of the privileges] but lykwayes ... had procured up the principall charters and priviledges granted by the kings of France to this nation to be keeped for the use of the royall burrowes', no record has yet been found of these documents or what they contained.[107]

The question of when the Auld Alliance was terminated, if not in 1560, is a matter for further study and debate. No formal document from the period has yet been uncovered that stipulated a Scottish break with France, and despite England's ongoing concerns regarding the relationship (explored below) neither the 1603 nor the 1707 union specifically provided for an end to the allegiance. There is some suggestion that the terms of the historic Franco-Scottish treaties remained valid until the Entente Cordiale. Writing in *Scottish Field* in 1967, J. Harvey MacPherson declared that 'many Scotsmen still possess rights and privileges in France granted under the alliance and still valid in French law'. French rights in Scotland were formally dissolved by Westminster only in 1906, but the French government declared that the terms of previous Franco-Scottish treaties remained valid for every Scot alive at the time of the Entente – meaning that a Scotsman born before 1907 would possess the full rights and privileges of French nationality.[108]

That the exact terms of the continuing Franco-Scottish relationship remained elusive to contemporaries suggests that the alliance did, inevitably, change from its original form. Robert Arbuthnot, Scottish factor in Rouen, wrote to the Duke of Hamilton in 1700 that

> your grace knows the ancient priviledges the Scots have had in ffrance formerly, the which within these threttie years by past have been clipt to a great degree, not by any publick authority, but rather by bringing them in desuetude, so that wee have as yet just title to pretend to them, and I have been assured here by such as pretend to know it that if a continuance of our priviledges was hansomly asked it would be granted provided our parliament renew'd the French priviledges in our country.[109]

There appears to have been no firm legislation to which mercantile agents could refer to support their claim to trading rights in France. This rarely mattered. That there had been 'no occasion to demand them' suggests a belief that they had continued inherently regardless of a lack of formal documentation. As later chapters will confirm, the continuation of these privileges lived on firmly in the hearts and minds of those involved in Franco-Scottish commerce, as well as those responsible for its regulation. Those participating in and regulating this trade followed a code of conduct that acknowledged the continuation of some kind of formal allegiance.

V.

Categorization of the Franco-Scottish relationship remains problematic, as establishing comprehensive terms post-1560 is unfeasible. The Auld Alliance in its medieval, military incarnation did not proceed unchanged, but both Scotland and France pushed for renewal of 'privileges' that included automatic naturalizations and mutually favourable trading conditions. The continuation of the Franco-Scottish alliance, even if no longer explicitly military, was fully recognized south of the Tweed. In 1570 Elizabeth I 'import[ed] no less than the manifest break of the auld league which has continued betwixt the crown of France and Scotland this aucht hundredth yeris and mair, without violation, and has been very profitable to Scotland'.[110] Two years later Elizabeth pursued a defensive alliance with Charles IX of France – an agreement that not only provided for the provision of soldiers for both sides but also included an arrangement for the pacification of Scotland (then in the throes of civil war).[111] Five years later, Francis Walsingham wrote of 'the amitie and good intelligence that hath bin of longe time established' between England and France.[112] Despite the ongoing relationship between France and Scotland, Henri III, while making clear that the maintenance of Scotland remained his priority, acknowledged that friendship with England was desired. Monsieur de Mauvissier assured Walsingham that

> the King of France only asks union and good understanding between those two Princesses, peace and quiet in Scotland with liberty and surety for the young Prince, and that he render all honour to the Queen of England, provided that it be not to the prejudice of the amity of France with Scotland, which will be so much more sure when it shall also be constantly maintained between France and England.[113]

A more cordial relationship began to develop between France and England in the latter part of the sixteenth century, and in 1590 an answer from English merchants to a complaint of a French merchant assured them that they had the same privileges in England as the English merchants had in France[114] – but as will become clear, these 'privileges' never emulated those of Scottish merchants.

It is unsurprising that England wished to counteract the continuation of an alliance that had historically been aimed against her, but though the political dynamic had shifted English fears regarding the Franco-Scottish alliance lingered. A letter to the Lord Chancellor of England in 1605 on the difference in payment between English and Scottish merchants in France highlighted that English merchants actively pushed for the same trading privileges the Scots enjoyed – suggesting not only a desire on the part of the English to foster a closer relationship with France, but also that Scottish privileges in France both continued to exist and remained significant enough to be covetable.[115] At the beginning of the eighteenth century it was reported in English governmental circles that a formal alliance was being considered between Scotland and France, although this was probably a symptom of perceptions of Scottish Jacobitism.[116] Though Anglo-Scottish, and therefore Franco-British, relations changed as the long seventeenth century progressed, the French authorities maintained clear distinctions in their relationships with the British Kingdoms, even after 1603 and 1707.

It is inevitable that the Auld Alliance evolved over time, adapting to changing political contexts both at home and abroad, but none of these junctures marked an end to the Franco-Scottish relationship. This association endured for monarchs, governments and merchants who consistently exhibited their belief in the continuation of their commercial privileges and a relationship that was fully reciprocal. Pertinently, the continuation and importance of the Franco-Scottish relationship is best seen not through official legislation or decrees, but through the actions of those directly involved in it. The contributions of commercial agents, be they merchants, skippers, dock-workers or officers of admiralties, shaped the continuation of Franco-Scottish trade links throughout the long seventeenth century, doing so against a backdrop of a historic alliance that remained at the forefront of the consciousness of its participants.

2 MARKETS AND MERCHANTS

The continuation of the Auld Alliance and the retention of Scottish trading privileges in France after 1560 have important ramifications for our understanding of Franco-Scottish trade in the long seventeenth century. So too does a reconsideration of the people involved in this trade at every level and a close examination of what and how they traded. Trade is habitually viewed as a national phenomenon – after all, trade routes start in one port and end in another, fostering exchanges between two (or more) foreign nations. The impact of this trade is consequently viewed at a national level, and often based on quantifiable evidence – which countries and ports do these routes link; what do these exchanges contribute to national revenue; does one country have a favourable balance of trade over another? Such an approach gives an overview of where primary trading routes were situated and the goods that were exchanged along these routes, and has contributed to attempts to calculate the revenue generated by duties charged and the contribution of overseas trade to the economy of the nations concerned.

An approach that prioritizes the people involved in commerce, though, provides nuances to these conclusions, and in some cases offers an entirely different picture. To understand how trade was conducted and thus how economies interacted and developed in the early modern period it is vital to consider fully the roles played by merchants and their networks. As discussed in the Introduction, the application of social methodologies to studies of international trade has yielded significant results in several contexts. In these contexts an understanding of trading relationships has emerged that cannot be gleaned from a focus on statistical records such as port books and customs records, but which stems from the prioritization of private records including merchants' accounts, journals and correspondence.[1] A top-down, politicized view neglects the people in international exchanges, preventing them being placed at the heart of economic or commercial histories, but an accurate depiction of the state of nations' commerce can only be based on all of the commercial endeavours of those nations.[2] As Sanjay Subrahmanyam suggests:

> Once one leaves behind the antiseptic realm of theoretical economic models, and enters into an historical world of flesh and blood, merchants appear not as faceless

facilitators, but as a social reality, an interest group, or even a class. Merchants thus do not appear as abstract individuals but as concrete collectives, indeed as merchant communities.[3]

Far from being incidental, merchants were central to economic development, exercising a great deal of influence – both directly and indirectly – on the cultivation of international trading links. The wider economic impact of international trade can only be fully appreciated if the mercantile networks that undertook so many of the exchanges that formed this commerce are also understood. Individuals including John Clerk, David Wedderburne and Archibald Hamilton – all of whom feature in this chapter – significantly contributed to the nature of Franco-Scottish exchanges in the early modern period, and their actions support the recent claim that non-governmentally controlled commercial networks were often more effective than ventures of companies or monopolies.[4] The networks within which these merchants worked, the commodities they exchanged and the trading methods they adopted were crucial in ensuring that Franco-Scottish commerce continued during periods of adversity. Such individuals played key roles both in maintaining and shaping overseas exchange, with their records exposing aspects of commercial relationships invisible in statistical figures. This chapter is concerned with the nature of Franco-Scottish trade and how it was carried out. It reveals what was traded, how it was exchanged and what impact merchant groups had on international commerce, thus providing the backdrop against which the continuation of such commerce during times of conflict is later examined.

I.

Trade between France and Scotland, particularly that which originated from the Biscay ports of La Rochelle and Bordeaux, has been seen as 'synonymous' to Scotsmen with salt and wine.[5] Many contemporary sources support this point of view. Scottish customs records from 1595 to 1599 confirm that primary export goods were the 'native commoditeis' of wool, cloth, fells and salmon, and Scottish port records show the most prominent imports from France to be wine, vinegar and salt.[6] The Dundee shipping lists for 1580–1618 detail cargoes from Bordeaux containing wine, woad and prunes, cargoes from Dieppe with 'cradilles of glas', cork and wine, and shipments from La Rochelle and St Martin de Rhé that invariably contained salt.[7] These commodities certainly formed a major part of Scotland's trade with France, but they all have something in common. They were transported on vessels passing through major ports, having (at least to some extent) their contents scrutinized and recorded, hence their appearance in records of bulk exchange. The picture gleaned from the private accounts of merchants involved in Franco-Scottish trade is strikingly different.

Far from participating in bulk exchange, John Clerk specialized in expensive, luxury items. In 1638 John Johnstoun commissioned Clerk to send him 'a watch or two for gentlewomen, of small value but small & handsome', which were purchased as gifts for his wife and daughter.[8] Clerk's customers in Scotland included William Kerr, the third Earl of Lothian, who bought books, book bindings, 'gold watches of the newest fashion', 'a reasonable faire ibeny cabinet trimmed with silver', and in June 1652 'a knyffe for cutting the corns on the feet' – all of these transactions being fulfilled during the British Civil Wars and Interregnum.[9] Goods sourced by Clerk for other customers included spectacles, decorative cases with knives and bodkins for dressmaking, clothes including gowns and petticoats, luxury cloths such as bukram, waskyne and romany, ebony furniture, atlases and diamonds.[10] Cloth was not only acquired for clothes; in 1664 the Laird of Pitfodels purchased '48 els of ritch scarlet coloured Avignon taffatie to line a bed ... 11 els of fine Callico of sam coulour to line the courtpoint ... 2 ounce halfe of silk of the coulour to stitch it' from Michel Mel, a Scottish merchant based in Dieppe.[11] In addition to fulfilling commissions, Clerk purchased lavish items for personal use – paintings, silver and musical instruments 'for the usse of my wyffe and childring'.[12] Clerk's son and namesake, following in his father's mercantile footsteps, was thanked by the Countess of Stair in 1718 'for your prettie cap and your brave big gooseberries', and a month later for his 'good big pears'.[13] David Wedderburne, a Dundee merchant, traded in wine, vinegar and salt, but equally prevalent in his records are commodities including violet powder from La Rochelle, comfits, sugar candy, syrup, aniseed oil and toffee.[14] Further, many transactions were not for vendible goods – loans of money were common in a period when many commercial agents acted not merely as merchants, bankers or factors but in various and fluid combinations of these roles, embracing 'a diversity of interests and talent'.[15]

There were many other types of transactions that played a role in international exchange. Ships themselves were bought and sold; between 1682 and 1696 the Admiralty of La Rochelle reported four English-built, but French-named and owned, ships being registered.[16] Once bought, vessels needed to be maintained and were serviced in foreign ports. In 1595 Mungo Mackall wrote to Robert Galbraith in Bordeaux to ask that if 'ony of your friends or acquaintance passis to saintmalloss I pray yow to send with thame sua mekill money as to by for me 20 boulttis of narrow canves the best can be gottin for topsails'.[17] And while vessels were refitted and repaired, merchants and skippers sought accommodation, food and local beverages in these foreign ports – all activities that contributed to the economies of trading centres.[18] The Scottish ship the *David* bought provisions in ports across Europe in 1713, including hiring a sail maker and a smith in Bordeaux.[19] Focus on trade as a national phenomenon has encouraged focus on bulk commodities, but private accounts suggest a far greater range of goods being exchanged. Rather than passing through trading centres private transactions bypassed these official channels, being sent instead in the care of family, friends or business associates. John Clerk continually fulfilled commercial commissions by sending goods home in the care of his friends or colleagues.[20] Yet although they were conducted in the private rather than the public domain, orders and accounts recorded by these commercial agents followed established patterns of exchange. Transactions were conducted through commissions, orders and accounts in the traditional manner, but without being recorded in the statistical sources that have formed the basis of conventional economic histories.

While the impact of these transactions or of merchants' spending patterns on nations' economies is almost impossible to quantify, this does not render it any less noteworthy. Indeed, the high profit margins of many of these transactions lend this activity economic significance. Further, the qualitative nature of this source material offers a new perspective on international trade; in the Franco-Scottish context, as will be explored in the following chapters, it allows us to build quite a different picture from the historiographical status quo. Such sources provide 'a remarkable bottom-up account of the maritime world', offering insights into the lives of individuals committed to maintaining international commerce even in the most hostile of circumstances.[21] While Clerk's plethora of records focus primarily on his business transactions, they also permit glimpses of deeper relationships with the people connected to his business networks. Most revealingly, Clerk writes passionately in a letter to William Rires of his feelings for a gentlewoman – Mary Gray – the daughter of his prominent business associate Sir William Gray, whom he later married.[22] Here, we have a unique insight into a personal aspect of this international merchant's life that can only be gleaned through examination of his private correspondence.

Initially this may seem tangential to the issue at hand, but as we will see throughout this volume merchants' personal circumstances played a huge role in shaping their commercial activities and thus in the development of international trading routes. The social and cultural, as well as economic, aspect of trade is worth exploring in two directions. First, economic exchange was not needed for contribution to Scotland's social and cultural development. In 1669 John Hutcheson wrote home from France of a game, stating that 'this bilzard table is neither difficult neither dear to erect, the clubs may be mad by any wright, and the balls also, otherwise as your wish desired I wold have sent of them home, & yet with this letter I could not for they are not posts cargo'.[23] Second, the cultural and social contexts within which mercantile agents operated had marked effects on the ongoing development of the Franco-Scottish commercial relationship, as explored in detail in Chapter 7. To echo Subrahmanyam, merchants should not be viewed as faceless facilitators – they were the heart of international exchange.

II.

In order to understand how these individuals functioned and were thus able to influence trade, it is essential to consider the nature of the expatriate Scottish merchant community in France. Throughout Europe, Scottish commercial communities established themselves in the nations with whom they traded. Research into Scottish communities in Stockholm, Gothenburg and the Netherlands has shown that in these locations such communities were supported by established institutions – the Scottish trading staple in the Netherlands has been described as a 'centre for market advice and commercial intelligence' and 'invaluable to merchants abroad' because of the social support network it offered in providing accommodation, advice and financial assistance to both visiting and settled merchants.[24] Andrew Russell, James Gordon and other merchants in the Netherlands were bolstered by the presence of the Scottish Kirks in Rotterdam and Veere,[25] and there was obvious institutional support for the Scottish merchant community based at the staple in the form of a resident chaplain, whose stipend was 'payed by a contribution to be imposed upon the merchands goods that cummes to Camphear and no utherwayes'.[26] When the Convention of Royal Burghs ratified the re-establishment of the trading staple at Dordrecht in 1669 provision was made for a Scottish Reformed church and apothecary.[27] In the Dutch Republic Scottish exiles formed a distinct temporary community in the second half of the seventeenth century, based largely around Rotterdam.[28] In Stockholm, Scottish entrepreneurs became embedded in institutions such as the nobility, councils and parliament.[29] In Gothenburg two seats were reserved on the city council for Scots and Thomas Cunningham, Scottish Conservator at Veere, married into the local oligarchy.[30] Throughout the Netherlands and Sweden coherent expatriate Scottish communities mirrored life at home, offering individuals who were part of them a secure and distinctly Scottish environment in which to operate.[31]

There were Scots who became embedded in civic institutions in France. Thomas Kirkpatrick was working as secretary to Louis XIV when he applied for a Scottish birthbrief in 1670, and in 1672 James Pringle also applied for a birthbrief, giving his occupation as Councillor in Rennes.[32] In Bordeaux Scots worked for the Admiralty of Guyenne, and following the end of the War of the Spanish Succession Robert Gordon testified on behalf of several countrymen applying for passports to enter France or to go back to Scotland.[33] Though these people integrated themselves into civic life – some, notably Robert Gordon, provided support for fellow Scots after doing so – the same level of established institutional support for Scottish merchants found elsewhere in Europe was not emulated in France. The support that was available was more commonly of an independent and unofficial nature. In July 1655 James Mowat wrote to John Clerk: 'I am much pressed by your advysse of my freinds to taik a great lodging to lodge out countrymen, and others when they come'; providing support, but not an officially established institution.[34] In comparison with other locations, the Scottish commercial community in France operated through widespread networks, rather than within geographically close-knit communities, with less institutional support and more onus placed on the actions of the individual.[35] This was a merchant community that was transient, which was not confined to one geographical area but which fostered connections throughout the early modern world. Thus in order to function Scots with mercantile interests in France drew on a range of connections and relationships to allow their business to prosper.

One vital connection exploited by merchants was their relationship with overseas factors. These were individuals employed throughout Europe for their expertise in business, languages and knowledge of local markets – and who commonly charged a commission for their services (usually 2.5 per cent).[36] Official factors were used to great effect by Scottish merchants trading with France. Though there is evidence of complaints against factors who abused their position,[37] prompting the Council of Aberdeen to stipulate in 1634 that no factor could be employed by any merchant unless they had been authorized by the Convention of Royal Burghs,[38] such complaints are rare in merchants' personal records and the use of factors was widespread. Despite assertions that 'it is astonishing to find how few they were in number ... John and Richard Gordon, for example, seem to have managed almost all the trade to Bordeaux', there were a great number of individuals acting in this capacity, speaking to the sustained health of Franco-Scottish commercial links.[39] William Popple and Robert Stewart, factors in Bordeaux, were used regularly by Scotland-based merchants with commercial interests in this port. The Aberdonian Robert Gerard wrote to Popple and Stewart in 1681 that 'som frinds & I intends to send a small vessel for wyns brandy vinager', asking them to send him the rates for these goods. They also, in addition to these bulk commodities, asked for the price of stockings and tallow.[40] Archibald Hamilton regularly employed Stewart (among others) to facilitate his trade in Bordeaux.[41]

In addition to using official factors, the Scottish merchant community in France operated through personal networks that fostered kith and kin relations and within which connections were passed down through generations of families; a phenomenon common in expatriate communities in many spheres throughout the early modern world. The longevity of the participation of certain commercial families in trade contributed to its survival throughout the turmoil of the long seventeenth century – both in the specific Franco-Scottish context and throughout Europe more widely.[42] In the Franco-Scottish context the Macmath family provides one example. The first Macmaths found involved in Franco-Scottish trade were Edward and James, who in the 1590s pursued business with Robert Galbraith, an Edinburgh merchant based in Bordeaux.[43]

Their descendants appear in Franco-Scottish transactions throughout the seventeenth century. Alexander Macmath, merchant burgess of Edinburgh, complained to the Privy Council in 1612 that James Dundas owed him 26s. 8d. in exchange for 400 livers French money in Bordeaux.[44] Between 1635 and 1637 twenty-five letters survive written by Hector Macmath from Dieppe, Rouen and 'St Jermains' to John Clerk in Paris, further stretching our knowledge of the extent of Clerk's connections, and David Macmath acted as a witness for the closing of an account between Clerk and Michel Mel in September 1652.[45] That merchants' contacts were passed down through generations is unsurprising – as is regularly asserted, trust and personal acquaintances were the foundation of seventeenth-century commercial relationships and these were developed not overnight but over generations.[46]

Ostensibly, one of the strongest personal ties was that of family. Many successful merchants relied on family members, and the inherent trust between them, to undertake business on their behalf. David Wedderburne commissioned his uncle, Peter Imrie, in 1593 and his nephew, Alexander, in 1614 to travel to Europe to exact his business.[47] Despite claims that 'all merchants were dependent on the good or bad fortune of the members of their family',[48] however, permanent settlement of a family on the Continent, or their prolonged success, was not indicative necessarily of success for all future generations. The Hope family was prolific throughout Europe in the early modern period, being present on the Continent from at least 1548 when Alexander Hope wrote from Dieppe to his father, John Hope, a burgess of Edinburgh, detailing a consignment he was planning to send home. Henry Hope, who we will meet again shortly, was well established as part of John Clerk's network in the mid-seventeenth century. In the late eighteenth century, members of the Hope family were still present but their fortunes seem to have taken a turn for the worse. In the 1780s James Hope wrote from Amsterdam to his sister Anne in Edinburgh to lament his displeasure at his work, his dislike of the weather, and his aversion to his fellow lodgers. Central to this correspondence, though, were his fears at having upset Mr Henry Hope, writing that he did know what he could have done to deserve the treatment he received from him. James seems to have been on the Continent due to family precedence, but was excluded from the mercantile networks that had made his predecessors so successful.[49] In James Hope's case exclusion was the cause of his misery; for others, exclusion may have been preferable to dealing with misguided family members. In 1642 John Dougall wrote to John Clerk from Paris that 'sore against my will I am forcet to goe doun to Newheaven for ther ar arryvet tuo of my fathers barks, truly I cannot cleanse myself of ingratitude'.[50] The family elders did not always know best; earlier in the year Dougall had written to Clerk that although there was no market for salmon in Dieppe, his father demanded that he stay there until all that he had was sold.[51] For all involved in mercantile activity in this period, 'employing family was far from always being a sound idea'.[52]

Some merchants found out to their cost that the success of family members was not always reflective of future generations' success. In 1643 Charles Erskine began dealing with John Clerk, following a recommendation from Henry Hope.[53] When Erskine asked that Clerk also assist his brother, William, while he was on the Continent, Clerk obliged – William benefitting from his sibling's reputation. Unfortunately for Clerk, William failed to live up to the family name. In 1644 William wrote to Clerk thanking him 'hartile for the paynes ye have taken to furnish my coffer I doue not dout of your carr of it ... as for my monies I am confident my brother will put that in order schortlie'.[54] This particular venture proved ill advised, however, and money lent to William in the 1640s had still not been repaid by 1669. Clerk stated in one of his account books in that year that 'I keep thir letters – that if I ever see his face; to see iff he will repair any off my great losse of the 4444 livres Bot I fear the worst'.[55] James Mel used his elder brother Michel to gain access to an established commercial network, acting as factor for the Edinburgh merchant James Graham in Rouen in the 1680s.[56] Graham, however, petitioned the Privy Council in 1686 complaining that Mel 'having stayed a long time without giving the petitioner any satisfaction or security ... is shortly to goe from this place without securing the petitioner as to what is duly resting him'.[57] The 'implicit contract of family' espoused by Yoram Ben-Porath suggests that family members would be more trustworthy than other people, but this was not always the case in the Franco-Scottish context and neither was it throughout the early modern world.[58]

It was vital, then, that merchants had other routes into established commercial networks, and rare was the merchant who confined their activities to family members or to those who shared their religious or political beliefs. As Henriette de Bruyn Kops observes, 'the risks associated with early modern trade would make it imperative for any merchant to be part of a network with as many layers and connectors as possible, so that the weakness of one segment could be absorbed by the mobility and elasticity of the other components'.[59] Credit and reputation have been described as 'elusive but the fundamental key to success in early modern commerce',[60] and for younger merchants social credit obtained through association with older, more experienced and well-trusted individuals was the precursor to financial credit.[61] Recommendations were vital for commercial agents at all stages of their career, and successful merchants such as John Clerk were well placed to provide these recommendations to both inexperienced and established Scots. In October 1644 Clerk wrote to Michel Mel to introduce

> Robert Fletcher sonne eldest to Sir Andrew Fletcher ... on off the lords off the session: the gentlman with him is Mr Piter wederburne whom ye knoue weill in my

name I bessich yow offer to doe them any pleaser you can: I have wreatten to Jhone dougall younger to give them sum money for my Accompt.[62]

While James Mowat had long been established in France in his own right, he continued to seek advice from John Clerk, writing in 1654 that

> I hav found ... that M[onsieur] Dourny was a good friend butt not fite for my business, for this six months bygone I have not one lyne from him ... If you know of any merchand that would taik peines for me in my bussines, I would pay what he desyreth. You will infinitely oblidge me to give me advise.[63]

Once established within a network, future business opportunities became available following previous success. Henry Lavie, another factor based in Bordeaux, acted on behalf of a cartel of Glasgow merchants who formed a bond of co-partnery to control the import of the 1674 Bordeaux vintage.[64] Lavie's previous work for John Cauldwell, who headed the cartel, put him in a prime position to be employed again, highlighting the importance of experience, prior contacts and a gleaming reputation whatever the stage of merchants' careers.[65] Despite the ongoing commercial privileges Scots enjoyed in France, recommendations and reputation remained essential for success. John Snodgrass, writing to Andrew Russell in 1678, commented on the 'vain conceit' held in Scotland that 'it is almost sufficient to obtain employment and credit ... that he have lived in France were it but for two days'.[66] This alone was not sufficient, and Scottish merchants trading with France relied on their contacts to allow them to pursue successful commerce.

Recommendations not only helped merchants to kick-start their careers and gave them access to future business opportunities – they could also be instrumental in offering them protection. Laurence Fontaine argues that the credit system was designed to foster leniency; that merchants were encouraged to display disinterestedness. Indeed, Jacques Savary in *Le Parfait Négociant* (1697) emphasized that it was essential to adopt a gentle approach with debtors: 'one should not make too much of debtors who are unable to pay their debts because their business has failed; this is a time when one should treat them gently, so as not to force them into bankruptcy'.[67] As a consequence of such attitudes it often happened that the first to be hit by bankruptcy were the most recently established merchants who were least well-integrated, even if they were not the deepest in debt; those who had high levels of support could escape bankruptcy even if their level of debt was high.[68] An established reputation was an asset to any merchant, and as we will see this became particularly important during periods of conflict.[69]

III.

Trust and reputation were the bedrock of commercial networks, but their wide geographical spread inevitably fostered problems. In 1651 Henry Lavie wrote to Annabella, wife of Lord Lothian, that he was

> disappointed of the confidence I had in the Mr boullay of Nantes who I thought would not refuse mee the favour I desire of him (in messers Broune & Inglis name) towards payinge your lady the £500, he hath been pleased to answer mee that he cannot doe it at all, in soe much that I am now forced to tell your lady plainly that I know noe way ... to satisfie your lady's desire.[70]

Being let down by others was a common complaint, as was lack of commercial opportunity. In 1675 Thomas Smith wrote to Andrew Russell from Bordeaux: 'I have bein heir neow a meownth and ther is not eney apereinc of my lodeing for my merchen heir seyed that he knoes not of on town of guwdes yeit to peit a bord of us bowt seir I heve down all that I can do heir'.[71] Two years later Thomas Dinmuir wrote to Russell from Nantes that 'I am lying heir on the river of nantis & hes bein heir neir four weiks, & ame not readie yet for at first my merchant wold not weill acept me nor answer me'.[72] In all of these cases Lavie, Smith and Dinmuir believed that they could rely on their business associates, but they were proved wrong.

Mistakenly placed trust – either in implicitly trusting family and business associates or as the result of taking an unsuccessful recommendation – was one of the most common causes of loss or inconvenience. Advising John Dougall in March 1645, Clerk urged him to 'mak a formall protest' of a bill of exchange drawn by Sir William Gray on Gilbert Pape. Clerk stated that

> heir is no faveur to be shown in such busyness ... which I am sure will no wayes tend to Mr Pape his weill not his credit for which am sorie: Sir William is too fare a dealing man to be used; those that ar not willing to pay finds many excuses.[73]

Clerk's intervention in this case seems to have been as mentor rather than as an invested party, but in defending an individual's interests Clerk inherently defended the system within which he operated – for these networks to be successful, all participants must operate under the same code of conduct.

When an individual did not adhere to this code of conduct, networks had their own methods of meting out punishment, seeing appeal to authorities as a last resort. In the same month Clerk wrote to Sir William Gray regarding a 'difference betwixt your Worship and [Michael Mel's] son'. Describing Mel junior as 'basly wicked and malitious' and 'the most abominable man', Clerk asserted that 'he wil never end that busienes in fair termes'. He also suggested that 'if it draw to a sut or action in lawe it wil draw verie long'. In an effort to avoid lengthy (and costly) litigation, Clerk asked David Blackburne, 'a friend and a verie able man' – and fellow merchant – to undertake the case on his behalf, as he was unable to stay in Rouen for the two or three months the negotiations were expected to take. Clerk emphasized the benefit of this course of action, as 'marchants that ar able men ar mor fitting to judg on thes differences then all the lawiers in France. It wil be the best way and soonst endit'.[74] The damage caused to the reputation of the transgressors was likely to be great, thwarting their chance of gaining future credit or business within this prominent network as well as elsewhere. The highly personal nature of these networks made recourse to legal action superfluous – with his reputation tarnished beyond repair, no-one would trust the transgressor with their business.

A merchant of Clerk's experience was able to provide advice and references – a highly valued commodity – but providing, as well as receiving, such advice could have negative consequences. In September Clerk wrote, exasperated, to Lady Pittendrum regarding her son, Robert, who had undertaken a 'neidles … expenssive and dangerous' voyage to Italy, despite Clerk giving him 'my advysse to which he hath given no ear at all'.[75] Two months later Clerk lamented, 'I wish he had taken lesse money & more off the counsell I gave him'. That Robert did not heed his advice caused Clerk to fear for his own reputation. He wrote to Lady Pittendrum that her son was denigrating him, as he 'sits in his owin light and doth much wrong me to wreat to everie man he knowes heir off my ingratitud to him and off my abuzeing off him so wyldlie'. Clerk was content that 'what he hath said or wreatten off me they doe not beleve him in respect they have bein eye witnesse that I have allwayes indeavored that he sould do that which wold have most tendit to his weill & credit', but his concern for his reputation, despite his senior position, confirms how imperative trust and status was at all levels within international commercial networks.[76]

IV.

Personal relationships in commerce have been criticized as a disadvantage. They allegedly reduced the clarity of the business at hand, clouded or delayed rational decision-making and provided 'no contractual coordination' as there would have been between strangers.[77] Further, it has been argued that social and political obligations lay behind the granting of credit (for example to family members or patrons) at the expense of the consideration of economic imperatives, and that family members were granted special terms such as no-interest credit.[78] The success of a network, though, cannot necessarily be viewed by the economic return of each transaction. As Sheryllynne Haggerty has argued with reference to trade in the British Atlantic in the later eighteenth century, business culture was 'socially embedded and did not allow for pure profit maximizing … [merchants] were not atomized, profit-maximising, rational economic men', they were men who 'internalized and emotionalized to a large extent'. Indeed, Haggerty defines 'strong' ties between commercial agents not necessarily as those providing the greatest financial value, but as those that were the most 'emotionally-intensive'.[79]

Most merchants saw the advantage of longer-term, lower-return relation-ships as opposed to transactions that were lucrative in the short term but which might damage future business. They invested in their reputation and in relation-ships to allow them to take advantage of opportunities at a later stage – including Henry Lavie, whose service to Cauldwell in 1674 led to him being re-employed a year later, as we have seen. When considering merchants taking 'risks' one imagi-nes a direct correlation between risk-taking and level of profit, with bigger risks yielding bigger rewards; taking chances on unfamiliar or uncertain markets, for example, or in buying perishable commodities with no guarantee of sale.[80] Risks were also taken when trusting recommendations and lending money, which as we have seen did not always pay off. Risks were not always taken, though, in pursuit of financial gain. Merchants also took risks in order to cultivate high profile recommendations, which would enhance their reputation and be more beneficial in the long term, increasing their chances of successful business ven-tures in the future. In 1680, Thomas Thomson, a Scottish merchant in Bordeaux who was part of John Clerk's network, sent 200 crowns to Robert Kerr, fourth Earl of Lothian. Thomson sent this money, drawn on a Mr Ellison in Newcastle, although Lothian confessed that he 'had neither bill nor letter of credit which should have come from Rosline, cam somewhat slow'. Despite this, Thomas 'immediately returned me all I desird', prompting Lothian to write to his wife that 'I never saw such a discreet and obligding marchand as that Mr Thomson is'.[81] Though forwarding a large sum of money without a copy of the bill or a letter of credit was a risk, if a calculated one, Thomson benefitted from this transaction as it ensured a recommendation from Lothian, a high profile figure in Scotland, would always be favourable.

Moreover, though the nature of commercial networks was personal, this did not mean that merchants were not shrewd in their business. Those involved in Franco-Scottish trade adopted a level of professionalism even when dealing with family members. In 1590 a list of 'debtis awin me' made by Wedderburne included a sum of £5 27½ merks owed by 'Lady our mother' (Lady Westhall, Wedderburne's mother-in-law), and another list from the 1590s included 'Robert my brother' for £3 and 'James my brother' for £5.[82] The Edinburgh merchant John Charteris noted in his memorandum book money owed to him by his mother, and Pierre Petit, a Bordeaux merchant, listed in 1688 'all the money that has been between my mother and me'.[83] Frequent references to international exchange rates, trading practices and banking methods evidences the professionalism of these commercial agents, despite the private nature of their operation.[84] As already explored, private transactions were recorded in an official manner, even though they did not pass through official channels. Though family members or close acquaintances may have had high expectations of each other, Haggerty argues that these expectations were of a similar nature to all business associates – 'to follow procedural norms, to pay on time, and to give some leeway where necessary'.[85]

Early modern merchants – the successful ones at least – were extremely sophisticated in their understanding of commerce,[86] and the methods they habitually employed in times of peace contributed to their ability to conduct business during times of war. It was unusual for the seventeenth-century merchant to confine themselves to a single market, either in specializing in one commodity or focusing exclusively on one port. Instead, they diversified the commodities they traded in and the locations they traded to in order to take advantage of opportunities as they arose. Alexander Charteris wrote to John Clerk in 1654 that he 'made a journey to Bordeaux, Rochelle and other places in these quarters where I stayed three months much longer than I intended', prolonging his stay to take advantage of unforeseen commercial opportunities.[87] This was common practice throughout Europe, and merchants who thrived in the seventeenth century did so precisely because they did not specialize in a single commodity. In a period before marine insurance became widely used, it was diversification that minimized risk, and it was not until the eighteenth century that specialization in commodities became the norm.[88] Even for merchants who prioritized a certain commodity diversification remained key, seen most clearly in the Franco-Scottish context through evidence exposing the activities of wine merchants. Though Franco-Scottish trade has been seen as synonymous with wine, it has been suggested that in the 1620s Spanish wines were equal in popularity with French wines in Scotland.[89] The Watson brothers of Kirkcaldy imported French and Spanish wines apparently indiscriminately, testifying to the health of the market for wines from both destinations in the 1660s.[90] Those who purchased wine arriving in Leith on the *Rowland of Hambrough* in January 1673 did so from a variety of merchants – though the wine was part of the same cargo. Thus if one importing merchant were to default on an agreement, not all would be lost. Similarly, those who bought wine from this cargo did so in relatively small quantities, having additional interest in other cargoes imported throughout the year (Appendix A).[91] This practice continued throughout the century, and Scottish merchants purchased a range of both French and Spanish wine in the 1680s, including the Marjoribanks family of Edinburgh and Leith who bought wine from Bordeaux and Cadiz.[92] This behaviour complicated merchants' activities but provided an essential guard against loss in a period when international trade remained somewhat unpredictable.

It was not unusual for merchants' commissions to offer a range of commodities or a choice of ports, allowing the merchant to adjust their plans as variances in market or weather conditions dictated. In February 1591 David Wedderburne sent a last of herring to Peter Man 'to be sauld quhair he happenis to mak mercat to my proffit'.[93] Similar instructions were given in August 1593 to Alexander Rankine, entrusted with parcels of bleached linen, and to Wedderburne's uncle Peter Imrie, who was assigned barrels of powder.[94] Writing to Margaret Gray in May 1645 regarding a commission for clothes and textiles, Clerk noted that she 'did not mak choyse off the cullor ye loved best to be your petticot the which being left to my choyse I have sent that which did most content my self', in the same month writing to her mother that 'your Lady did not wreat at what pryce and off what hight ye wold have the pearling for your owne gown, that which I have sent is prettie and weill made and shall be sorie if it be not to your Ladys mind'.[95]

The willingness of Scottish merchants to utilize contacts in a range of locations and their reticence to specialize in a single commodity has led to Scotland's overseas trade being described as 'not so much a policy as a complex ad hoc response by producers and traders to a changing market situation'.[96] More cuttingly, this approach has encouraged evaluations of Scotland's overseas trade as unregulated and opportunistic.[97] The ability of merchants to adapt their itineraries and to take advantage of opportunities as and when they were present, however, contributed to continued success in times of adversity. That this ability suggested sophistication, rather than disorganization, was voiced by Daniel Defoe, who noted in his *Essays upon Projects* (1697) that

> ships are sent from port to port, as markets and merchandises differ ... [exchange of information] and travel makes a true-bred merchant the most intelligent man in the world, and consequently the most capable, when urg'd by necessity, to continue new ways to live.[98]

That merchants were able to make major decisions not only on behalf of themselves but also of their clients is indicative of the need to adapt quickly to changing market situations, but confirms that trust bolstered all of these personal relationships and thus underpinned international exchange.

Business and private associations necessarily merged, but though it is tempting to see 'personal connections' as fostering something akin to our modern understanding of acquaintance or even friendship, this was not always the case in the early modern world. John Clerk did indeed know many of his business associates, preferring to travel frequently to oversee transactions personally. Between 1644 and 1645 he travelled to Edinburgh, London, Dieppe and Paris, with his accounts for this period recording money spent in a great number of locations throughout Britain and France. On several occasions Clerk emphasized his desire to remain mobile, in August 1644 writing, 'I thought to have pairted from Scotland long agoe: I find great scairsty of money but godwilling about the first of September I will be ready to pairt for London whair I intend not to be long'.[99] Personal presence was, Clerk believed, essential to success, and he voiced this belief in November, writing to Sir James Lockhart that 'being present it may be I wold get more done then any uther wold doe in my absence'.[100]

Clerk was one of those merchants who 'carried out every stage of their trading operation personally',[101] but the very nature of the environment within which these traders operated and the ways in which business was managed across large geographical areas meant that a purely individual approach was not always practical. While his extensive movement allowed Clerk to oversee his business matters directly, it also necessitated time away from the heart of his network. Writing after his return to Paris from Edinburgh in May 1645 Clerk lamented that 'since I cam to this kingdome last I have gotten litle rest, my long stay in Scotland by my expectation ocasioned pains and trouble at my returne: which I am wynding my selff out off peice & peice [*sic*]'.[102] Merchants seldom acted entirely alone, instead relying on networks of contacts both at home and abroad. Contrary to Clerk's approach there is no evidence that David Wedderburne ever ventured to any of the European countries he traded with, or that he met any of the factors that facilitated his business; the same is true of the Edinburgh merchant Archibald Hamilton.[103] Wedderburne and Hamilton preferred to remain at home in Scotland, making extensive use of trusted intermediaries to act on their behalf. Whichever method was adopted the large geographical spread of commercial networks meant that a high level of trust, built on credit and reputation, was essential for success.[104] In July 1644 Michel Mel was urged by Clerk to 'pay non of thos billis to any whatsoever unless you knoe the man to whom you pay them'.[105]

Business relationships were based not on friendship or even personal acquaintance, but on commercial reputation. Though based in Rotterdam Andrew Russell facilitated many contacts between Scottish merchants and the factors Popple and Stewart in Bordeaux, and it did not seem to be a concern for merchants that Russell was not geographically based within a community in France. There is no indication that all Scottish merchants trading with Bordeaux ever travelled to Bordeaux themselves, or met Popple and Stewart – or other factors – personally.[106] Despite his willingness to travel, Clerk's approach is not an indication of reticence to trust; his continental commercial networks were extensive, spreading not only back to Scotland but throughout France, Britain and across Europe. Even merchants who handled much of their business in person were dependent on reliable correspondents whom they may never have met in order to make the most of business opportunities, facilitate new contacts and cultivate existing links.[107] Jacques du Cornet acted as Clerk's banker in Bordeaux, enabling business between Clerk in Paris and Scots on the west coast of France: Robert Brown in La Rochelle, Adam Mitchelson in Rouen and William Monteith in Bordeaux.[108] In the space of just three months from January 1644 Clerk, acting as a banker, lent more than 720 livres to Sebastien Jauffray, 422 livres to Monsieur Belm and 145 livres to Jean Perouet, all on recommendations from Henry Hope to whom he also provided finance.[109] There is no indication that Clerk knew these individuals; he explicitly trusted Hope's recommendations. It seems that the use of networks of trusted individuals led to what was described by Defoe as 'strange and universal intelligence' by which 'a merchant sitting at home in his counting-house, at once converses with all parts of the known world'.[110]

V.

Personal relationships were central to commercial networks, and correspondence and recommendations allowed them to be maintained across large geographical areas and over long periods of time. The abilities and methods of the merchants and factors who participated in these networks, coupled with a determination that their activities should not be curtailed by the political climate, contributed to the preservation of Franco-Scottish trade during times of conflict. In pursuing the range of opportunities on offer these merchants acted primarily in their own interests; though unsurprising, this behaviour has contributed to the characterization of such trade as damaging to the state. In 1630 the Convention of Royal Burghs complained of

> the grit hurt the natioun does suffer through occasioun of the factoures abroad who haiveing thair meanes and educatioun frome the merchandis of this countrey yit proves so unthankfull that they becum altogidder negligent of all deutye ather to thair native cuntrey or merchandis, that hes imployed theme, and by maryeing with straingeris becumes altogether alienants and straingeris.[111]

Following the culmination of the Nine Years' War government officials in Rouen voiced concerns that

> since the sole purpose of merchants is to make profits and become wealthy without regard to the welfare of the state, their actions may prove prejudicial to the nation as a whole. The Council [of Trade] therefore, should endeavour to ascertain (and then to encourage) whatever lines of trade are likely to prove most beneficial to the state.[112]

In the aftermath of the War of the Spanish Succession the *Flying Post* reported that 'the private Interest of a few Men' corrupted British trade with France, as there would always be some that 'value nothing but private or particular Gain', which would 'bring a general Calamity upon Trade in all its parts'.[113]

Though the physiocrat François Quesnay contributed to this school of thought and accused the merchant in his *L'Analyse* (1766) of trying to 'make his gain as high as possible at the expense of the nation: his individual interest and that of the nation are opposed',[114] self-oriented merchants did have a positive effect on their native economy even if they may not have intended to do so. On the other side of the eighteenth-century debate, Adam Smith was a supporter of private enterprise:

> By directing that industry in such a manner as its produce may be of greatest value, he intends only his own gain, and he is in this, as in many other cases, led by an invisible hand to promote an end which was no part of his intention. Nor is it always the worse for the society that it was no part of it. By pursuing his own interests he frequently promotes that of the society more effectively than when he really intends to promote it.[115]

As Smith was well aware, merchants directly boosted their home economy through the repatriation of capital back to Scotland. While at times this was incidental to their primary strategy, Scots throughout Europe made deliberate provisions in wills and testament for their homeland, repatriating their wealth posthumously.[116] Much repatriation, of course, took place on a relatively small scale, but larger repatriations are also evident. John Black traded in the *Temperance* of Anstruther between Boston in Lincolnshire and Bordeaux between 1602 and 1603, and in February 1603 shipped 200 quarters of malt and beans from Boston to Leith. His earnings from months of Anglo-French voyages were therefore repatriated to Scotland in kind – demonstrating the economic benefits that Scotland could glean from the commercial activities of her subjects even if they were not directly part of her own national ventures.[117] If we assume that Black was not the only individual to embark on such ventures and eventually return with his earnings to Scotland, Scotland's trading account must have been substantially enlarged as a result. John Clerk's purchase of the barony of Penicuik in 1654 came as a direct result of money he made in France, from beginning as an apprentice in 1634 to returning home a wealthy man over a decade later.

Merchants' methods of trading affected local business practices, influencing the ways in which economies functioned.[118] In 1701 the Aberdeen merchant Robert Gerard wrote to an 'RA' in Bordeaux highlighting the importance of that French port to the manufacture of cloth in Aberdeen, asking his correspondent to 'advise me if thow please what may be most vendible with yow at this tyme'; the types of cloth manufactured in Aberdeen being directly influenced by French trade.[119] Merchant communities developed commercial techniques including double-entry bookkeeping, interest loans and the bill of exchange; the latter began as a way for merchants to exchange vendible goods but later became a practice adopted by governments to move money both domestically and internationally.[120] Thus the effect that expatriate merchants had on their home countries occurred in a variety of ways and may not have been as detrimental as some contemporary commentators suggested. This, too, suggests that these 'flesh and blood' merchants deserve attention, as their activities had a very real impact on economic development and the maintenance of international trade.

VI.

That Scots operated within personalized networks in France and prioritized their own interests is unexceptional, but the issues considered in this chapter offer new perspectives on the Franco-Scottish commercial relationship. Though it has been portrayed as disorganized and *ad hoc*, despite appearances the Scottish merchant community in France had as one of its most striking attributes a high level of organization.[121] The Scottish mercantile community in France did not need to operate within a distinct geographical sphere to be successful. This was not a static community and does not seem to have had the same level of institutional support found elsewhere in this period, but it comprised individuals whose skill ensured that Franco-Scottish commerce continued during the 'crisis' of the seventeenth century.

These skills were twofold. First, these were individuals who were knowledgeable about their business and who were adept at modifying their methods when circumstances dictated. They were used to adapting itineraries at short notice, and their approach to risk saw them avoiding commodity-specific specialization. Second, merchant networks used a range of tactics to allow them to continue to trade during periods of conflict. Clandestine tactics were adopted – including the acquisition of false passes, sailing under 'flags of convenience', or claiming neutral domicile.[122] When the Dutch declared themselves neutral during the British Civil Wars, British ships used Dutch ports as safe havens and traded under Dutch protection.[123] During the Second Anglo-Dutch War both the Edinburgh merchant Henry Wilkie and the London merchant Thomas Culter employed a Swedish ship, the *St John of Congelfe*, to trade between France and Scotland.[124] In addition to using flags of convenience themselves, Scottish vessels were in a unique position to provide them to English ships wishing to travel to France. In 1619 the Privy Council suggested that the best ships of Scotland were unavailable as they were continually employed in the service of Frenchmen. Due to the 'somewhat indeterminate diplomatic status of Scotland', France and England both used Scottish ships to enter waters unavailable to their own nationals.[125] Further, 'the greater affability of the French towards the Scots' provided 'an obvious explanation of the English willingness to employ them in Anglo-French trade'.[126] This reveals an interesting perspective on Anglo-Scottish relations post-1603 as Scottish vessels, drawing on their continuing favourable status in France, provided a service otherwise unavailable to their apparently dominant southern neighbour. We saw in Chapter 1 that in 1607 it was clearly stipulated that the benefits enjoyed by Scottish merchants in France were privileges 'the English cannot atteine'.[127] The ramifications a reassessment of Franco-Scottish trade has for our understanding of Franco-British and Anglo-Scottish relations are explored in the final chapter of this book.

Before attention is turned to specific conflicts, one more element of early modern commerce requires further analysis. The devastation apparently wrought by warfare on trade originated from a combination of legislation including declarations of war, prohibitions on trade and the raising of customs and excise rates. Merchants involved in Franco-Scottish commerce in the long seventeenth century may have been experienced and knowledgeable about their business, but prohibitive legislation provided a seemingly insurmountable obstacle to trade.

3 'THE CUSTOM HOUSE OFFICERS ARE SO AGOG OF SEIZING': LEGISLATION AND COMMERCIAL POLICY

Though the merchants involved in Franco-Scottish trade operated within informal networks, they nonetheless adhered to a set of established traditions and codes of conduct. In addition to these informal rules, their activities were subject to a plethora of official regulations, all of which affected their ability to do business. During the early modern period commerce was regulated in a number of ways – financially through customs and excise rates, and more practically as activity was limited by prohibitions and restrictions on commodities or bans on travel to certain places. In wartime the role played by this legislation was more prominent, as it could be used as a tool by which the exchange of commodities and the movement of people to enemy nations was controlled, either by direct embargoes or through raising customs rates to such a level that they were prohibitive to trade. The very act of declaring war initiated such legislation; at the beginning of the Nine Years' War in 1689 the Scottish Privy Council stated, in declaring war on France, that they forbade 'all the leidges of his Majesties antient kingdom of Scotland to trade, corospond or have any intercourse or medling with the said French King or any of his subjects'.[1] It seems obvious that such legislation would have a negative impact on commerce – indeed the 1689 embargo, coupled with further restrictions on trade, has led to the view that Franco-Scottish commerce was virtually ruined thereafter.[2] The Nine Years' War is examined in detail in Chapter 6, where an alternative assessment is offered – one that sees Franco-Scottish commerce continuing in spite of these restrictions. This reinterpretation relies on, among other things, a considered view of the effectiveness of legislation and commercial embargoes.

Before this assessment can be drawn, a closer understanding must be gleaned of the types of legislation that ostensibly controlled commerce in the early modern period, which have been seen as so instrumental in governing the development – or stifling – of trade links. This chapter delves into the range of motivations behind the implementation of legislation, particularly that which was apparently detrimental to trade. Even during wartime, motivations were far more complex than a desire to cause damage to an enemy's commerce; as already discussed in the Introduction, this was not a period in which war was 'total'. It should not, therefore, be assumed that embargoes on trade were intended to be absolute. Bi-lateral approaches to international trade – examining trade on a national rather than local level – have not always taken regional disparities in commercial regulation into account. The complexities that arose from these inconsistencies inevitably gave rise to confusion among both merchants and authorities concerning how legislation should be implemented. In many cases this confusion was no doubt genuine, but in others merchants took advantage of this lack of clarity, quickly identifying loopholes through which they might profit. Further, although modern observers generally assume legislation to be something implemented from above without recourse to the wishes of those it affected, the merchants and commercial agents with whom we are concerned were not silent bystanders unable to resist the might of the state. Instead, they exercised potentially great levels of influence on national commercial policy; invaluable at times when their business was threatened by wartime restrictions. Finally, the context of the period itself will be considered. In addition to legislation affecting specific elements of commerce, the rise of protectionism profoundly affected the circumstances in which commercial agents pursued trade, playing a crucial role in the maintenance and development of trade routes.[3]

I.

'Prohibitions' or 'restrictions' evoke overwhelmingly negative connotations, particularly during periods of conflict when this negativity was bound up in hostile relations. Many declarations of war – such as the 1689 example cited above – did indeed block trade to enemy nations, and embargoes including that issued by the French on all trade with adversaries in 1703 introduced significant obstacles to merchants.[4] It is, inevitably, possible to identify prohibitive commercial legislation that directly targeted political enemies, including the ordinance passed in France in 1691 'forbidding subjects or foreigners importing goods from enemy countries'.[5] As war progressed, though, it was seen as expedient to avoid inflaming volatile political situations by imposing complete embargoes, instead raising taxes to a level prohibitive to trade. Such attempts to maintain ostensible neutrality while pursuing a specific agenda did not pass unnoticed. The Committee for Trade in the Scottish Parliament in 1698 commented that France

> of late have prohibited the import of Scots goods by Scots men either directly or virtually by impositions equivalent to ane prohibition & as a remedy it is proposed That the import of ffrench goods be discharged until the scots preveledges be restored & those incumberances & havy impositions be taken off.[6]

As the above demonstrates, retaliation was one stimulus for the implementation of commercial legislation. Prior to the outbreak of the War of the Spanish Succession, the Scottish Parliament passed a 1701 act stating that 'tradeing with France may be discharged until they take off the prohibition of importing our herring and imposition upon Salmond and Scots ships there'.[7] Contemporaries recognized the problems caused by retaliatory legislation, and the Deputies of the Council of Trade created by Louis XIV were concerned with the wider impact of these policies, commenting that to forbid imports from England simply because England forbade imports from France 'would be like cutting off both our arms in order to deprive ourselves of the use of one hand'.[8] Though such legislation points towards a context in which prohibitions, particularly in times of conflict, were issued out of malice, many restrictions reflect domestic economic concerns more accurately than international relations, regularly influenced by increasing adherence to mercantilism and protectionist policies.

Trade in several of the bulk commodities that formed a part of Franco-Scottish trade in this period was affected by such policies. In the late sixteenth century, bans on the export of coal (1563) and wool (1581 and 1597) were implemented in Scotland, legislation apparently affecting the country's export trade, economy and overseas commercial relations.[9] These policies though, rather than being aimed at any nation in particular, were a mercantilist device to encourage domestic manufacture by banning the export of vital raw materials.[10] Scotland's salt trade – a major part of the country's trade with France – was controlled by similar strategies. What has been described as a 'golden age' in Scottish salt manufacturing began in the 1570s.[11] As salt production was expanding – and the quality of this salt improving – importation of French salt was controlled in order to encourage further expansion in domestic manufacturing. Fuelling this expansion further were the production struggles experienced by both the French and the Dutch, who had previously been sources for salt imported into Scotland. Though a decline in the importation of salt from France coincided with a perceived cooling of political and diplomatic relations following the events of 1560, this pattern was determined by economic developments – as Edgar Lythe argues, Scotland would have bought less French salt whatever had happened to her crown or church.[12]

As Scotland's salt production fuelled export trade, a dearth of salt available within Scotland led to rising prices and further legislation. On 30 April 1573 Parliament took action against 'the great and exorbitant prices the small salt is lately risen to within this realm' by ordering that 'no small salt be transported out of this realm at any time hereafter, at the least for the space of three years ... providing always that the pain of this act extend not against strangers of Norway and others of the east parts who bring in timber in this realm'.[13] As a prelude to later discussion, it is worth noting that this ban was neither total nor widely adhered to – exports were maintained at record levels from the mid-1570s until

1582, with Scottish shipments of salt to the Baltic peaking between 1576 and 1578. Complaints continued to be made about a 'derth of small salt within this realme' as those involved in production sought 'privat lucre' rather than concerning themselves with the national economy. For salt-makers, desire for revenue from the export trade unsurprisingly remained a greater priority than concern for domestic supplies, and the peak period for the exportation of Scottish salt in the early modern period came in the 1620s and 1630s.[14]

Following this peak market conditions in Europe altered, and by the mid-seventeenth century focus in Scotland had shifted to the question of the importation of foreign salt. The Portuguese Revolt in 1640 'burst the Baltic and Low Countries "bubbles" for the Scots', the Dutch regained control over the international salt carrying trade, and Scots feared being shut out of England as the Tyneside producers' anxiety over Scottish competition led to prohibitively high tariff rates. As a result of the loss of these overseas markets Scottish saltmasters sought to sell a larger proportion of their salt in Scotland.[15] The saturation of the domestic market with Scottish salt led to restrictions on importation, causing problems for several sectors of Scotland's economy that relied specifically on the foreign product; Biscay salt, for example, remained the optimum salt for curing Scottish fish.[16] The Council of Aberdeen sent commissioners to the Convention of Royal Burghs in 1652 with instructions 'to obtane ane libertie for bringing home of salt ... this toune is singular for the mater of salting of fish and speciallie salmond which cannot be saltit without French salt'.[17] By the end of 1665 Scotland was committed to a protectionist policy, adding £12 Scots to each boll of foreign salt imported and stating that only Scottish salt may be used for domestic purposes.[18] Despite this, by 1671 the Council of Aberdeen had succeeded in obtaining permission for foreign salt to be imported as long as it was used only for the curing of fish intended for export.[19] This was reiterated by the Privy Council ten years later, who 'seing the salt manufacture of this kingdom will abundantly serve for all domestick uses' stipulated that 'no forrain salt be allowed to be imported from France except for curing of salmond and Spanish salt for curing of herrings'.[20] During the reign of Queen Anne concerns regarding the effect of this protectionism on various sectors of the economy continued. George Flint wrote to the Earl of Morton, 'I hear the Fishery of this Country is like to be quite lost this year for want of Foreign Sald; & that they intend to apply to the Government for leave to import Foreign Salt from Irland'.[21] Despite coinciding with the War of the Spanish Succession, difficulties in importing foreign salt were affected more by domestic policies than by war with France.

These patterns are reflected in Scotland's wine trade. In February 1650 the Council of Aberdeen, when discussing an 'act anent our wyn customes', stated that 'we will onlie get allowit to us ane hundredth tunes in all ... for ane year' – the amount of wine permitted to be imported was restricted, but trade in the commodity was not prohibited entirely.[22] Similarly, an act drafted in 1701 regulated the amount of French wine that could be imported per annum rather than completely preventing its importation, ceding that wine could be brought in with 'a speciall license from the Lords of his Majesties theasurer'.[23] Though it might seem from the political context that this was conceived as a precursor to the hostilities with France that broke out in 1702, that the embargo was not absolute and that the legislation could be circumvented suggests more complex motivations for its implementation. Trade in a range of commodities was increasingly controlled by protectionism: in 1579, although 'our said soveranis lieges may be first servit' with domestic fish, if 'abundance occurit ... they micht be sellit and transportit',[24] prioritizing domestic consumption by restricting exportation. In 1649 'An Act for Relief of Feltmakers and Hat-band-makers against Aliens and Strangers importing such Wares to the hindrance of their Manufacturers' was passed in order to protect domestic manufacture, and the exportation of native commodities including wool and bear (a hardy variety of barley) was prohibited in 1662.[25]

Regulation of the domestic economy, rather than concern with international relations, was foremost in the formation of economic policy on both sides of the Channel. In 1625 Charles I proposed a new custom on coal exported in foreign vessels but this had little to do with commerce, instead being intended as an additional tax to raise domestic revenue. Unsurprisingly, the owners of the coal-houses on the Forth vehemently opposed the custom, and concerns that trade would fall if this tax was levied led the Convention of Royal Burghs to reject the proposal.[26] In 1638 the Provost, Baillie and Council of Banff ordained that no merchant should 'carrie away furth of the said burgh any merchandice or merchand wair to any landwart pairt to be sold be them except it be to public mercatis and fayres',[27] regulating the ways in which commodities could be traded and thus influencing the development of domestic markets. Louis XIV's first attempt to stimulate France's domestic commercial activity by enforcing payment of the *taxe des éstrangers* (a 2.5 per cent tax on the value of foreigners' goods) in 1643 robbed foreign factors of their commission and reduced their motivation for doing business in France, but the aim of this policy was to eliminate competition to domestic factors rather than being directed explicitly against the foreign factors themselves.[28] Similarly, when the mayor of Bordeaux forbade foreigners from dealing with anyone in France except French merchants in 1653, this was an attempt to protect natives by ensuring that French merchants were involved in every transaction, thus maximizing the return to the domestic economy.[29] In November 1687, a year before the Nine Years' War broke out, a 'Judgement of the King's Council, controlling the entry of foreign draperies into the Kingdom' was passed in France. The importation of foreign cloth was regulated, but no political motives for doing so were cited. Instead, the declaration explicitly sought to eliminate counterfeit goods from the market, as 'foreigners do prejudice the manufactures of the kingdom by making counterfeit linen of the same quality and measures'.[30]

Concerns for domestic economy, manufacture and consumption thus underpinned many pieces of commercial legislation, including those issued during periods of war. Although such legislation was overwhelmingly concerned with commerce, on occasion social concerns played a significant role in its conception. In July 1593 an act was passed preventing the exportation of animal skins from Scotland. One motivation was economic, attributing this legislation to 'how necessary and profitable the schurling skynis ar for lyning cuschenis making of pokis lyning powchis [and] gluiffs', again aiming to stimulate domestic production. Also noted, though, was the use of these commodities for the 'clothing of the puir', highlighting social as well as economic concerns.[31] Shortly before the outbreak of the 1627–9 Anglo-French War, a 1626 act prohibiting the importation of French wines was passed. Obvious motivations included the build-up to war itself, as well as retaliation for the seizure earlier that year by the French Governor of Guyenne of a fleet of 200 English and Scottish vessels transporting wine from Bordeaux,[32] but the reasons cited suggest the influence of social concerns. These included anxiety over the scarcity of money in Scotland, as well as 'the wraik of mony poore people, who, neglecting that trade and calling whairunto thay ar called for winneing of their leving, does unthriftilie spend the most pairt of their meanis in drinking of wyne', and the prohibition was implemented explicitly 'for preventing of whilk abuse'.[33] In 1641 an act prohibiting the exportation of eggs did so as 'it bringis not any considerable moneyes into the country ... Considering the dyet of poore labouring people and servants who eat only bread and drinke water if egges were restrained might be bettered by getting eggis ... at an easir rate'.[34]

Perhaps the most prevalent social motivation for closing trade links was disease. In 1629 the Privy Council of Scotland considered potential danger as Denmark, Sweden, Bordeaux and other places in France, Orkney and Shetland were 'visited with the contagious sicknesse of the pest'.[35] In 1664 Sir George Downing wrote to Henry Bennett from The Hague referring to Scotland's decision to prohibit all trade with the United Provinces for fear of contracting plague; the timing coinciding with the build-up to the Second Anglo-Dutch War but being motivated by public health concerns.[36] The French also acted to counteract dangers from disease, in September 1712 passing an ordinance 'with regulations, on the precautions to be observed in the Ports of France in order to prevent the communication of the contagion which reigns in the North', citing problems in Denmark (Copenhagen in particular) and Sweden, but also following European precedent as 'England and Holland had by decrees of 4 & 16 September 1711 taken precautions to prevent vessels, crew or goods from the North Country spreading disease'.[37] Though enacted during the War of the Spanish Succession, these restrictions represent social concerns rather than political, wartime tactics. Concern for social well-being played at least an osten-sible role in the implementation of these commercial policies, even when the context might suggest political, conflict-driven motivations.

II.

If motivations for developing commercial legislation were complex, so too was its execution. In 1762 the *Universal Dictionary of Trade and Commerce* lamented, 'what a maze our merchants must be in about customs duties ... it is no easy mat-ter for any merchant in this country to be master of this branch of his business'.[38] Though written in the mid-eighteenth century, this sentiment can be applied just as usefully to the period under consideration here, as legislation was not standardized either in motivation or in implementation.

The least surprising complexity is that the same commodities imported from different countries incurred inconsistent charges. In 1644 the import duty on a pint of French wine was 1s. 4d., while on the same amount of Spanish wine it was a comparatively hefty 2s. 8d.; by the 1680s, the excise duty on a tun of French wine was £36, compared to £54 per tun on Spanish.[39] Perhaps more surprising is that rates differed depending on the intended use of goods. In 1657 Spanish wine was liable for import duties of £9 per tun, non-Spanish for £6; all of which was to be paid by the buyer of the wine. If, however, the wine was being bought for the purpose of selling it on, the retailer was liable for a reduced duty of just £1 15s. per tun.[40] Similarly diverse rules applied to other commodities. Following the protectionist policies on salt discussed above, an act of 1681 'anent the prices of French and Spanish salt' stipulated that in order to 'prevent the unnecessary importation of forreigne Commodities and the exorbitant prices that may be exacted from the Leiges', 'the Inland Salt of this Kingdom is sufficient for all other uses except the cureing of Fishes and Beeff exported ... all Importers of French Salt or Retailers thereof ... shall not ... exact more ... then Five punds Scots for the Linlithgow boll of French Salt'. Conversely, 'Importers and Retail-ers of Spanish salt shall not exceed six punds for the Linlithgow Boll'.[41]

That customs rates differed by nation is unsurprising, but there was inconsist-ency at regional and local levels too, with regulations varying between different ports in the same nation. In the case of France this was particularly prevalent, as France did not have a single unified economy but operated explicitly through a number of regional economies.[42] The implementation of legislation differed between these regions, governed by both local tradition and particular cir-cumstance.[43] In July 1605 discussions between the English and Scottish Privy Councils concerning the appointment of two Scottish and two English agents to be sent into France to report on the relative privileges of the Scots and the English stipulated that this included 'all trade with France distinct from the

Bordeaux wine trade'.[44] Bordeaux's political situation, being formally annexed to France only at the end of the Fronde in 1653, explains why rates on imported wine from that port might differ from elsewhere before mid-century, but there were also variances in regulations on wine originating elsewhere in France. In 1573 the Scottish Parliament stipulated the maximum prices imported wine could be sold at; figures that differed depending on the wine's origin (see Table 3.1).[45] This was influenced by the quality of the wine, not simply by location, but whatever the reason the difference in charges presented complex considerations for Scotland's wine merchants.

Table 3.1 Maximum prices imported wine could be sold at in Scotland.

Origin	Maximum price per tun	Maximum price per pint
Bordeaux	£24	12*d.*
'Haultpoyis' (a town in the Bordeaux region)	£22	12*d.*
'Cunyeak' (Cognac)	£20	10*d.*
La Rochelle	£16	8*d.*

Source: 30 April 1573, *Records of the Parliaments of Scotland to 1707*, online at http://www.rps.ac.uk, A1573/4/3.

This pattern continued into the seventeenth century. Rather than stipulating rates on imports 'from France' as a single national entity, in July 1596 the Convention of Royal Burghs discussed 'the lait impost at Deip', which 'is ceissit sen Maij last',[46] suggesting both that this impost was temporary and particular to this port. A commissioner sent to France by the Convention of Royal Burghs in 1601, charged with 'doungetting of the customeis rayssit in France upoun the guide passand thairto further of this realm, contrair the preveldgeis grantit to this natioun and by the auld custome payit of befoir', was instructed to consider goods being exported from Scotland to specific ports, namely Calais, Saint-Valery-sur-Somme, Le Tréport, Dieppe, Le Havre, Rouen and the fledgling French colony of Cayenne.[47] Ports having a particularly significant Scottish presence are notable for their absence – including Bordeaux and La Rochelle. Again in January 1612 the Convention of Royal Burghs suggested the placement of Scottish collectors at French ports, yet only considered ports in Normandy, naming Rouen, Dieppe, Le Havre and Caen.[48] By the mid-seventeenth century, customs discrepancies remained in duties depending on the origin of goods, even those sourced within the same country, as demonstrated by customs charges of 1643 (see Table 3.2).[49]

Table 3.2 Customs duties on goods imported into Britain, 22 July 1643.

Commodity	Amount	Customs duty
Venetian, Florentine or Milan gold and silver thread	12 ounces	3s. 4d.
French and Paris gold and silver thread	11.5 ounces	2s.
Bridges silk	16 ounces	2s.
Paris silk	16 ounces	9d.
Callicoe quilt	1 item	2s.
Satin or silk quilt	1 item	6s. 8d.
French quilts	Dozen	4s. 8d.

Source: Schedule of Commodities to be taxed, 22 July 1643, C. Firth and R. Rait (eds), *Acts and Ordinances of the Interregnum: 1642–1660*, 3 vols (London: H. M. S. O., 1911), vol. 1, pp. 208–14.

Though France's regional economies played some part in these complex regulations, legislation was similarly inconsistent in British ports. In 1633 Charles I granted Edinburgh and Glasgow alone an exemption from wine duty.[50] In England in January 1644, it was specified that the excise on domestic salt had to be paid by the maker, whereas in Scotland the first buyer of the salt was liable.[51] Though these pre-union differences between England and Scotland are unsurprising, they nonetheless contribute to a picture of early modern commercial legislation that is particularly complex. Not only did customs duties differ depending on the commodities imported, the origin of those commodities, or their future purpose, but even depending on the person who physically brought the goods into British ports. In 1647 a tun of wine brought into London by an Englishman was charged £4 10s., whereas the same amount of wine brought in by an alien was charged £6 – similarly, wine brought into any other port by a native was charged £3 per tun, for an alien this was £4 10s.[52]

The complex nature of commercial legislation in this period unsurprisingly gave rise to confusion among both merchants and authorities. In some cases, clarification of regulations was sought. When the Edinburgh merchant George Veitch and his associate James Clerk – son of the prolific John Clerk – sought to import books into Scotland in 1686 they petitioned the Privy Council concerning a duty that had been imposed on bound volumes in 1681. The Council replied that

> it was not understood that the forsaid imposition imposed upon bound books imported was to be exacted off any lawfull books that are out of print or scarce to be had within the kingdome, and therefore the saids Lords does hereby allow the petitioners from time to time to import into this kingdome all lawfull books.[53]

As following chapters will demonstrate at greater length, confusion regarding regulations provided loopholes for merchants seeking to circumvent regulations on the commodities they traded, or the locations to which they traded. Some misunderstandings were perhaps genuine, with Scottish merchants being 'apparently oblivious' to embargoes implemented from London designed to inhibit imports to the British nations from France in the second half of the seventeenth century.[54] It is, however, unlikely that individuals with such sophisticated understanding of their business would be unaware of these restrictions. Rather, Scottish merchants maintained an inherent belief in their continued privileged trading position in France that led them to feel wholly entitled to preferential treatment. As such, Scottish merchants sought to clarify their privileged position in relation to other nations. In the midst of the War of the Spanish Succession the French Board of Trade granted an extension to the passports of Dutch traders, who were at this time the direct enemies of France. Although the same favour was not granted to Scotsmen, several Scottish shipmasters believed that these decrees were applicable to them and in 1712 appealed for the privilege of freely exporting their herring to France as 'the Dutch had this priviledge before the war and we were very unjustly refused it since that the Scots much more than a hundred years agoe were and are all naturalized in France beside the benefit they may demand of a free Commerce'.[55] Not only were merchants aware of their continued privileged position post-1560, they believed that the Franco-Scottish relationship, and specifically its commercial privileges, remained in force after 1707.

Authorities, too, were confused by the multitude of regulations controlling trade, leading to complaints from merchants who felt that they had been treated unjustly. In 1607 Thomas Inglis, merchant burgess of Edinburgh, complained to the Privy Council concerning the difference between the 'bind of Burdeaulz and heich cuntrey wynis'. While importers of the latter had always received 'every fyft tun in the payment of their impoist',

> the takkismen of the customes burdynnis the said complenair with the hail impoist of certane canarie wynis broght hame be tham within theis kingdom, craving als mekle for the canarie as for wyne seck, albeit it be of treuth that the pype of canarie is sevin gallonis les not the pype of seck, and thairfoir the lyke consideratioun proportionallie aucht to be had in the impoist of thir wynis as is had in the impoist of the cuntrey and tun wyns of France.[56]

Such objections persisted. The Aberdeen Council received a complaint in 1676 that merchants were being charged 'with generall letters of horneing when not guiltie' and denounced 'wherby they ware debarred from persutes and defence of their lawfull actions and were forceit to suspend and relax or to compone with the collectors'.[57] Into the eighteenth century merchants continued to criticize what they saw as unlawful actions of authorities. George Flint complained of the ruination of the wine trade of Scotland, as 'the Custom house officers [are] so agog of seizing, that no sooner a Wine ship approaches a porte; But the first that can get aboard seizes her right or wrong, for Importing French Wines'.[58] In addition to grievances regarding misinterpretation of legislation, or overzealous seizure of goods, there were protests over lack of action. In 1608 the Scottish Parliament talked of 'the bipast negligence in not seiking the executioun' of acts against the exportation of coals and 'barkit ledder', as a

> grite nowmeris of personis preferring their privt gayne to the obedience of the law ar not effrayed privatlie and publictlie to transports the saidis commodities To the grite hurte of the commounweele. Thairfore the estaities presentlie conveyed ordains new intimatioun and publicatioun to be maid of the saidis actis.[59]

Legislation was potentially at its most harmful to trade when it was being implemented incorrectly or inconsistently – but this inconsistency benefited merchants who sought to circumvent regulations. In a period where regulations changed rapidly and new legislation was frequently passed, a common excuse for those caught flouting the rules was that they had been ignorant of them, or that they had departed on their voyage before the law had been ratified. In many instances, they were afforded the benefit of the doubt. In 1595, following an Act of Parliament regulating the prices of imported wines, merchants and skippers who had brought wines home that year petitioned the Privy Council to be allowed to sell their goods at the old prices, claiming that they had embarked on their voyages with no knowledge of the change – this was permitted.[60] During the Anglo-French War in 1627, in contravention of an act prohibiting the importation of French wines, several merchants claimed to have brought home these wines 'before ... this restraint could be made known to them', and the wines were permitted to be sold, provided that the customs were paid.[61]

In other contexts the level of punishment received by a transgressor was based on a mixture of luck and circumstance. During the First Bishops' War in 1639 the Marquis of Hamilton seized a Scottish ship laden with salt from La Rochelle. Hamilton asked Sir Henry Vane for advice regarding how the master of the ship should be dealt with, stressing that he found him to be 'a verie honest man swears he neid subscryved the countries covenant and most willingly did sweare and signe that oath and the oath of supremacie'.[62] On this occasion the severity of the treatment received by the merchant would be influenced by his testimony of political loyalty. Though French goods were being transported, that this question needed to be decided at all was a result of domestic hostilities rather than having anything to do with the state of the Franco-Scottish relationship.

III.

Why legislation was conceived, how it varied and how it was interpreted are essential elements to this analysis, but just as important is consideration of who developed it. By definition legislation was implemented by governmental bodies, rather than the wider population affected by it, but merchants, manufactures, retailers and consumers played significant roles in influencing and altering legislation affecting their commerce in this period. They wielded this influence at a number of levels, through petitioning representative bodies such as the Convention of Royal Burghs or the Privy Council but also through direct involvement in policy-making and repeals of prohibitive legislation.

Many commercial agents made use of petitions to voice their disquiet over certain policies. In 1672 the Masters of the Soap Works in Leith protested to the Parliament of Scotland that despite the establishment of domestic soap works and a prohibition on the importation of soap from abroad 'forraigne soape is brought in als great quantitie as ever ... the manufactories of the country is therby absolutely discurraded and ruined'.[63] Despite striving for permission to import foreign salt to cure their fish, and receiving this in 1671 as discussed above, a decade later the saltmasters of Aberdeen submitted a petition to the Council of that port 'craving that all forraine salt may be discharged to be imported except for the curing of fish ... and that they themselves may onlie import quhat is needful for fish'.[64] In the same year the petition of the weavers, spinners and rural domestic producers against exporting wool to France considered both social and economic implications, acting to protect their own ventures but also voicing apparent concern about the state of their nation's society and economy. They maintained that by exporting wool to France and elsewhere Scotland had 'exposed the inhabitants to all manner ofe meanes sillieness vice and debaucherie throw idleness, so we have robbed the poor of their bread and given it to strangers'. The petition cited a 'neglect to improve the product of our oun nation', and the danger that

> the French will set up manufactories with our wool and by stealth import it unto England, And we our selves shall receive our oun back with a heave ... the French in time will fill all the places wherewith we and the English trade in woollen manufactorie.[65]

In this instance, the petition eventually bore fruit; in 1701 Parliament 'discharged the import of cloth that the manufactories at home may be encouraged and the poor rightlie employed'.[66]

A common issue broached in petitions was the perception that domestic conventions did not always support legislation. In 1685 the Incorporation of Tailors of Edinburgh sent a petition to the Privy Council concerning the Act of Parliament forbidding merchants to import foreign cloth, questioning that there was 'noe prohibition nor restraint as to the *wearing* of forraigne cloaths [emphasis added]'. Furthermore, they stated that authorities 'upon pretendit commissiones ... cary away what they find at ther pleasure, soe that by this means your petitioners trade is absolutely ruined, for none will adventure to put any cloathes in their hands'; dissatisfaction being expressed regarding the ways in which these regulations were enforced.[67] Yet there were previous acts restricting the wearing of certain clothes, including that of 1672 'against all persones quha wearis silver or gold leafe silver buttons or louping, striped silks etc ... non of the said commodities ar to be imported ... The said act is to reatche womenis apparel als weill as menis'.[68] That the Incorporation of Tailors of Edinburgh believed this not to have been the case says something further about the effectiveness of the implementation of legislation.

It has been claimed that the most merchants could do was to try to keep commercial objectives to the fore through actions such as petitioning, and that 'even the most powerful merchant groups had no direct control over the state or policy'.[69] Throughout this period, though, individuals at all levels were directly involved in the formation of commercial legislation through both action and consultation. When Louis XIV succeeded to the French throne in 1643 the textile sector was in the midst of a crisis marked by falling sales, dwindling profits and declining production levels. In order to minimize production costs and stimulate the industry, the Languedoc merchants took it into their own hands to transfer the majority of their cloth production into rural areas and out of the hands of urban artisans who were allegedly damaging the quality of cloth – a system of 'putting out' which not only improved manufacture but promoted cheaper manufacturing in the countryside.[70] By taking this initiative the Languedoc merchants contributed to the reinvigoration of an economic sector whose recovery has previously been accredited to the policies of Jean-Baptiste Colbert. Other mercantile groups, on either side of the Channel, acted as consultants, involved at the sharp end of the formation of commercial policy. In 1681 merchants in Scotland were invited to participate in the commercial proceedings of the Privy Council.[71] Similarly the Councils of Commerce established in France by Colbert in 1664 and Louis XIV in 1700 involved members of the commercial classes; Louis XIV appointing thirteen men with 'experience in commercial matters' to act as deputies and advise the controller general and the secretary of the marine.[72] Throughout the following chapters there are examples of merchants succeeding in having embargoes or prohibitions on wartime trading overturned, helping to ensure that Franco-Scottish trade persisted regardless of the political context.

IV.

In addition to acts or ordinances that sought to regulate specifics, developments in approaches to commerce more broadly impacted on trade and both Scotland and France modified their economic policies as the trend towards protectionism continued.[73] In France, of course, mercantilist policies have long been synonymous with Colbert, though there were advocates of this approach in the latter half of the sixteenth century. Many reforms later attributed to Colbert have been identified in Antoine de Montchrestien's *Treatise of Political Economy* (1614) and later in Cardinal Richelieu's *Political Testament* (1624).[74] Henri IV worked towards the development of the silk industry of Tours by prohibiting the importation of Italian silks, though the resistance of the Lyon merchants encouraged him to relax this policy – another example of merchant influence.[75] This was not the only one of Henri IV's policies to be overturned by popular pressure. In 1605 Isaac Bernard, one of Henri's court officials, was granted a ten-year monopoly on the transportation of exported brandies from Nantes. The following year, the municipal authorities sided with the local producers when they protested against this monopoly, and Henri was forced to renounce this privilege.[76]

Although the policies of Henri IV and Maximilien de Béthune, first Duke of Sully, were not always successful, they initiated an economic policy of statebuilding that provided impetus for the mercantilism of Richelieu and Colbert later in the period.[77] In November 1626 Richelieu presented an economic programme to the Assembly of Notables in which he praised the Dutch for their ability to pool resources, blaming the French merchants' lack of success on their propensity to carry on overseas trade as individuals. He concluded, 'we must require merchants to enter large companies, and give them great privileges as [the Dutch] are'.[78] However, his encouragement of trading companies, later emulated by Colbert, met with resistance and ultimately failed – adding fuel to the debate already outlined regarding the relative success of non-governmentally controlled commercial ventures and those of national trading companies.[79] Alongside this failed attempt to prioritize trading companies, Colbert effected many changes in France's domestic economy as he strove to standardize business practice in France.[80] His 1673 *code savary* (code of commerce) detailed rules for apprenticeships and the admission of masters, regulations for bankers and brokers, and instructions for the formation of companies, partnerships and instruments of credit. Colbert also limited rates of interest on loans, hoping to encourage investors to put their money directly into business or commercial enterprise rather than acting individually as bankers or brokers.[81] To consolidate this approach, and in line with the policy of Sully that had been so unpopular under Henri IV, Colbert reduced duties on imports of raw materials and exports of manufactures, instead levying high duties on exports of raw materials and the importation of manufactured goods.[82] The level of Colbert's success, and his effect on French commerce, has been hotly debated elsewhere.[83] In attempting to tackle one of France's biggest problems – her finances – Colbert precipitated economic recovery in some sectors. Notably, when he came to office in 1661 the royal income was approximately 32,000,000 livres p.a., while expenditure was 53,000,000 p.a. At Colbert's death in 1683, income had risen to 94,000,000 p.a. and expenditure fallen to 40,000,000 p.a. Some of the successes attributed to Colbert, however, would not have been possible without the intervention of the commercial classes. Though he has been heralded as ending the crisis in the French textile industry,[84] the intervention of the Languedoc merchants in this sector precipitated recovery, as noted above.

Colbert's reforms caused some problems for France's overseas trade, and his domestic policy must be considered alongside the wartime policies examined in the following chapters. Foreign ships had become accustomed to the advantages of trading with France on the numerous occasions when authorities, prioritizing dynastic or political success, seemed willing to sacrifice the interests of their native merchants and shippers.[85] Under Colbert, this changed as protectionist measures temporarily closed ports, though native mariners continued to suffer as a 'hot and cold' shipping policy damaged French interests.[86] In fact, although external war later in the century disrupted trade to some degree, it has been argued that the nationalistic economic policies developed by Colbert had by this time already affected Franco-Scottish trade – for example, the abolition in 1663 of the exemption granted to Scots from the 50 sous per ton levy imposed on foreign imports.[87] Theodora Keith describes Colbert's implementation of his mercantilist system as the moment from which 'the exemptions which the Scots had formerly enjoyed were gradually disregarded', suggesting that Scottish trade with both the French and the Dutch 'suffered severely' as a result of these policies.[88] The new tariffs imposed by Colbert at the conclusion of the Franco-British war of 1666–7 were not wartime policies, but apparently affected both Scottish and English merchants' activities as almost all duties were increased significantly (Appendix B).[89] England, however, was the target of these tariffs. In 1698 a French memo emphasized that the tariffs were specifically applicable to 'the entry into France of goods and commodities from *England* or from the *English* trade [emphasis added]'.[90] As we will see, French attitudes towards British commerce during conflict are testament to the fact that Scottish and English merchants were treated independently. While the deputies of the 1700 Council of Trade maintained that Colbert had helped overseas trade by simplifying tariffs, subsidizing shipping and shipbuilding and challenging the maritime supremacy of the Dutch and English, they believed that merchants should be granted more freedom and disagreed with Colbert's policy of regulation and control as 'commerce is presently too constrained both internally and externally

... it is this lack of freedom rather than a shortage of capable merchants which cripples overseas trade and navigation'.[91]

Though France and Colbert are particularly implicated in the rise of protectionism in early modern Europe, Britain's own economic policies played their role in influencing European trade patterns, as already considered in relation to her salt trade. Charles I's liberality with corporate monopolies, particularly in staple domestic commodities such as salt and malt, caused discord among independent commercial agents; this was a trend begun under James VI who had granted 700 monopolies by 1625.[92] James VI endeavoured to bring Scottish practice in line with English, attempting at his final Privy Council before he went to London in 1603 to prevent merchants from freighting foreign bottoms. Following his continued desire to bring Scotland and England under a common rule, in 1615 James proclaimed again that only native vessels should be used as British shipping was not being utilized to its full capacity, resulting in ships laying idle in port. Though supported by the Privy Council in the belief that this legislation would bolster the shipping industry,[93] his proclamation was met with protest from Scottish skippers. The Royal Burghs objected that other countries, notably France, might retaliate to such legislation. In response, James argued that the French would still need to sell wine each year and so would not refuse to send it to Scotland on Scottish ships.[94]

In this incident the wishes of Scotland's mercantile agents appear to have been all but ignored, and under Cromwell and the aggressive mercantilism that followed Scotland, was not, apparently, treated as an equal. The English protectionist lobby succeeded in having the Scottish marine reassigned 'alien' status in a new series of acts including the 1660 Navigation Act, the 1662 Act of Frauds and the 1663 Act for the Encouragement of English Trade, excluding foreigners from the import trade of England except as carriers of their own commodities. Though aimed particularly at the Dutch these acts excluded Scottish traders from further participation in English colonial and domestic trades and imposed inflated duties on the movement of cattle, sheep, corn and salt from Scotland to England.[95] Scottish retaliation, in the form of the Scottish Navigation Act of 1661, included import embargoes and colonial and fishery schemes but 'failed to produce a workable homespun version of mercantilism'.[96] Later in the century, attempts in Scotland to harden mercantilist policy included further bans on the co-ownership of vessels with foreigners in an effort to resurrect the domestic shipbuilding industry. In 1681 the Privy Council compelled any Scottish owners of multinational ships to 'sell their partes to forraigners or forraigners their partes to Scotsmen'.[97] In the same year a Council of Trade was revived under James, Duke of York, the Lord High Admiral of Scotland, intended to recover Scotland's prosperity by stimulating an export-orientated carrying trade while actively discouraging imports with heavy customs tariffs – bringing Scotland in line with the developed European mercantilist system.[98]

Though this system apparently disregarded Scottish desires and hindered the country's commerce, Scots acted to evade those policies with which they disagreed. Despite the continued discouragement of the acquisition of foreign ships by the 1660 Navigation Act, a large number of Dutch ships were purchased, and Scottish skippers had foreign-built ships registered as Scottish.[99] There was precedent for such practice: in July 1626 several Scots who owned Flemish-built ships had them inspected by the Master and Brethren of Trinity House in England and certified as Scottish,[100] and in 1629 the *Seaventure* of Kirkcaldy was recorded as a 140-ton Yarmouth-built vessel.[101] Again, however, economic policies were altered when they were deemed to cause too much harm domestically. In 1663 restrictions were issued on the importation of Scottish and Irish cattle into England. The following year the English Council of Trade recommended that these regulations be relaxed as they apparently damaged the English market. Scottish cattle continued to be imported and in 1667 were officially freed from the earlier restriction.[102] Major legislation such as the Navigation Acts has been assumed to have been implemented fully, but this was not the case, due in part to merchant influence and in part to governmental awareness of the importance of domestic economic stability. As examination of Franco-Scottish trade during specific conflicts will show in practice, Scottish merchants did not heed these exclusive, mercantilist policies; they continued to pursue multinational trading ventures in ships of all origin, prioritizing the accomplishment of lucrative commerce over national economic strategies.

We have seen the scope of merchants' activities and influence in shaping the legislative framework, but even more crucial to our understanding of commercial development were the social and cultural contexts within which trade took place. Though assessments of the historic Auld Alliance emphasize France's dominance as the superior partner in this association (particularly from an economic point of view), at the beginning of the seventeenth century France remained 'tragically underdeveloped' with a 'tiny and ineffective' merchant and war fleet and disparate regional and local economies.[103] In addition, negative attitudes prevailed in France towards participation in trade. While the *noblesse* were never officially excluded from commerce, entrenched attitudes discouraged their participation until at least 1664, when an edict was passed that permitted nobles to enter the East and West India Companies and the customary laws of Brittany and the privileges of Lyon recognized that nobility and business were compatible.[104] Despite this progress – fostered under Colbert and reiterated formally in 1669 – these attitudes still prevailed in France at the turn of the eighteenth century, at which time one of the deputies of the Council of Trade noted that 'one has only to become a merchant to be held in contempt'. By contrast, noted the deputies, the English (and the Scots) had a much healthier attitude to trade, with nobles frequently apprenticing their younger sons to merchants. It was not uncommon for these sons to become wealthier than the eldest, who had inherited the family estate.[105]

Further, though France was fortunately placed geographically, with a long coastline and a large sea-faring population, her infrastructure was not conducive to successful mercantile activity.[106] The French crown manipulated the coinage, spent little on roads and canals, and distrusted the middlemen who would have allowed trade to extend into the countryside – hence why the textile merchants of Languedoc took matters into their own hands in outsourcing cloth production to rural areas after 1643. Historically, the protectionism exhibited by the guilds in France was condoned, and as a consequence goods were heavily taxed, competition was limited among manufacturers and the price of French goods remained high and therefore unattractive to potential foreign buyers.[107] The willingness of the French to allow their strongest economic competitors – the Dutch – a monopoly over the carrying trade in the first half of the seventeenth century was arguably an effect of France's inherent economic weakness, though under Louis XIV this monopoly was countered and with the exception of Baltic traffic most French commerce (including colonial trade) was being carried in French ships by 1690.[108] In the regions in which France did have some success in commerce and manufacturing this was limited and often temporary – Lyon was the focal point for European finance and Italian trade in the sixteenth century, but her status declined following the Wars of Religion and the development of more accessible financial markets elsewhere.[109] Trading centres such as Rouen, Nantes, Bordeaux and La Rochelle could arguably not compete with those of Antwerp, Lisbon, Seville and Amsterdam, and none of the merchants in France generated enough business to have a significant impact on regional or national economy.[110] Though the Auld Alliance has been portrayed as one-sided, with the more economically powerful France contributing more than Scotland, this disparity is perhaps less apparent than previously thought.[111] The continuation of Franco-Scottish commerce after 1560 must be considered against this context.

V.

A range of legislation governed early modern commerce, from prohibitions and embargoes to customs charges. Though such legislation may seem to be particularly commensurate with conflict, a range of motivations shaped its implementation. These motivations were not always borne out of international affairs; even when restrictions coincided with conflict they frequently reflected domestic concerns. Legislation that outwardly restricted trade incites conclusions that commerce was necessarily hampered as a result, but whatever lay behind its implementation it was not always upheld. Failure to apply legislation successfully was brought about in part by the complexities inherent in regulations, allowing both merchants and authorities to take advantage of loopholes to pursue or encourage trade at times when exchanges were banned. More significantly, merchants were not idle bystanders who could do little to prevent the impact of legislation on their business, but were active participants in its formation who influenced policy-making to their own ends. That merchants wielded this influence is indicative of governments' tractability, as well as the interdependence of early modern economies. Indeed, rulers tolerated – even encouraged – the continuation of 'illegal' trade during the conflicts of the long seventeenth century because they recognized the importance of constancy in international commerce to domestic stability.

Previous conclusions regarding the impact of conflict on international trade links, particularly in the Franco-Scottish relationship, need to be refined. A linear approach to exchange necessarily relies on national circumstance, but regional variations suggest that we might learn more from consideration of local as well as national patterns. Indeed, throughout the coming chapters the importance of appreciating the local context becomes increasingly apparent. More immediately, in prioritizing the activities of the people at the centre of international exchange – the merchants, skippers and factors at the coalface – a different picture emerges, one in which the realities of trade do not reflect the apparent truths revealed in official legislation or trading figures. The following chapters apply the frameworks introduced throughout Part I to specific conflicts, reassessing traditional interpretations of the impact of war on Franco-Scottish and -British trade in the long seventeenth century.

4 'FIRE THAT'S KINDLED WITHIN DOORES': THE BRITISH CIVIL WARS AND INTERREGNUM, 1639–1660

The London merchant James Battie wrote in 1648, following a decade of civil war in Britain:

> Now there is no greater enemy to Trade than War, be it in what Countrey it will ... Yet forraigne war is not so great a disturber of Trade, nor halfe so destructive, as intestine; For as the fire that's kindled within doores, and in the bed-straw, as it were, rageth more violently: so civill War ruines Trade faster than any other.[1]

Battie's claim that trade was ruined by warfare is one that has persisted into the modern academy, contributing to a generation of scholarship asserting that the seventeenth century was one of 'general crisis'.[2] As discussed in the Introduction to this volume and developed throughout Part I, however, not all sectors were affected in equal measure by the events of this period. As Part II will now demonstrate, despite the inclement political context and the numerous wars that raged, international commerce not only continued but remained robust and lucrative. This owes much to the actions and abilities of mercantile agents themselves, as they not only worked to maintain business links but acted to influence governmental policy regarding commerce. Equally, it is worth re-emphasizing that this was not an era in which political leaders sought to destroy international commercial links – to do so would be counter-productive. Early modern national economies were interdependent and motivations for implementing economic legislation, even during periods of war, owed as much (if not more) to domestic than to international concerns. There are many examples in the analyses that follow of mercantile agents receiving formal support for their actions, even if this contravened official wartime policy. Though Battie, at least for the purposes of his polemical pamphlet, believed that war was trade's greatest enemy, mercantile agents and networks had other ideas, ideas that were frequently sanctioned by authorities.

Subsequent chapters will examine the extent to which 'forraigne wars' disturbed trade, but first we will consider more closely Battie's assessment of the effect of 'intestine' wars on foreign exchange. Both France and Scotland experienced significant bouts of internal strife during this period. In France, this included the Wars of Religion (1562–98) and the Fronde (1648–53). The former arguably 'killed the only major centre of international commerce and finance' and 'paralyzed French economic initiative in the critical latter half of the sixteenth century',[3] while the latter has been described as going hand in hand with severe economic crisis in France.[4] In March 1596 the Scottish Parliament outlined its concerns that

> Quhill now of lait that sindrie Impoistis and Exactionis hes bene rased of the guidis of the saidis maircheantis of this realme, be ressoun of the civile trouble and Insurrectioun quilk hes Intervenit within the cuntrey of france thir divers yeiris bigane, be the qlk forme of doing his majestie finding the said auld league tobe sumquhat infringeit and alterit and the saidis maircheantis of this Realme thairby gritlie prejugeit.

These concerns prompted instructions to John Lindsay of Balcarres, James VI's secretary, to go to France 'to procuir at his said darrest brutheris handis a speciall discharge of the saidis impostis and exactionis and to have the auld liberties and previlegeis of the saidis mercheantis of this realme observit'.[5] Despite the potential effect of France's civil wars, belief in the Auld Alliance and the ongoing benefits it fostered persisted. Merchants' activities reflected this persistence. David Wedderburne, who featured in Chapter 2, observed early modern merchants' adherence to diversification and had a number of outlets for his business, his account book indicating links with Norway, the Low Countries, France and Spain.[6] Though he had clear alternatives to use if needed, Wedderburne did not avoid exchanges with France and instead maintained productive business interests there throughout the Wars of Religion. Using known contacts and networks, the commodities Wedderburne exchanged and the places in which he did business remained constant during times of peace and war.[7]

During the Fronde, too, perceived economic impact prompted the concerns of Scottish merchants with business interests in France. In 1653 Michel Mel wrote from Dieppe to Sir Gilbert Menzies of Pitfodels that

> heir we have the civill wars the prince of condi with a strong army cum near al saith but has retired & we houp sal not harme uss any more ... at see the dangers ar much great for we have nothing bot taking of schips ... the marchands have nead of a more setled tyme god graunt it.[8]

Despite Mel's concerns regarding the impact of the Fronde, this is the only time he mentions the conflict in this correspondence, instead prioritizing business discussions.[9] As will be seen throughout this chapter, mid-century events in neither France nor Scotland brought a halt to economic exchange. Mel himself, as seen throughout Chapter 2, maintained a lucrative business regardless of such occurrences. The dearth of references to conflict in Mel's correspondence follows a pattern found in other collections of mercantile records from this period, in which mention of the impact of warfare is rare. Throughout both the Wars of Religion and the Fronde Scottish merchants found ways to continue their business in France, ensuring that Franco-Scottish trade remained healthy.

While more could be said about the impact of events in France on trade with Scotland, the focus of this chapter is on domestic events within Britain, as a precursor to discussion of the broader British elements to Franco-Scottish trade in Chapter 7. It is inevitable that a lengthy, widespread conflict such as the British Civil Wars impacted on overseas commerce, but the nature and extent of this impact requires detailed consideration. This chapter first considers the British Civil Wars, identified here as the period between the outbreak of the First Bishops' War in Scotland in 1639 and the execution of Charles I in 1649. Obstacles that presented themselves to merchants as a result of this conflict are considered, before the realities of continuing trade are presented. In addition to considering the direct impact of this conflict on Franco-Scottish trade, consequences for the continuing political relationship between Scotland and France are explored further. Indeed, as advocated throughout this volume, the impact of any conflict cannot be fully understood without taking the wider context into consideration. As Mack P. Holt writes in reference to the French Wars of Religion, 'the principal difficulty in assessing the economic impact of half a century of civil wars is distinguishing between what was the result of civil wars and what was simply the result of half a century'.[10] Following investigation of the civil war period, this chapter turns to consider the impact of the Interregnum on Scotland's overseas trade. Though not a period of 'conflict' in quite the same way, between 1649 and 1660 there were numerous changes in domestic government, creating periods of uncertainty in which mercantile agents were forced to revise their approaches to trade as the parameters within which they operated were adjusted.

I.

Contemporaries and modern scholars alike have considered the British Civil Wars as economically detrimental to Scotland. The local effect of the wars made itself evident – the Council of Aberdeen petitioned central government in 1654 lamenting that as a result of the debt created by war 'this place is become so miserable that almost ther is non in it that can subsist or have any liveing'.[11] Financial repercussions of 'the late troubles' remained prevalent in this port city until August 1675, when thirty-two noblemen and heritors of Aberdeenshire consented to a tax on ale, beer, wine, brandy and strong waters 'for relief of the publick debts' that had resulted from the conflict.[12] Voltaire focused on the impact of civil war south of the Tweed, commenting that 'this civil war ... prevented England for a time from interesting herself in the concerns of her neighbours, she lost alike her prosperity and her reputation; her trade was suspended'.[13] Modern accounts focusing on Scotland see the Civil Wars as having 'retarded national industrial development'.[14] Indeed, in some regions Scottish trade did stagnate during the civil war years. While an average of ninety-eight Scottish ships per year sailed through the Scandinavian Sound between 1625 and 1630, this figure significantly dropped to fifty-six between 1644 and 1649.[15] Closer to home, trade through the commercial centre of Aberdeen fell in the 1640s from an average of 126 ships per year between 1620 and 1625 to just eighty-three between 1643 and 1649.[16] This trend, replicated across Aberdeen's entire import and export trade in this period, was reflected in voyages to and from France (see Figure 4.1).[17] These figures suggest a notable fall in exchanges between Aberdeen and all locations in France during the civil wars.

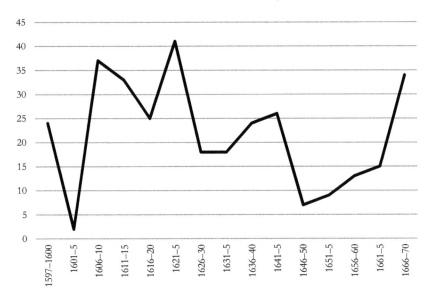

Figure 4.1: Voyages between Aberdeen and France, 1597–1670.

In recent years focus on the impact of the British Civil Wars has moved away from questions regarding the consequences of fighting a conflict on home soil for economic, industrial and demographic development and towards consideration of the effect of naval conflict. Recent research has given much needed attention to the threat posed to the flow of trade by the actions of contesting parties, as well as to the involvement of foreign powers in what was a domestic crisis.[18] In November 1639, a ship belonging to Gilbert Aikman was 'taken by the Irish frigatis and dunkirkeries' who had worked together since the beginning of the conflict; Ireland's privateering armada was almost exclusively composed of Dunkirk frigates.[19] Though this lost him a cargo worth 3,000 merks, plus an additional 16,000 merks worth of salmon, Aikman was not deterred from pursuing his trade. Nine years later his determination was rewarded with more suffering when his ship, containing fifteen lasts of salmon, was taken.[20] These personal losses contributed to public declarations of concern, including a report made to the Council of Aberdeen in 1640 of

> the imminent danger we now stand in, we thought gude first to let yow know that the Englishe (whether freebuitters or the kingis ships we know not) have takine sindrie of our Scotishmen comming from Holland and France and have confiscate ther gudis and schippis stript ther men naked and used them with all kynd of hostilitie.[21]

These dangers were reported at regular intervals throughout the 1640s. In 1645 Thomas Cunningham observed that Scotland's staple ships were 'affrighted from comming to Sea because of the many Irish and other men of warre, and for want of convoyes from Scotland', the net result being 'the great prejudice of trade not only to the Staple but also to France and other places'. When Cunningham visited Scotland in 1648 he observed 'a very great quantity of all sort of native commodities lying upon merchants hands ready to spoile in Scotland, for not daring to venture them in regard of the many Irish, and Dunkirk pirates'.[22]

The danger described here manifested itself in personal losses for some mercantile agents. The case of John Slowane and Adam Mitchelson was heard in the Scottish Parliament on 16 April 1644, following their supplication to the Convention of Estates. Both merchant burgesses of Edinburgh, they had loaded a ship belonging to James Reddie, skipper in Burntisland, with wine in Bordeaux. On their way back to Scotland the ship was taken at St Martin by John Tisone of Dartmouth, who was 'imployed and direct out be his majestie'. The ship, wine, skipper and all of the ship's company was 'takin by his majesties warrant be reason of the common cause now in hand, covenant and reformation' to Dartmouth; Slowane and Mitchelson suffered personal losses of £18,124 Scots. Though the Estates declared that 'his majesty's rents, customs and casualties are and shall be liable in payment to the supplicants of what shall be found they have lost by the taking of their ship and goods', Slowane and Mitchelson were nonetheless severely inconvenienced by this incident. Their financial losses may have been reimbursed, but their business was interrupted by the rigmarole of petitioning for reparations and awaiting an outcome.[23] As the wars progressed these incidents continued to be reported. In 1648 the Dunkirkers sank a ship belonging to Gilbert Andersone that was en route to Bordeaux, Andersone losing twenty tuns of wine 'caste away in Bichebay'. In the same year, Andrew Burnet's 'schip belonging to the Forth' was taken to Dunkirk with forty-five lasts of salmon and the merchandise ransomed for 26,000 (currency not specified).[24]

The effects of these incidents on Scottish commercial activity were compounded by retaliation. In July 1649 John Gillespie was given a commission by Parliament 'for pursueing the Irish friggots and uther enemys of this kingdome by sea' in his vessel the *Elizabeth* of Kirkcaldy. His commission permitted him to 'protect secur and defend all the merchand schips of the kingdome in the exercesing of thair laufull trade from the violence and wrongs of the Irish frigotts and piratts and all other pirrats and sea robbers whatsoever'. The granting of this commission was justified due to

> the great losses susteaned by diverse merchandis of his kingdome through the taking of thair schipps by irish friggots Pirrats haunting upon the coast of this kingdome and elswhair to the obstructing of the trade merchandize and utter ruine of many merchands.[25]

Merchants of all of the British nations targeted, and were targeted by, each other during the Civil Wars. Periods of ceasefire were equally fraught with danger, as ships that had been deterred from sailing during the conflict suddenly took to the seas. In October 1640 there was 'ane cessation fra Warres both be sea and land for tua moneths and libertie to pass and repass during the said space',[26] prompting a report that 'mony schippis tane the seas being very full'.[27]

It was not only direct threats to their vessels, cargoes or persons that caused concern for Britain's merchants as civil war raged. The need for men and ships to contribute to the war effort hampered commerce as the Covenanted Parliament pressed merchant ships into service as troop transports, victualling ships and convoy escorts. In order to ensure the availability of shipping, William Keith, sixth Earl Marischal of Scotland, ordered in April 1640 that ships in Aberdeen should be stripped of their sails in order to keep them in port. However, those reliant on their shipping for their livelihoods had other ideas, as reported by John Spalding: 'under feir the tounes covenanteris wold flie ... many tounes men, heiring of Marischallis cuming to the toune, takis the flight'.[28] Despite its limited initial success, this policy continued throughout the conflict, becoming particularly prevalent following the signing of the Solemn League and Covenant in 1643. After February 1644 the Committee of Both Kingdoms, the executive body of this confederation, officially took responsibility for all foreign policy including military and naval matters.[29] On 21 February an ordinance was passed 'to enable the Lord High Admiral to press Mariners, Saylers, and others for the service of the Navy' seemingly indiscriminately:

> the Lord High Admirall of England ... may at any time or times from the date hereof, unto the first day of January 1645 ... raise, levy, and impresse such and so many Marriners, Saylers, Water-men, Chirurgions, Gunners, Ship-Carpenters, Caukers, and Whoymen, as also Carmen for carriage of Victuals etc. as shall be requisite and necessary for the service aforesaid.[30]

Those who evaded impressment encountered problems of their own that threatened commercial activity. In attempts to suppress rebellion within Britain, freedom of movement was curtailed. In 1645 the Scottish Parliament cited the specific concern of domestic uprising in decreeing that 'no person whatsoever [may] transport themselves forth of this kingdome to Ireland, or any other place, without a sufficient passe granted by the Committee of Estates'.[31] The motivation behind such legislation was emphatically domestic, but restrictions on travelling to 'any other place' presented problems for merchants and skippers whose mobility was key to their success. Furthermore, the actions of soldiers damaged the state of trade at home, as 'under the pretence of the libertie that suldiors claims to traid in any part of the thrie dominions all sort of unfrie people have usurpit the libertie and priviledgs and traid at ther pleasur and bear no part of the common burdens'.[32]

Though the requisitioning of men and ships provided some of the paraphernalia necessary for war, money was needed to fund the cost of fighting in a period in which this cost was increasing.[33] The merchant class was an easy target from whom to extract the necessary revenue. In September 1643 an ordinance was laid 'for the speedy raising and levying of moneys by way of charge and new-impost, upon the severall commodities ... for the maintenance of the Forces raised for the defence of the King, Parliament, and Kingdom, both by Sea and Land'.[34] Four months later a new excise was raised on both native and foreign commodities 'for the maintenance of the Armies raised in defence of the King and Parliament ... the Navy cannot be sufficiently maintained out of the Revenue of the Customes'.[35] This included new rates on wine, strong waters and salt, commodities familiar to Franco-Scottish exchanges. Once raised, armies needed sustenance, leading to constraints on the export of victual. In 1644 it was decreed that

> all meanes be used for provydeing of victual for maintenance of the armies ... [Parliament] doe thairfore ... inhibit All his majesties subjectis of what ranke and qualitie soever That nane of them presoome nor tak upon hand efter the date heirof To transport out of the Kingdome anie maner of victual wheat beare oatis meale or ry.[36]

The implementation of new excise taxes to raise revenue for war was a regular occurrence, by 1649 being seen as 'the most equal and indifferent levy that can be laid upon the people'.[37] Presumably, merchants saw the increased costs to their business as neither equal nor indifferent.

Perhaps unsurprisingly, commercial agents abroad retained an interest in the development of conflict at home. John Clerk wrote to John Murray from Paris in 1640 that 'sum agreement is past Betuixt the noble men of England, and the Scotts commissioners at Rippon in England sum 4 myles fra Boroubrigs. First, a Cessation of Armes by Both Armies. Second, a trade to be made open for both kingdoms'. He added a postscript that 'in respect that nou the passage is open to Scotland, Letters will cum more frequently as Before ... If I had knouen all this tyme whair ze had Bein I wold have wreatte more frequently: off the passages of our Countrie'.[38] Though retaining an interest in events at home and suggesting commercial benefits of a potential ceasefire, Clerk was primarily concerned with interruptions to correspondence, rather than trade. Problems with the exchange of information plagued Clerk throughout his residence in France, though at no other point are these blamed on the political context. It is, indeed, worth reflecting that not all of the problems merchants had to contend with during the civil war period were caused by the wars themselves.

Instead, many issues were symptomatic of the very nature of conducting international business during the early modern period. Writing from Edinburgh to Dieppe-based Michel Mel in 1644, John Clerk bemoaned that

> the first and second bill ... ar miscairied and I cannot learne what is becum of them so they have assingd me only to the third bill which I have in my hand and cannot send forward till I cum my selff fearing they be losd also then I have nothing to showe for the money.[39]

The miscarriage of this paperwork was not attributed to ongoing civil strife. Delays were not uncommon, particularly when goods were carried in person as was the case with many of Clerk's transactions. In May 1645 Clerk wrote apologetically to Lady Pittendrum that, for 'the want off a bearer', the goods she commissioned took so long to send to her.[40] Six months later Clerk experienced further problems in the exchange of information, writing to Janet Gray that he had

> resavet a letter fra Mr William Rires date at Newliston, 6 September last, in which he wreat that long ago he had wreatten to me & then sent a letter ye wes pleasd to honor me with. I have never sein it, sorie it is unhapily miscairied, since I beleve it wes the first. At this tyme I have wreattein to Mr William to informe me how and what way and with whom he sent his letters, to the end I may use means to discover them.[41]

Though the civil wars had some impact on commerce, not all problems experienced by commercial agents can be attributed to continuing conflict. The nature of doing business in the early modern period, particularly across international borders, presented its own challenges that merchants were fully adept at dealing with. As already suggested in Chapter 2, this ability stood merchants in good stead when seeking to continue their activities during periods seemingly hostile to commerce.

II.

Drawing on their aptitude for dealing with adversity, mercantile agents ensured that Franco-Scottish commerce continued during the 1640s despite the obstacles explored above. Though some ports experienced a fall in the volume of overseas trade during this decade, including Aberdeen as we have seen, patterns were not nationally uniform, emphasizing once more the importance of considering regional variations. There was little change in the amount of trade passing through Dumbarton during the civil war years compared to the 1620s. Indeed, there was a slight increase in activity with eight ships on average per year being recorded between 1643 and 1648, compared with seven on average from 1620 to 1625.[42] In some larger ports, too, merchant activity remained healthy. In order to receive full commercial privileges (including the right to import goods from Europe), merchants were required to be registered as guild brethren. Figures for these registrations in Glasgow suggest that the civil wars did not deter merchants from pursuing overseas trade. Between 1610 and 1615, 101 merchants registered as guild brethren in this port. Between 1645 and 1650 this figure was slightly higher at 104. Thereafter, the number drops slightly, to ninety-nine between 1675 and 1680 and ninety-eight between 1700 and 1705.[43] The number of merchants participating in Glasgow's trade thus remained fairly constant, and these figures are suggestive of the continued optimism maintained by the trading classes regarding the viability of commerce despite sustained conflict at home.

In addition to continued optimism that their typical trade was able to continue, opportunities arose for commercial agents to profit as a direct result of conflict. Some, like John Gillespie, turned to privateering; others offered assistance to the government in other ways. Many who fought in the British Civil Wars, particularly in Scotland, were veterans of European conflicts who needed to be transported from the continent back to Britain.[44] This facilitated opportunities for merchants, as those transporting soldiers on behalf of the state were permitted a return journey custom free.[45] Among the merchants to profit from this provision was Michel Mel, as John Dougall reported to John Clerk in 1642, 'he hes fraight the ship that is heir cum over with the souldiers to goe to the Rochell for salt and also one uther ship that is coming from Scotland heir to goe to St Mallos or any uther pairt aux environs to load with cornes if they are cheap'.[46] Those in military or diplomatic roles sought other services provided by expatriate merchants and bankers. In 1643 William Douglas, a captain in James Douglas's regiment, borrowed 670 francs from Robert Murray, a merchant in Paris.[47] The French ambassadors, too, made use of these services – in 1647 Montereul reported to Cardinal Mazarin that 'I offered Sir Robert Moray to pay him at present four thousand crowns, which M. du Talmon, merchant, has kept ready for me', though Moray did not wish 'to receive the money before the bill of exchange falls due'.[48] Opportunities to profit from the conflict continued following Charles I's execution. In April 1651 James Bruce wrote to the Earl of Lothian from La Rochelle that 'he had procured a cargo of materials for his majesty's army, which would be sent upon the engagement that it should be paid in Scotland, with the freight of the ship'.[49] Bruce offered his assistance to the Royalist cause in supporting Charles II's claim to the British thrones, but ensured that he would benefit from his contribution whatever the outcome.

Though there were opportunities to profit as a result of the war effort, the majority of merchants continued to achieve financial success by operating within the commercial networks and communities they had previous ties to. In addition to keeping Clerk abreast of activity within his network, John Dougall was one of several itinerant Scots who embarked on commercial missions despite hostilities in the British Isles, and like so many merchants in this period he was not averse to changing location in order to achieve the best profit. Letters to John Clerk in 1636 see him at Rouen, but in 1643 he is in Dieppe, and correspondence from later in that year places him in Le Havre.[50] Similarly, William Erskine, the individual who proved such a disappointment to John Clerk, appeared in Orleans, Angers, Geneva, Marseille and Lyon in the space of eighteen months between February 1644 and October 1645, though given his history it might be speculated that this movement was to evade pecuniary accountability rather than to pursue legitimate business opportunities.[51] Either way, Scottish merchants remained active throughout the 1640s, facilitating trade along Franco-Scottish routes as discord persisted at home.

Charter parties and commissions continued to be drawn up regarding imports of commodities from France into Scotland. In the brief hiatus between the Pacification of Berwick (1639) and the outbreak of the Second Bishops' War (1640) Alexander Dick, collector of customs at Burntisland, acknowledged the payment of customs on salt from La Rochelle by skipper burgess Robert Angus.[52] As the wars persisted, so too did Franco-Scottish exchanges. Michel Mel settled an account in June 1643 with Andrew Beaton, who had been in Paris but since returned to Edinburgh.[53] Two months later Lord Ross acquired furnishings including satin, taffetas, a black trellis and a 'toile de rouan blanche fine' from a merchant in Toulouse.[54] David Dunbar in Garmouth entered an agreement with the partnership of Alexander Farquhar in Aberdeen and James Browne in Findhorn in 1647 for Bordeaux wine, again with no mention of any particular difficulties or special considerations to be made due to ongoing civil war.[55] Thomas Cunningham, while reporting on the effect conflict in Britain had on trade through the staple, acted to circumvent this problem by obtaining

from the Admiralty of Zeland a ship of warre, not only to carry me over ... but to stay there upon my returne and to follow my orders, so as thereby I gave warning to all the merchants who presently laded their commodities, and they were safely convoyed, to the number of 12 shipps full of Staple goods.[56]

Franco-Scottish trade continued in the same manner and in the same circles as it had done prior to the Civil Wars. Though arms and ammunition inevitably became more prevalent, there was little variation in the range of goods sought in France by Scottish agents. The numerous letters and accounts between Henry Hope and John Clerk continued to discuss the exchange of the types of luxury goods identified in Chapter 2; in January 1644 Clerk recorded that Hope owed him 17 livres 'payit to a goldsmith for setting your ring & for gold'.[57] Throughout the following year, at a time when the Montrosian Civil War raged in Scotland and the wider British conflict continued, Clerk consistently sent such commodities home. He wrote to Lady Pittendrum from Paris in April to inform her that sixteen gowns and petticoats were being sent with William Paton.[58] The following month, she received a packet 'conteining divers callors off worsit [worsted]' and a ring, 'tyed with A Bit off bleu ribbon to on off the little pacquets'. This transaction complete, Clerk prepared future exchanges, enquiring as to 'what hight ye wold have the pearling for your oune goun', adding that he had 'bein verie desireous to have found out sum prettie stuff to be A waskyne [vasken] for your Lady'.[59] In September Lady Pittendrum received '1 grein etuise [French case] with sheirs botkin and knyffe'. Lady Pittendrum was not the only recipient of goods from Clerk during the civil war period; in the same letter-book are copies of letters to Lady Newliston and to Janet, Margaret and Mary Gray, Clerk's future wife, to whom Clerk sent similar merchandise.[60] Goods exchanged by Clerk and James Mowat in 1647 included 'ane sute of blak clothe for Robert Gray & the compt off A gray drap de Berrie [French design] casak for my self'.[61] Sir Charles Erskine frequently sent home gifts with his letters, including a watch and clothes for his wife Mary's brother, Sir Alexander, a pair of 'Romon' gloves from Paris for Lord Haddington and a 'sticke of black silke stufe' and 'tuoe glasses' for his wife.[62] Significantly there is no indication that any of these exchanges were made more difficult by the context, nor was the conflict mentioned within this correspondence.

Scottish commercial emigration to France continued during this period, being the subject of a report of the Council of Aberdeen in 1646:

> Many of our neighboures quha haid best estates and greatest traffique have removeit themselffis, and ar setlit in forrein countries as in France, Mr Alexander and Robert Irwingis, David Inglis, Thomas & Alexander Mengzeis, Mr Alexander Burnet, Mr Gilbert & George Paipes, William Robertsone ... and many others have quytt thair burgess richts and gone, sum to the south otheris to the north to dwell.[63]

The Inglis, Burnet, Pape and Robertson families all played a significant role in the networks that engaged in trade between France and Scotland.[64] It is plausible that some relocation was motivated by a desire to escape from events at home, and the loss of these individuals from Scotland may have had a negative impact on her domestic economy. In settling in France, however, these merchants became better placed to facilitate commerce with Scotland. In addition to contributing to the continuation of Franco-Scottish trading activity, that France was the chosen destination for these commercial agents suggests the strength of this continuing relationship. Existing networks of merchant Scots facilitated the continuation of commercial activity throughout the 1640s despite the inclement political context.

III.

Though the British Civil Wars were ostensibly a domestic crisis, the involvement of foreign nations had consequences, both positive and negative, for Scotland's merchants. The involvement of the Dunkirkers enhanced Irish privateering capabilities, providing a naval dimension to the conflict and an obstacle to commercial voyages. More positively, the Dutch were instrumental throughout the Civil Wars in providing British ships with false papers that allowed them to continue to trade despite naval conflict. The States General declared the United Provinces neutral, facilitating the acquisition of these papers as well as affording foreign ships refuge in Dutch ports; the Dutch in turn benefited from their neutrality by selling arms and ammunition to all sides, as well as by the rise in the number of English ships paying anchor money at Veere after rebellion broke out in Ulster in October 1641 and the First English Civil War erupted the following January.[65] For their part, the French believed that it would be profitable to entwine themselves in British affairs. On succeeding Richelieu as the principal agent of French government and diplomacy in 1642, Cardinal Mazarin pursued policies that promoted French involvement in British matters. In 1645 Jean de Montereul, the French ambassador, observed that 'the king's party being reinstated, France will have full time to consider how she can interpose to assure the peace of these kingdoms'.[66] Two years later his colleague Pompone de Bellièvre spoke of his intention to 'continue to influence matters here as much as I can'.[67] French intervention continued throughout the conflict; it was at Mazarin's behest that Montereul spent the majority of 1646–8 in England and Scotland meeting the King, the Scottish Covenanters and the English Parliamentarians, under a remit to persuade the Scottish Covenanters to stand by Charles I and to urge the King to consider acceptance of the National Covenant.[68]

It was thus by their own design that France featured prominently in British foreign policy from the moment the First Bishops' War broke out in Scotland in 1639. Both the Covenanters and the Royalists – the latter through Charles's queen, Henrietta-Maria – approached France for assistance. In 1639 John

Elphinstone, second Lord Balmerino and a principal adviser of the Covenanters, voted in Parliament for the necessity of a defensive war. He subsequently
wrote to Louis XIII to implore assistance against the 'tyrannical proceedings'
of Charles I, significantly citing the ancient alliance between France and Scotland as reason for Louis's involvement.[69] The Royalists, buying into the patriotic
rhetoric of the Covenanters, were wary of the continuation of the Franco-Scottish relationship. Secretary Coke wrote to Secretary Windebank in May 1639
that 'you will understand what heavy burden the French begin to lay upon our
[English] merchants, and how they favour the Scots after the old manner'.[70] In
September the Covenanted Scots remained 'hopefull of powerful assistance
from abroad if we should have required it. France would not have failed to have
embraced our protection'.[71] By 1645 the Covenanters were no longer 'the masters of the settlement of affairs in Great Britain', but were nonetheless assured
by France that 'the union that has always existed between the two kingdoms'
would be willingly maintained.[72] The Franco-Scottish relationship persisted,
was recognized as specifically commercial, and caused concern in England on
both economic and political grounds.

Following the agreement reached between the Scottish Covenanters and the
English Parliamentarians in 1643, French support extended to those belonging to the latter group. In 1644, the English Parliamentarian Thomas Ellis was
'forced for safety, being sought after by the Cavaliers to be apprehended ... to fly
towards France, carrying such commodities as he could procure'.[73] The Cavaliers
recognized the support offered to Charles's opponents in France. The English
Royalist Sir Thomas Allin worked under Prince Rupert, Charles I's nephew.
Allin was advised in 1644:

> when you have taken any prize from any of the rebels against the King of England
> ... keep all your prisoners safe aboard your own ships; suffer none of them to remain
> in the prizes, till you may conveniently send them on shore in England or France
> after that the goods are sold and the whole fleet put out to sea, to prevent noise and
> discovery.[74]

Despite their apparent support of the Solemn League and Covenant, however,
as well as the assurance given to the Covenanters of French commitment to a
Scottish alliance in 1645, the following year the French intervened in an attempt
to bring the British Civil Wars to a close in favour of the King:

> Our negotiations will place the king at the head of more than four thousand Scottish
> cavalry, and assure him of one of the best fortresses on this island, which will render it
> necessary evidently for the Scottish Government to interpose in order to make peace
> on some tolerable terms.[75]

By early 1647 Charles himself sought the protection of the French ambassadors, as he 'did not see a single place within the three kingdoms where he could remain in safety'.[76] He proposed to Jean de Montereul that the French ambassador 'publish loudly here that he [Charles] was right in not sanctioning the Covenant, and in not establishing Presbyterianism, and not doing the other things that were demanded by the Scots'.[77] Despite their continued support of Scottish merchants the French ambassadors made sure to voice their apparent frustration with the conduct of the Covenanters to the reigning monarch. Montereul informed the British king of 'the unwillingness of the Scots and the little trust he ought to place in their statements', writing to Mazarin that

> the treatment that he [Charles] was at present receiving from the Scots gave him no reason to wish to do anything towards releasing them from their promises ... The King of Great Britain manifested his approval of what I said, and stated that he would act accordingly.[78]

By the spring of 1647, France's vacillating allegiance had caused previous accord with the Parliamentarians to give way to antagonism. As Bellièvre reported,

> The shelter given in the French harbours to the ships that keep the sea with commissions from the Prince of Wales make them [the Parliamentarians] look for an opportunity of avenging themselves on the French, which they propose to do on the first opportunity, by giving letters of marque to their traders, who say they have not been able to obtain justice in France for the wrongs that have been done them there ... the principal members of Parliament are in favour of granting reprisals.[79]

That spring, the 'St Malo incident' further fuelled British mistrust of France. A ship sent by the English Parliament to Ireland laden with cloth for soldiers' uniforms was captured by a French frigate and taken to St Malo. Bellièvre felt that 'although those who are acquainted with such affairs know well that this cannot have taken place as it is related, such rumours produce the worst possible effect on the public mind'. He asked for more information, to prevent 'what may impair the good understanding that ought to exist between these two kingdoms', further demonstrating French resolve to maintain civil relations with the English Parliamentarians.[80] Ultimately, though reluctantly, Bellièvre wrote that

> Parliament has ordered today that ... this ship laden with uniforms, which they say has been taken to St Malo, [be] restored to them ... it will obviate great complaints ... I cannot engage to prevent the letters of reprisals that have been spoken of for some time from at last being granted.[81]

France's vacillating political loyalties did not go unnoticed by the Scots, and concerns were expressed regarding French motivations. The *Scottish Dove*, a populist news-book produced throughout the mid-1640s, reported in August 1646 that the desires of France were granted before they could be asked! ... The French Ambassador and Montrill [Montereul] are conceived to doe hutt [hurt] not good ... and it is believed our Brethren of Scotland will ... not be stirred either by large promises nor greatest threats.[82]

Despite evident desire to consolidate their historic friendship with Scotland, the French government remained acutely aware of their diplomatic position in Europe more broadly. In 1645 Montereul reported that France had an interest in preventing Charles I from coming to terms with the Independent party because any such alliance would result in the ruin of the Scots, whom France should 'maintain as a power she will one day be able to oppose to England'.[83] Montereul considered that 'France would thereby secure an advantage for herself, since she would thus separate Scotland from England'.[84] Support for Scotland at this juncture was in part borne out of historic allegiance but was additionally – and unsurprisingly – self-serving. Two years later Montereul argued that France should 'endeavour to maintain the monarchy, which being a means of dividing England and Scotland, is also a matter that may contribute to the interests of France'.[85] While the French monarch had obvious motivations in protecting the institution of monarchy in Europe there was a belief that France would have less to fear from an England under Charles I than from a Republican England that might threaten France's declining naval strength.[86]

Alongside concerns for the political balance of Europe – particularly their own place in it – key to French motivations in involving themselves in the tumultuous events in Britain was pursuit of material gain, and their quest for British troops for French service was prioritized. Even before conflict had broken out in Britain France had sought to levy Scottish troops to fight in France, no doubt seeking to bolster her military strength following entry into the Thirty Years' War three years earlier.[87] Mazarin wrote to the Comte de Harcourt on 1 January 1644 imploring him to ask the King of Great Britain to facilitate the raising of 2,000–3,000 troops from Ireland.[88] There was some limited success. In June 1646 Montereul wrote to Mazarin, 'I believe it will be possible to send from here four or five hundred men, who have formerly served the King of Great Britain, but I fear there may be some difficulty in obtaining passports for them'.[89] In March of the following year Bellièvre confirmed that he had 'the verbal assurance of the leaders of Parliament and of this Committee ... that the ships in the service of Parliament on the coast of Ireland [would] allow the ships sent there from France to convey the soldiers to pass and repass'. In addition to being allowed to collect Irish soldiers, French ships delivered arms and ammunition to Ireland. In doing so, suspicions in Ireland concerning the Franco-Irish relationship were increased, as correspondence 'affirm[ed] that the ships for which we are asking passports are laden with arms and gunpowder for Ireland'.[90] In 1647 there were additional attempts to recruit Scottish troops,[91] further cementing the military relationship between the two nations.

Rather than acting selflessly to assist its historic ally during the British Civil Wars, France was concerned primarily with its own interests. Despite this, however, French overtures seeking to re-formalize their historic relationship with Scotland continued throughout this period, as seen in Chapter 1. Even as Montereul was instructed to act in order to protect the institution of monarchy and thus support Charles I, he was simultaneously entrusted with reviving the Auld Alliance. What is demonstrated by this diplomacy is that events at home cannot be separated from Scotland's relationship with France – and vice versa. Though France remained primarily concerned with her own interest, events throughout the following decade continue to testify to the strength of the Franco-Scottish relationship, and particularly the commerce that formal associations explicitly protected.

IV.

By April 1654 the domestic situation in Scotland had changed radically. Charles I was executed on 30 January 1649 and a year later the Covenanting army, under the Earl of Argyll, was defeated by Oliver Cromwell at Dunbar. In 1651 the Royalist Army met its fate at Worcester, precipitating the Cromwellian conquest of Scotland. Scotland was incorporated first into the English Commonwealth and then the Protectorate, before an ordinance on 12 April and a proclamation on 4 May 1654 made republican union between England and Scotland official. The Earl of Loudoun proclaimed England's dominance in this union, believing Scotland to be 'under the power and force of the armie of the Parlament of the pretended Comonwealth of England'.[92] Some modern scholarship concurs with Loudoun's assessment, observing that 'Ireland and Scotland, after being conquered, were forcibly incorporated in a military state totally dominated by England'.[93] Conversely, there is scholarship that has questioned this dominance, and particularly the 'forced' nature of this Anglo-Scottish relationship.[94] There were elements of English foreign policy that did affect Scotland after 1651, including being drawn into the First Anglo-Dutch War from 1652. It is important to note, however, that Cromwell did not sacrifice the well-being of Scotland on the altar of a wholly English agenda, but on occasion deliberately acted to defend the commercial interests of his northern dominion. In May 1657 Cromwell wrote to Frederick III of Denmark-Norway concerning two Scottish ships captured between Dunkirk and Norway – the *Greyhound*, captained by William Adamson and the *Comfort*, captained by John Robertson. Upon receiving letters from the captains concerning the incident Cromwell voiced his support of the Scottish ships, requesting that Frederick III punish the behaviour of those who captured the vessels and asking that an example be made of them.[95] Of course, rather than necessarily indicating affection for Scotland, this intervention allowed Cromwell to assert his power within Europe.

However the mid-century Anglo-Scottish relationship is read, the upheaval caused by changes in domestic government fundamentally altered the context within which Scottish merchants did business. Under Cromwellian government Scotland was supposedly 'ill-prepared for the importation of aggressive mercantilism'.[96] Foreign trade, it has been argued, was unable to prosper. Christopher Smout suggests that Scotland was too 'enfeebled [by] years of anarchy' to take advantage of the opportunities – such as free trade across the Anglo-Scottish border – offered by Cromwellian Union in 1654, and Theodora Keith states that 'trade, both inland and foreign, had decayed, and showed little sign of recovery'.[97] There were, indeed, tangible consequences of this upheaval. Looking again at the Sound Toll Registers, we see that Scottish trade through the Sound declined during the 1650s to a greater extent than it had during the 1640s. Just twenty-six Scottish ships on average per year sailed through the Sound between 1653 and 1658, compared to an average of ninety-eight between 1625 and 1630 and fifty-six between 1644 and 1649.[98] The picture was particularly bleak in the Scottish ports of Glasgow and Dundee. No ships at all were recorded entering the Glasgow ports in 1651, the year following the Scottish defeat at Dunbar and the Cromwellian occupation of Edinburgh,[99] and the port of Dundee continued a decline in trade, albeit one that had begun before the 1650s.[100]

Merchants involved in Franco-Scottish trade experienced problems that they attributed to domestic changes. Three months after Charles I's execution Andrew Hay wrote to his kinsman Archibald discussing at length the political situation in Scotland, stating that 'I am not able to do anything with this new state ... it is not possible yet for a little tyme to procure yow a passe to goe to France, becaus they doe so much search into mens actions'. This was no doubt inconvenient, but provided incentives for commercial expansion. Immediately after relaying these troubles Andrew wrote that 'I have enquyred for shippes going to Barbados, ther is on going within ane moneth from the west countrey to barbados, and ther is on going from Leeth presently to Virginia'.[101] Some merchants had already been pushed towards other trading destinations following the turmoil of the 1640s. In February 1642 Benjamin Fletcher, a Scottish merchant in Rouen, sent an account to Alexander Hayes in London concerning a shipment of cotton wool from Barbados.[102] These episodes confirm that merchants were adept at turning to alternative destinations and different commodities when circumstance dictated. Significantly, despite his shift in focus Fletcher continued to act within Franco-Scottish trading networks, seeking alternative locations in addition to, not at the expense of, links with France that were the bedrock of his business interests.[103] In expanding their business horizons such individuals fundamentally enhanced Scotland's overseas trading patterns, contributing to the increasing globalization of their nation's commercial interests.

Indeed, despite dismal outlooks for Glasgow and Dundee it has been argued recently that the Cromwellian Union was not disastrous either for Glasgow or for the port of Aberdeen, as both towns quickly re-established the level of commercial operations that had prevailed before the civil wars.[104] In the Glasgow port of Dumbarton, sixteen ships per year on average are recorded for the period 1654–9 (both entries and departures), a 116 per cent increase from 1643 to 1649. Aberdeen also displayed a marked improvement in traffic under the Cromwellian regime, with 119 ships on average recorded between 1654 and 1659, a 43 per cent increase on the previous period. Figure 4.1, which shows a fall in Aberdeen's trade with France during the civil war years, also shows it recovering during the Interregnum, particularly following the 1654 union, suggesting that Scots were not enfeebled and that their trade had not decayed.[105] The French ports of Dieppe and Le Havre witnessed continuing British trade through the second half of the Interregnum and into the Restoration period – although these records frustratingly stop in 1656 and 1664 respectively, preventing analysis of trading patterns thereafter.[106] Gilbert Pape, a Scottish merchant enmeshed in John Clerk's French network and the same who emigrated to France during the Civil War, appears in the Dieppe records at regular intervals, in three consecutive Januaries between 1654 and 1656, plus twice in March 1654.[107] The records of La Rochelle depict further Franco-British trade, with English, Irish and Scottish merchants continuing their business apparently unhindered by concern over events at home.[108] In many transactions in this port merchants of the three British kingdoms worked together, suggesting the lack of impact of domestic conflict on business relationships, and the case of La Rochelle is considered in Chapter 7.

Discernible falls in Scottish trade may owe more to European alliances than to domestic events, supporting claims that in the seventeenth century 'stumbling foreign policies had repercussions on domestic affairs'.[109] When the First Anglo-Dutch War broke out in 1652, Denmark-Norway was bound to assist the Dutch by a 1649 alliance. They fulfilled this duty in 1653, placing an embargo on all British ships passing through the Sound.[110] Accordingly no Scottish or English ships are recorded passing through the Sound in either direction in this year, contributing to an overall fall in average figures.[111] Domestic policies were influenced by broader events – an act of 1652 'for calling home Seamen and Mariners and Inhibiting such to serve abroad without License' reflected a need to recruit men for the war effort against the Dutch.[112] Such policies might speak more to the wider European context than to the effect of domestic upheaval, but they contribute to a broader debate on whether Scotland was subjugated by her more powerful neighbour, having her commerce annihilated in the process.

Despite the impact of England's foreign policy on Scotland's affairs, Scottish merchants continued to pursue commerce during the Interregnum as they had during the Civil Wars, with largely positive results. Continued optimism among the merchant classes immediately following Charles I's execution was epitomized by John Clerk's network; the desire and ability to source and send home luxury goods remained evident. Despite returning to Scotland for personal reasons in 1646, Clerk remained involved in French trade, supporting the notion that geographic location was not central to successful participation in Franco-Scottish commercial networks.[113] In January 1650 James Mowat assured Clerk that 'Madam Selon hath maid and delivered your six hats to Mr Houp [Henry Hope]', and that 'Monsieur Peronet hath maid you 8 hatbands ... according to your order he gave them to Monsieur Houp'.[114] When John Clerk sent 'a knyffe for cutting the corns on the feet' to the Earl of Lothian in 1652, he also claimed remittance for items including hose, silk hose, knives with tortoise shell handles, ivory handles and combs.[115] Business continued to flourish to such an extent that twice in 1650 Mowat wrote to Clerk regarding continuing business opportunities in France. His first noted that

> any merchand ther in Paris, with whom you hav haid to doe with before would send you [goods] upon your simple leter, for says often to me that they mutch mor wish you send your commisones for waires, and that you should not pay one pennye moor as if you were in persone yourself.[116]

Five days later Mowat wrote again that business opportunities were rife, imploring 'good Mr Clerk' to

> taik once moor a triall of it, and you shall be most heartly welcome ... if you find your owen securitye you may deall with gentlemen at home, and remite your moneys hier and fournish them, and maik good profite you know the way before.

This letter had an additional dimension. Rather than encouraging Clerk to participate in a distinctly Scottish network, Mowat told Clerk that 'theris many english and severall Scots that you might deall with'.[117] Despite domestic squabbles Mowat thought nothing of mentioning trade with both Englishmen and Scots, indicating that for the merchant classes commercial concerns were more important than political or national divisions.

Just as they had in the civil war years, Scottish merchants traded successfully with France despite the political context. The improvement in Aberdeen's commercial fortunes during the Interregnum can be gleaned through merchant activity as well as through shipping figures. John Donaldson, burgess of Aberdeen, drew a bill of exchange on Michel Mel in Dieppe in November 1650 to be paid to John Irving. Though Donaldson submitted a complaint that Irving had forged this bill there is no indication that domestic politics were responsible for the failure of this, or any other, transaction. Donaldson used his good reputation to his advantage in this case as Thomas Melville, former Dean of Guild, Alexander Alexander, burgess of Aberdeen, Alexander Davidson, advocate, and former bailies George Morrison and Alexander Lumsden all testified that Donaldson was 'a man of good credit and honest and of good estimation within the said burgh'.[118] William Robertson, an Aberdonian who acted as both a merchant in La Rochelle and a factor in Le Havre enjoyed a prolonged period of success during the Cromwellian regime. Business documentation from 1651 detailing a joint venture with John Forbes, provost of Inverness, Patrick Leslie, an Edinburgh merchant, and Alexander Keith, gives no hint of the ubiquitous domestic crises and changes in government in Britain.[119] Robertson's business interests survived the Cromwellian period; in 1662 he appeared in La Rochelle in a commercial capacity.[120] Other networks continued to operate despite events at home. Annabella, Countess of Lothian, wrote from La Rochelle to her daughter Lady Lothian in 1651 advising her to send letters by her merchant, John Inglis, who travelled frequently between Scotland and France with no apparent impediment.[121] Inglis maintained a number of contacts throughout France and his business survived the Cromwellian period: he wrote to George Maine in 1659 of his 'correspondent in deip [Dieppe] mester biger'.[122]

The merchants who remained active in Franco-Scottish commerce in this period adopted familiar methods. As we saw in Chapter 2, Alexander Charteris adjusted his itinerary in 1654 to spend three extra months in 'Bordeaux, Rochelle and other places in these quarters', letting his itinerary be dictated by commercial opportunities that seem to have been plentiful.[123] Merchants based in France continued to provide finance to fellow Scots in a number of different spheres, this sector similarly unperturbed by events at home. Evidence from 1662 records activity six years previously: Sir Thomas Hay of Park borrowed money from Thomas Crawford in Edinburgh and Francis Kinloch in Paris to finance his 'travels in France and England preceding the month of December 1656'.[124] During the Interregnum, as it had during the British Civil Wars, Scottish overseas trade continued to flourish despite some inconveniences. Merchants operated within the same circles as they always had and there remained both a demand for and supply of goods from France. Indeed, local burghs remained concerned with local issues, rather than tackling broad difficulties arising from Britain's new rule. The Council of Aberdeen, for example, continued its long-running campaign to gain permission to import French salt for the curing of fish, with apparently no expectation that this was any more unlikely under the new government.[125]

V.

The British Civil Wars and Interregnum combined to generate a prolonged period that was likely to be hostile to trade. Increased danger at sea, increased duties in order to raise wartime revenue, the impressment of men and ships for service and bans on travelling abroad all impacted on merchants' ability to carry out exchanges along traditional routes. Certainly merchants voiced concerns; Andrew Hay bemoaned the 'new state ... search[ing] into mens actions' as well as describing difficulties in procuring passes for France following Charles's execution.[126] Some, like Hay, voiced these concerns privately; those in positions of authority, like Thomas Cunningham, voiced them publicly. Though these concerns were at times reflected both in the trading figures of certain ports and in some individuals' experiences, such occurrences are not representative of broader trends. Patterns of trade were not uniform across all ports, emphasizing the need to look to local or regional patterns in determining the state of any nations' commercial activity. Further, the continuing commercial activities of mercantile agents themselves say more about the effect of the conflict in real terms – both positive and negative – than trading figures alone. When all of the evidence presented here is taken together, there appears to have been no general drop in Franco-Scottish trade as a result of this period of turmoil in Britain. Many merchants continued to pursue their business with great success – though others, like Slowane and Mitchelson, would take little comfort from that.

When patterns of trade were affected as a result of conflict the effect was not overwhelmingly negative. In seeking new opportunities elsewhere men like Andrew Hay contributed to the globalization and development of Scottish trade, widening commercial horizons while maintaining their former interests. The continued optimism exhibited by those who continued to participate in Franco-Scottish exchanges was fully justified. Merchants drew on their well-honed skills in adapting their trading activities when obstacles arose, allowing them to maintain established links. For some, not much changed – evidence of continued activity within John Clerk's network suggests no significant deviation from the norm as a direct result of conflict; the same people remained involved and the same commodities continued to be exchanged. Though Clerk returned to Scotland during the Civil Wars, there is no suggestion that this was as a result of the conflict; indeed he stayed deeply integrated in the commercial activities of this network, being frequently encouraged to return and remaining informed of continuing commercial opportunities. Significantly, that Clerk's movements continued to be motivated by personal circumstance rather than the political climate confirms that conflict did not necessarily infiltrate or dictate all aspects of commercial life. Merchants operating during the mid-seventeenth-century upheaval appear to have been impressively resilient to political change, prioritiz-ing personal gain over national strategy.

Questions already raised regarding broader British and European dimensions to the Franco-Scottish relationship continue to gain prevalence as this study progresses. That falling trade figures in the early 1650s can be attributed more clearly to broader European contexts than domestic events emphasizes the need to widen our investigation beyond bi-lateral Franco-Scottish links. Further, that patterns of trade and domestic policy owed much to the outbreak of the First Anglo-Dutch War broaches the question of whether Scotland was becoming more subsumed under English control as the century advanced. We will return to both of these issues in later chapters, but there are already hints that Scotland maintained vestiges of her independence despite the changing political situa-tion at home. In 1649 the importation of wine, wool and silk from France was prohibited in England and Ireland, but not in Scotland. Perhaps this is indicative of the different political situations north and south of the border, with Argyll's Scotland rejecting the regicide and declaring for Charles II, but it might equally be attributed to continuing Franco-Scottish accord.[127]

It is inevitable that changes within Britain in some ways affected Scottish relationships with foreign powers. The French maintained a level of political neutrality, using their diplomatic talent to full effect – mirroring, in some ways, Scotland's responses to overtures from the French that were explored in Chapter 1. Despite both political and material motivations, however, France maintained her desire to reassert formally aspects of the Auld Alliance, and Secretary Coke was right to lament the ongoing favour offered to Scottish merchants in France. Regardless of the regime in charge, domestic upheaval did not extinguish either practical Franco-Scottish commerce or notions of the Auld Alliance. James Battie, of course, saw things differently, but despite his opinion that 'civill war ruined trade faster than any other' the British Civil Wars did not herald signifi-cant damage to Scotland's overseas trade – with France or elsewhere. Whether there was 'no greater enemy to Trade than War' is the subject of the following two chapters, as we move on to consider the impact of international conflict on Franco-Scottish commerce.[128]

5 'IN PURSUIT OF HIS MAJESTY'S ENEMIES': FRANCO-STUART CONFLICT, 1627–1667

As we have seen, merchants pursued Franco-Scottish commerce throughout the British Civil Wars and Interregnum via both open and covert channels. International conflict, bringing with it trade embargoes, commercial legislation and increased dangers from privateers, perhaps provided an even tougher arena in which to compete. This and the following chapter examine several of the conflicts that saw France and the British nations on opposing sides, assessing the impact of these wars on Franco-Scottish trade. Here, focus is on conflicts fought against France by the Stuart monarchy; Chapter 6 considers the impact of wider European conflict in the post-Stuart age.

With the exception of the Interregnum, the interests of the House of Stuart dominated British foreign policy until 1688, but the two conflicts considered here emerged under different circumstances. While the 1627–9 conflict was concerned with relations directly between the Houses of Stuart and Bourbon, the conflict that broke out in 1666 was a part of the wider Second Anglo-Dutch War. The marriage of Charles I to Henrietta-Maria, Louis XIII's sister, in June 1625 provided Britain with a strong ally against Spain once hostilities were officially opened in September, but the Anglo-French relationship soon began to fracture. Following the Duke of Buckingham's behaviour and Charles I's refusal to alter his religious policies at Louis's request, by April 1627 the Stuart Navy was preparing to sail to La Rochelle to assist the Huguenots against their monarch.[1] In 1666, on the other hand, Britain and France became enemies by default as a result of broader European issues. Louis XIV was bound to assist the Dutch by a treaty of 1662, and when hostilities broke out with England the Dutch duly enlisted Louis's support, which was reluctantly offered.[2] Louis was governed primarily by his long-term political aims, rather than by a sense of loyalty or empathy for Dutch interests or hostility towards Charles II. The death of Philip IV in September 1665 triggered the issue of the Spanish Inheritance, and Louis hoped that in declaring war on England he would secure the support of Johan de Witt in his plan to annex portions of the Spanish Netherlands.[3] Certainly, Louis appeared somewhat apathetic to pursuing war actively against Stuart

Britain. His Court was allowed to express freely their reluctance to enter the conflict and he permitted his sister-in-law Elizabeth, the daughter of Charles I and Henrietta-Maria, to continue her correspondence with her brother, retaining the channel of communication that would be used after 1667 to reconcile the British and French kings and initiate the negotiations that culminated in the Secret Treaty of Dover in 1670.[4] The Dutch suspected France of remaining sympathetic to Charles II despite its involvement in the conflict – a report in the English Parliament in 1664 stated that the Dutch 'begin to be somewhat suspicious & jealous as if his Majestie & the French King did too well understand one another'.[5] Descriptions of the Franco-Stuart wars as 'unnecessary' (1627–9) and 'reluctant and half-hearted' (1666–7) indicate the lack of dogged determination for conflict on either side.[6]

Though the context within which each of these conflicts erupted was very different, there are parallels in the ways in which commerce was affected and in the means used by merchants to maintain Franco-Scottish trade links. Conflict with France under the Stuart monarchy has been thought to have had a detrimental effect on Franco-Scottish trade.[7] Edgar Lythe states that the £400,000 raised in Scotland in 1625 for war against the French represented 'active participation' on behalf of Scotland and was the 'last straw on the back of the Auld Alliance', with the 3,000 troops sent to La Rochelle under the Earl of Morton in 1627 signifying the moment that the old economic alliance ended.[8] There is evidence to support these claims – the records of the Admiralty of Le Havre record no ships going to or coming from any of the British nations between 9 July 1627 and 11 April 1629.[9] In the case of war against France as part of the Second Anglo-Dutch War in 1666–7, there is similar evidence to suggest that Franco-Scottish trade suffered – an entry book for Kirkcaldy from November 1666 to November 1667 records no voyages between this port and France.[10] Nevertheless, as we examine the wider context, it will become clear that commercial agents prioritized their business interests and strove to protect and to expand them during these conflicts, just as they had during domestic crises. Moreover, as explored in the previous chapter, war presented opportunities as well as taking them away.

This chapter examines the ways in which the Franco-Stuart conflicts of 1627–9 and 1666–7 affected Scotland's overseas commerce. The increased presence of privateers, prohibitive embargoes and the possibility of impressment contributed in both contexts to an environment hostile to commerce. Despite this, merchants utilized the methods examined in previous chapters to pursue their business, continuing to benefit from their commercial endeavours in a variety of ways. Crucially, trade embargoes were not effectively implemented and merchants were able to use their influence to shape economic policy, raising further questions regarding the nature of early modern warfare and its apparent

effect on commercial activity, as well as on the nature and construction of commercial legislation in this period. Finally, the question of England's dominance
over Scotland is once again raised, in preparation for detailed discussion of this
issue in the final two chapters of this volume.

I.

Rivalry at sea was one of the most obvious ways in which international exchange
was damaged by conflict, and both Scottish and French merchants suffered at
the hands of enemy privateers during the Stuart period.[11] Traditionally French
privateers have been seen as particularly harmful, and, unsurprisingly, during
the Stuart wars they targeted Scottish shipping.[12] This included the arming of
the frigate *l'Ermine* under commission of the Duke of Beaufort in 1666 against
'the English and other enemies of the state', which included Scottish and Irish
vessels.[13] Scotland's privateering armada in the early modern period, however,
has recently been demonstrated to have been stronger than previously thought,
and the strength of the French privateering fleet has been questioned.[14] During
the wars of the 1620s, Scottish privateers had success against both French and
Spanish shipping.[15] In September 1628 a fleet of five ships, two of the Royal
Navy (the *Unicorn*, captained by David Murray and the *Thistle*, captained by
William Duff) and three privateers (the *Grace of God* of Dysart, captained by
David Robertson, the *Alexander Bucephalus*, captained by David Alexander and
the *Gift of God* of St Monans, captained by James Binning) captured the *Jonas*
of Dunkirk, skippered by Albert Jansonne of Calais.[16] David Alexander appears
again in November 1629 in the *Gift of God* alongside two other Scottish men-
of-war off the coast of Shetland, having captured the *Green Drake*, a Dutch ship
from Alkmure captained by Cornelius Peterson, as it sailed illegally from Gothenburg to Bayonne in France carrying masts, tar, deals and copper.[17] The skipper
argued that they had sailed for Bayonne before Charles I had issued his proclamation against trading with France; the case appears not to have gone before
the Admiralty Court, suggesting that it was dismissed and the ship released.[18]
David Alexander appears a third time in May 1629 in the *James* of Anstruther,
having captured the *Houpe* of Calais, skippered by Jacob Hanson, bound from
Norway to Malaga with deals and tar.[19] Though these commissions were granted
as part of the 1627–9 war with France, it was not only French shipping that
was damaged. Dutch ships participating in exchange along French routes and
French ships engaging in trade elsewhere in Europe were targeted, indicating the
repercussions of such activity on commerce beyond the immediate protagonists.

This pattern is less surprising during the later conflict, when the Dutch and
the Danes, their allies, were specifically targeted. Commissions reflected this
state of affairs – Patrick Logan, captain of the *James* of Leith, was granted a let-

ter of marque in February 1667 'against the ships and goods belonging to the French King, the King of Denmark and the State of the United Provinces and to their subjects or inhabitants'.[20] The open threat to Dutch shipping prompted adjustments in sailing patterns. Already by the end of 1664, before war had officially broken out, the Dutch were ordered to avoid using the Channel and sail around the north coast of Scotland instead.[21] This practice became so common that English authorities discussed the possibility of having forts built in Shetland to prevent it,[22] perhaps as a way of forcing the Dutch back through the Channel and making them easier prey. As war continued most of the Atlantic trade of northern Europe began to round Scotland rather than sail through the Channel, avoiding a route that ostensibly presented a higher capture risk.[23] This evasive practice may have been unpopular with English government officials, but Scots with commissions became wise to changes in sailing patterns and seized the opportunity to prey on foreign shipping. As the *London Gazette* reported in June 1667:

> a great store of [Dutch] prizes lately brought in daily by Scottish vessels and of late scarcely a day hath passed in which there had not been two or three prizes sent in, so much that the harbour [Burntisland] is so thronged that they are forced to send several of them to other places.[24]

This activity had broader repercussions for Franco-Scottish trade in a period when Dutch shipping was used extensively by all trading nations. As a result of these actions French products remained in warehouses in French ports, damaging merchants' interests.[25] There were some positive consequences, however, of what is easily perceived as an overwhelmingly negative activity. The disappearance of the Dutch shipping fleet from Scottish waters encouraged more Scottish merchants to consider owning their own ships, providing impetus for the development of Scotland's commerce.[26] Scotland's merchants were encouraged to expand their personal investment in overseas trade and, as a by-product, helped to promote Scotland's commercial significance in Europe.

There were mariners who capitalized on the promise of financial gain that privateering offered. William Ramsay, captain of the *Alexander*, hired Richard Binning of Yarmouth in May 1627 for a passenger voyage to Nova Scotia. The ship sailed in September 1628 but Ramsay changed his plans after departure, putting his passengers ashore at Loch Ryan on the west coast of Scotland and going to sea 'in pursuit of His Majesty's enemies'[27] on 24 September. This gamble seems to have paid off – on 28 September, just four days after being granted his letter of marque, he captured a Lübeck ship laden with salt and later captured two French barks carrying fish.[28] Though Ramsay's profit materialized, such a return was not guaranteed. To obtain a privateer's commission initial investment of £2,000 sterling surety was required – payable even if no prizes were taken.[29] Patrick Crowhurst has argued that except for a few spectacular successes, most privateers failed to make any profit.[30] Despite this, applications for letters of marque were frequent and Steve Murdoch has estimated that the total amount held in escrow by the state in the Second Anglo-Dutch War was between £160,000 and £240,000 sterling[31] – of benefit to the state, perhaps, but not directly to the merchant class. It was perhaps low expectations of return, despite some success stories, that led some to flout the strict regulations that controlled privateering ventures, resulting in unregulated threats to continuing commerce. In September 1665 a French captain was arrested for using an English letter of marque against the Dutch, his compatriot French and even the English themselves.[32]

When prizes were taken, it was not guaranteed that they would be judged legitimate. Three French ships taken by Scottish naval vessels in 1627 had to be returned as they had been seized while under the convoy of a Dutch man-of-war.[33] The conduct of those acting under privateering commissions was regulated, and even if a prize was judged legitimate there might still be consequences for the victors. In 1629 John Anderson and John Daw captured two Calais vessels, the *St Michael* and the *St Peter*, while they were at anchor off Molde, Norway.[34] The captured skippers and crew brought cases against the Scots for cruelty. Several members of the crew, including Anderson and Daw, were indicted on these charges. Despite this, they were cleared of the unlawful taking of the vessels as they had been acting under a commission from William, Earl Marischal, and the prizes were declared lawful in Leith.[35] Scant consolation, perhaps, as the French vessels had already been freed, though just two years later Daw may have been more grateful for the intervention of authorities. Daw had been in waters just off Bordeaux when he and his ship were taken by Leveane Rickleman. When Rickleman appealed to the Admiralty Court for permission to return to Bordeaux his passage was granted only on the condition that Daw was released, a bargain that was upheld.[36]

Though the individuals discussed here experienced problems as a direct result of war, recent research has qualified the effect of privateering during the Stuart conflicts, indicating that there was 'limited impact' in terms of prizes taken with both the Scots and the French sustaining a relatively small number of losses at each other's hands.[37] Indeed, the apparent danger posed by privateering did not manifest itself frequently in records kept by merchants and mariners. The Elie skipper Alexander Gillespie sailed to France during the 1666–7 war, yet his logbook for this period mentions neither concerns nor problems with the privateers he encountered. The exchanges he had with them seem to have been civil: 'Monday the 13th of September we saw ... ane small caaper (privateer) whom we spoke'. The source is silent on how he negotiated this encounter, but it speaks volumes that the exchange warranted no further comments, and that Gillespie and his crew continued with their journey.[38]

II.

As already noted in the domestic context, it was not only violence that threatened merchants' business during war, as ships and men were pressed into government service in a variety of capacities. In preparation for the 1627–9 conflict all ships already on voyages were recalled to Scotland in 1626. In July the Privy Council wrote to the Council of Aberdeen asking how many ships could be assembled for the King's wars, what their burden was and the number of men they could hold. They also asked how many seafaring men were within the town, as men, as well as their ships, were pressed into service.[39] Two days later Gilbert Cullen was sent to Aberdeen as Commissioner to the Privy Council and a week later 'a nott of the schippis belonging to the toune of Aberdeen and of their burdenis' was produced.[40] These included Gilbert Anderson's *Bonacord*, which was reported to be fifty tuns in burden, and 'presently absent at hir voyage in France, whair shee hes almost being this year bypast'. This recruitment drive did not produce what was hoped for, however:

> none of these shippis caries any ordinance, except onlie the Bonacord, quhilk caries
> bot two taliounes; and they have not amongis thame all abone fyftie marineris to sail
> tham, quhairof their is bot fourtie belongis heir. The remanent ar hyred elsquhair.[41]

In August the Aberdeen Council were informed 'of the grit preparatiouns of a powerfull and forayne cuntrey to invade ... That a competent number of ship-pis providit with all weirlyke furnitour may be sett onto and maintained be the burrowes during the tyme of this common danger'.[42] On 27 September Thomas Haddington, Earl of Melrose and first Earl of Haddington, wrote to the Scottish burghs informing them that the King had ordered the Privy Council

> to make stay of all shippes bound for France, and commands to all such as are gone,
> to prevent the danger that some of them may happin to incurre by goinge to France,
> in regaird ... of some lait differences between him and the Frenche King; and at this
> same tyme all the serviceable shipps within the kingdome wer arrested for his Majes-
> tie, and at his command.[43]

In the same month the Privy Council noted that 'for defence of his awne domin-ionis and persute of the enemie [Charles] is to outreik his navyis and armies be sea and land, and to send royall supplies to his confederattis, in all whiche caises shippis ar necessarie above all things', permitting no ship to go abroad without a licence.[44] The impressment of these ships was more explicitly stated in the Privy Council two months later, though attributed to tensions with Spain rather than France:

> For the better praeventing and resisting of the Spanishe praeparationis whairwith this
> Iland is threatnit, causit stay and arreist all the shippis within his Majesties domin-

ionis, to the intent thay might be in reddines to be armed and send to sea as the necessities and occasioun of thair imployment and service sould require.[45]

In October these ships were

lying in the harbour, being six in number, an embargo laid on, by order of the Coun-cil, in pursuance of a missive from the secretary of state ... I [the Earl of Melrose] am comandet by his majestie to command yow in his name to take order preceislie that nain of your shippes sail any whair out of the dominionnes whill we have warr.[46]

Inevitably, the enlisting of merchant vessels for war was unpopular. When prep-arations were made for Scottish participation in the Second Anglo-Dutch War measures were taken to ensure smooth recruitment. The Scottish burghs could be fined 500 merks for each man they failed to provide for the Royal Navy, and when in 1665 Aberdeen had difficulty raising the fourteen men she was obliged to (as the seamen had absented themselves during the call for service) the withdrawal of brewing privileges from the wives of these men was threatened as an incentive.[47]

Though the impressment of both merchants and their ships for the war effort posed inconveniences to trade, some merchants were able to find ways of prof-iting within this environment. The services of merchant bankers were sought by those engaged in conflict – in May 1627 John Seaton of the *Garde Écoss-aise* acknowledged receipt of 11,000 francs from Andrew Beaton, a merchant in Paris, perhaps setting the precedent for similar activity during the Civil Wars.[48] Others assisted the government in transporting equipment, men or arms and, just as they did during the Civil Wars, benefited from the practice that 'shippes or boats serving the Countrey, or the Prince, have great prerogatives. For first they go free from all Imposts, Customs, and Arrestments, not only in forth-going but also in their return'.[49] Andrew Brown, master of the *Tyme* of Leith, transported sol-diers from Aberdeen to Glückstadt in September 1626. He intended, as ordered by the owners of the ship, to go from this Danish territory to Bordeaux and try for a cargo back to Scotland, taking advantage of being able to take a return freight custom-free. However, he was prevented from doing so 'by the outbreak of war between the King's majestie and the Kingdome of France'. In this instance, the conflict itself prevented Brown from taking advantage of this benefit, and he had to bring the *Tyme* home in ballast.[50] In April 1628 Archibald Douglas, captain of the *Lyon*, was slightly more fortunate. After being ordered to take the Earl of Morton to the Isle of Rhé for the La Rochelle expedition he was compensated with two barrels of peas and a barrel of herring on his return to the Isle of Wight.[51]

The practice of rewarding contributions to military transportation persisted into the 1660s. In October 1667 a contract was drawn up between Lord George Douglas, Colonel to the Scots Regiment, and James Mowat, the Paris merchant, for transportation of 300 men from Leith or Burntisland to Dieppe.[52] Mowat commissioned John Brown of Edinburgh to act on his behalf in Scotland and prepare two ships for this purpose. This instrument was endorsed in November, confirming that Mowat had fulfilled his part of the contract and that he 'should be free of all ... dampnadge interest & expenses'.[53]

III.

For those merchants who avoided the lure of privateering, the press or commissions to transport troops, it was business as usual, and there were a variety of ways in which they went about the pursuit of commerce. These included altering trading routes, hiring neutral ships, sailing under flags of convenience or using false papers. There is quantifiable evidence that commercial traffic between France and Scotland fell during both of the conflicts under discussion here. Figures for Leith show that as a percentage of all European trade through this port, French traffic fell from 41 per cent in 1611–12 to just 5 per cent in 1626–8. A look at the broader context suggests that merchants found ways to compensate. In the same periods the percentage of ships going to the Netherlands rose from 22.8 per cent to 37.8 per cent, suggesting that merchants continued to trade between Leith and the continent but adjusted their continental destinations.[54] As discussed above, upon reaching Europe goods might then have been transported overland, allowing merchants to facilitate exchange with France while avoiding the use of French ports that were ostensibly closed to them.

Available data from the 1660s allows us to consider this phenomenon for the later period. Eric Graham has compiled figures showing the number of ships entering the port of Leith from Europe in the mid-seventeenth century (see Table 5.1).[55]

Table 5.1: Place of embarkation of 'foreign-going' passages arriving at Leith, 1638–67.

Country of Origin	1638	1660	1661	1662	1663	1667
Norway	39	6	9	19	15	6
Baltic	20	6	7	5	7	11
Germany	0	1	0	1	0	6
Low Countries	28	6	8	7	6	27
England	13	8	10	6	7	21
France	35	10	12	25	10	5
Spain	4	0	4	0	1	0
American Colonies	0	0	0	0	0	2
Total	*139*	*37*	*50*	*63*	*46*	*78*

Source: E. Graham, *A Maritime History of Scotland, 1650–1790* (East Linton, 2002), p. 144.

Though there are gaps in this data, some speculative conclusions seem apparent. First, imports from France to Leith fluctuated throughout the century, falling prior to and during the 1666–7 war, suggesting some impact of the conflict on

Franco-Scottish trade. Second, there is a significant rise in entries from the Low Countries during 1667, initially suggesting that, similarly to the 1620s, merchants adjusted their trading destinations to account for a drop in trade with France. In the context of the Second Anglo-Dutch War, though, this is much more unlikely. Graham suggests that this increase in trade from the Low Countries occurred after the conclusion of the Treaty of Breda in 1667, and that these figures depict a 'drift in Scotland's foreign-going trade away from France and towards England and her colonies'.[56] It is hard to detect this drift, though, without comparable figures from 1665 and particularly 1666, or without dividing the 1667 data into pre- and post-Breda periods. Additionally, though the Treaty of Breda was signed on 21 July 1667, the restrictions on trade were not lifted until February 1668 and, as the remainder of this chapter will suggest, Scotland's foreign-going trade did not drift away from France as a result of this conflict. Third, the number of ships entering Leith from England had also risen considerably by 1667. While it is unlikely that this represents importation of French goods to England and thence to Scotland (as English merchants were operating under the same prohibitions), it does support the notion that Scottish merchants adapted their activities and expanded their commercial horizons when circumstance dictated. Fourth and finally, the total number of ships arriving in Leith was considerably higher in 1667 than it had been for the rest of the decade. Despite the aftermath of the Second Anglo-Dutch War, Leith's overseas trade remained buoyant.

In addition to targeting alternative destinations, merchants made use of neutral shipping to allow them to continue to pursue their trade. During the 1666–7 war, the neutral stance of Sweden made their ships particularly popular. Henry Wilkie, merchant of Edinburgh, freighted the Swedish ship the *St John* of Congelfe from Scotland to Bilbao, from Bilbao to Bordeaux and then back to Scotland, with 140 tuns of French wine and eleven bales of paper. Wilkie did not make it to Scotland – he was forced into the Thames for 'shelter from the Enimie' – and asked for permission, as some of the cargo was perishable, for a licence to enter and sell the goods in London.[57] In April of the same year Thomas Cutler, a London merchant, freighted the same ship from London to Leith, on to Gothenburg and Bordeaux and back to London. On the final part of his voyage the ship 'came to a disaster being cast ashoare neare the coast of ffrance', and Culter was forced to unload all the goods and repair his ship, which took almost three months, meaning that the 'ship could not arrive here within the time of his Majesties proclamation'. He therefore asked for permission to unload his goods after the trading embargo had been implemented.[58] In addition to demonstrating ways in which Scottish merchants could continue their trade, this indicates the boost given to Swedish shipping as a result of the conflict. When France and Denmark joined the Second Anglo-Dutch War in 1666 additional proclamations against foreign shipping and the hampering of the extensive Dutch carrying trade practically prevented trading in all but neutral Swedish ships.[59]

Though Swedish ships were used extensively to transport cargo by both sides during the Second Anglo-Dutch War, this did not provide immunity from the conflict. In September 1667 the *Flower de Luce* of Stockholm, master Joachim Burmaster, appears on a list of Swedish owned ships taken by Scottish privateers. The goods onboard the ship belonged to Dutch citizens and the steerman, timmerman and cook were all Dutch. The vessel went to France, despite its pass stating a different destination (we are not told where), and never having 'broke ground' in any Swedish harbour. Further, the pass cited salt as the cargo, but the ship was also found to be carrying wine, vinegar and pepper.[60] This is an example of Swedish shipping being utilized by Dutch merchants, who were acting contrary to their documentation. Ultimately, however, the vessel was taken, being unprotected by its neutral status, and Murdoch has identified further examples of neutral ships being declared prize during this conflict.[61]

Though neutral shipping was employed and false documentation used, there were merchants who simply continued trading as normal during both of these conflicts, apparently with no reprisal. It has already been noted that John Seaton received 11,000 francs from Andrew Beaton in 1627; this was furnished through a bill of exchange drawn on the Scottish merchant William Dick.[62] Beaton continued to act on Dick's behalf throughout the war, remaining active in Paris until at least 1638, suggesting that he navigated the conflict, continued to live in France and pursued commerce successfully throughout this period.[63] A month after Louis XIV's declaration of war in January 1666 Jean Mel appears in the records of the Admiralty of La Rochelle as the captain of the *Lion*, on a voyage from Scotland to La Rochelle with a loading of herring, salmon, butter and tallow.[64] These reports are not accompanied by any suggestion of contravention of legislation or mention of the political climate. In June and August 1666 the customs records for Kirkcaldy detail Patrick Angus importing French wine from St Martin, as well as 576 French hats brought home by James Broune, an Edinburgh hatmaker.[65]

The Edinburgh merchant Archibald Hamilton enjoyed prolonged success despite the political context. Hamilton continued to deal in French goods, primarily wine, between 1657 and 1679, using established mercantile networks to do so. Links with John Penston in the early 1660s manifested themselves in transactions in October and December 1666 for French wine, and though Hamilton appears to have specialized in this commodity he also purchased hoops and chairs from Andrew Johnston in April 1666.[66] This ledger suggests the breadth of Scottish commercial networks in France; in February 1665 Hamilton recorded a business transaction involving Michel Mel. This transaction comprised a 'voyage to deip in a French skipper, mr [scarlet] per convoyance of James Grame merchant debett 237:12 to stockings 237:12 for 9 dozen at 44s per dozen to be sold per mittchell mell for my acompt'.[67] Hamilton maintained his business relationships and his profit throughout the 1666–7 conflict, with no mention of any inconvenience experienced as a result of war.

IV.

In addition to using neutral shipping – or simply conducting business as usual – merchants directly influenced the Stuarts' commercial policies. When in 1627 Charles tried to prevent the sale of French wine already present in Scotland merchants protested so fiercely that the monarch relented, allowing the sale of this wine to continue.[68] On 5 February 1628 an embargo was placed on the importation of French goods in any ships. This embargo specifically reiterated the ban on French wines that had been in place since 19 December 1626, crucially removing a loophole that had allowed French goods to be imported in neutral shipping.[69] Scottish merchants informed the Privy Council three weeks later that 'upoun the occasioun of the troubles fallin out betuix the Kings Majestie and the Frenshe King, we out of our most humble respect to his Majesties interesse have dewtifullie forborne all trading in France', but asked that:

> for the better securing of our estaits there frome the danger of arreistment we gave ordour to our factouris to lift and imploy our stockes upon Frenshe commoditeis and to imbarque the same in Flemish bottomes the better to assure the transport thairof hither without challenge or impediment.

The concerns raised by these merchants were twofold. They expressed their desire to find a way of importing goods already in their possession in France, but also voiced apprehension regarding the wider implications of embargoes on French markets. Though Flemish bottoms were available, that these prohibitions encouraged merchants to pursue trade in Flanders was undesirable. Merchants would have to sell their goods in unfamiliar and uncertain markets, accepting in return 'suche commoditeis as they please give us' as the transportation of money to or from the Low Countries was forbidden.[70] While merchants were adept at adjusting their approaches to trade where necessary, this is not to say that they were always comfortable doing so. This group of merchants certainly harboured fears that they might be denied trade in unknown markets, placing their business in jeopardy. As we have already seen, merchants were most productive when operating within networks of people they knew and trusted.

Continuous protestations from merchants to the Privy Council, and the Council to the King, eventually culminated in a letter from Whitehall on 26 March 1628 conceding that all French goods already purchased by merchants may be brought into the country until 1 July.[71] This news reached Holyrood on 7 April:

the King has granted permission to all merchants who had stocks of wine in France at the time of his proclamation forbidding the import of the same, to import it before 1 July 1628. And that the wynes to be brocht home be them ar the returne of thers gudes within ffrance. By the end of April they must inform the Admiral of what wine they have in France, and the quantities they have, and thereafter may import only existing stock.[72]

This letter gave merchants the opportunity to import goods from France legitimately, but only temporarily; nonetheless the more enterprising merchants seized this opportunity to maximize profit. While the relaxation specifically permitted the importation only of wine already in merchants' possession, some apparently declared more than they had, then purchased the difference to gain maximum advantage from this respite. Following the granting of the concession there was a sudden spate of merchants making appeals to the Admiralty Court, declaring money abroad that 'could only be recouped by the purchase and import of wine'. The Glasgow merchants John Hamilton and William Hill declared that their factors, James Ligorie and Tobias Pedro in Le Croisic and Roger Lorentine in Bordeaux, owed them a total of 6,000 francs for goods sent to France in 1626. Hamilton and Hill specified that they needed to buy wine if they were to recover this money.[73] Two days later the Edinburgh merchant John Slowane declared that his factor in France, François Burse, held 5,000 francs as the proceeds of skins sent by him in 1626 and 1627, also stating that this money could only be recouped 'by the purchase and import of wine'.[74] It is unsurprising that the French factors supported these testimonies; without trade, the factors themselves made no profit.

Though these exaggerated claims seem to have been accepted, the time limit on the relaxation was enforced and in January and February 1629 imported wine was arrested.[75] Despite this action Scottish merchants continued to flout the prohibition, protesting that it should not apply to them. When in January 1629 the Earl of Linlithgow, the acting Lord High Admiral, rightfully arrested a consignment of French wines brought into Leith the Scottish merchants asserted that they were

encouraged to this kynde of imployment of their stockes by the exemple of the English who (as they affirme) wer daylie buying and sending over to England great quantitie of Frenshe wynes which had a free and uncontrolled vent there, without challenge or arrestment.[76]

Significantly, after continued pressure (and perhaps assisted by the claim that 'their factours had sent home these wynes for furnishing of the countrie at the tyme of your Majesteis muche expected heerecomming'), Scottish merchants succeeded in having the embargo on French wines lifted on 12 February 1629 – ten weeks before the formal declaration of peace at Susa on 24 April.[77]

While some embargoes were relaxed at the behest of merchants, other legislation was simply not implemented effectively. When several Scottish merchants complained in January 1627 that their shipments of wine had been confiscated Charles allowed the cargo to be restored, accepting claims that the merchants had been unaware of the embargo when they had first undertaken the voyage.[78] Two days later another Scottish merchant, who had imported French wine in a Flemish ship, was permitted to sell his cargo despite the embargo.[79] These are examples of permission being granted to import certain goods in specific cases; on other occasions a blind eye seems to have been turned to continuing Franco-Scottish exchanges. Andrew Watson, captain of the *Blessing* of Burntisland, brought a case to the Admiralty Court in April 1628 against George Scott, the former master of the ship. The case was settled, including £38 10s. to be paid to Scott for one last of Rochelle salt, with no mention of the prohibition on French commodities.[80] In September of the same year Patrick Baxter freighted the *Angel* from Leith to Dysart, and from there to his home port of Dundee.[81] The cargo was French salt, suggesting not only that this salt was imported during the war with France but also that French goods continued to be exchanged domestically despite the conflict. These patterns continued. In June 1628 James Smallat, merchant burgess of Dumbarton and master and owner of the *Providence*, complained to the Privy Council of Scotland that the goods aboard his ship were unlawfully seized and driven to the Kyle of Alloway on the Isle of Mull. More interesting than the details of the claim is Smallat's planned voyage. The *Providence* had taken on herring in the Clyde before proceeding to Ireland and loading the rest of the ship's cargo, including cloth, butter and cheese. Smallat then set sail to France. Despite trade with France from England and Scotland – and their dominions, which included Ireland – having been under prohibition since February, there is no indication that the Council considered the scheduled voyage illegal.[82]

The Privy Council received numerous petitions from merchants wishing to continue to trade with France during the 1627–9 war,[83] and authorities held some sympathy for those affected by international events. In the summer of 1625 Alexander Gray of Dundee, master of the *Falcoun*, William Black in Anstruther, master of the *Blew Due*, John Dow in Crail and 'some others' petitioned the Privy Council when, upon being in France pursuing trade, they were

> stayed at the Rotchell be commandement from Monsieur de Subyis and the governour and magistattis of the Rotchell, and commandit to attend thair directionis and service; quhairthrow your Majesteis saidis subjectis ar haiely distrest, thair voyage maid unprofitable, and thay thameselffis compellit to serve.

The Privy Council 'could not in so just a manner refuse thame', and recommended to the King that 'a coarse' should be taken for their 'comfort and relief'.[84] The Privy Council chose to act in Scottish merchants' interests on more than one occasion in the build-up to war with France. In December 1625 a Dunkirker took a ship of the Scotsman Gilbert Weddell, the *Mary*, which had been freighted to Calais with wheat. The ship and goods were 'made lawfull pryze'. Following this incident, however, Gilbert learned that his shippe had been sold to a Frenchman in Dieppe, before being 'happielie recoverit' by the King's vessels and brought into Plymouth. He asked that the ship be returned to him, and despite the ship having been classed initially as lawful prize the Privy Council acquiesced to his demand in July 1627.[85] Interestingly, successful appeals to the Council were made not only on the behalf of Scottish ships, but leniency was shown to French merchants. Two French barks, the *Hoip* of Rouen and the *St Johnne* of Calais, were sequestrated in Leith in January 1627 under the decree preventing the importation of French wine. Their masters, Jacques Ilkus and Paul Lupine, petitioned for their release, and this was granted on the grounds that the French authorities had liberated the Scottish portion of the British fleet arrested by the Governor of Guyenne the previous year.[86] Four months later Scottish merchants trading in France complained regarding the arrest of a bark of Calais and a hoy of Rouen (different vessels to those above), which were detained in Scotland under suspicion that they were Dunkirkers, 'his Majesteis profest and declaired enemies'. After being 'cleared to belong to Frenschemen' they were released.[87] Though merchants applied their own skills in pursuing continuing trade with France, they were assisted by the leniency of authorities, indicating recognition at the highest levels of the economic value of continuing trade in spite of deteriorating political relations.

V.

Although both were fought under Stuart monarchs, the Franco-Stuart wars of 1627–9 and 1666–7 were markedly different. Yet in many ways the effect they had on Franco-Scottish commerce was similar. In both conflicts Scotland involved herself in several guises; as a kingdom under duress, as an independent nation pursuing her own agenda, but also through the actions of individuals who saw opportunities to pursue personal profit despite the obstacles ostensibly presented by the wars, whether through commerce, privateering, or rewards for assisting the war effort. Those who pursued commerce did so by making use of neutral shipping or adjusting their destinations, but it seems that there were plenty of opportunities for merchants to continue to trade in the usual way, through their own networks, despite ongoing conflict. They were able to appeal to the authorities for changes in policy, particularly evident during the 1627–9 war, so that profitable commercial exchange could continue. Through both their actions and their negotiations merchants were involved in the shaping of Franco-Scottish trade links at every level during both of these inclement periods.

The continuation of commerce during these conflicts owes much to the actions of merchants themselves, but also raises questions over the dedication of Charles I, Charles II, Louis XIII and Louis XIV, as well as their officials, to the war effort. There is little evidence suggesting that either side was determined to pursue a war against the other, particularly during the 1666–7 conflict; instead it seems that they chose to pursue courses of action it was believed would deliver long-term political gains. Louis's apathy towards the conflict was evident in his January 1666 declaration of war, in which he paid lip service to severing all ties but allowed a generous leeway of three months for English merchants to move their belongings and families out of France. He did not decree that Scottish merchants were under obligation to leave.[88] Under the Stuart kings, war with France does indeed seem to have been half-hearted, and perhaps it is unsurprising that restrictions on trade were overturned by pressure exerted by merchants, or that merchants continued to trade without any demonstrable fear of retribution. This emphasizes further the importance of appreciating the context within which early modern conflicts were fought and resisting the temptation to import modern attitudes of the consequences of warfare. Early modern warfare was seldom about total destruction, but concerned with maintaining balance, particularly in commercial and economic terms. It was not until the Napoleonic period that the systematic and total destruction of an enemy became standard military strategy.[89] The patterns examined here were not unique to the Stuart period and despite increased dedication to conflict later in the seventeenth and early in the eighteenth century Scottish merchants continued to pursue commerce with France successfully. The following chapter explores the consequences of merchants' dedication to their activities, including their influence on European commerce, during the Nine Years' War and the War of the Spanish Succession.

Questions that have been developing throughout this volume come to the fore in the subsequent two chapters, including the issue of England's dominance over Scotland, and whether Scotland was disadvantaged by being drawn into England's conflicts against her own interests. Certainly the terminology used to describe the wars of the 1620s and 1660s – the *Anglo*-French War, the *Anglo*-Dutch Wars – suggest that these were England's wars. As discussed above, Edgar Lythe saw the 1627–9 war as a turning point in Scotland's economic alliance with France, with Scotland's involvement in the conflict triggered by union with England: 'after 1603 survival [of Franco-Scottish trade] was at best problematic, after 1625 its collapse was inevitable'.[90] The prohibitions placed on trade with France have been cited as specific reasons for the unpopularity of the 1627–9 war in Scotland.[91] Scotland's later antipathy towards Charles II's wars was identified by contemporaries: a 1664 report from the English Parliament stated that 'Scotland is very much against the war with this country & that his Majestie must expect nothing from that kingdome nor Ireland towards the maintainance thereof'.[92] Though Scots were included in legislation ordering seamen to return from abroad to contribute to the war effort, William Coventry reported to Secretary Bennett in November 1664 that he 'believes the Scotchmen at Yarmouth may be found on merchantmen, where they have run for great wages'.[93] Despite this antipathy, recent research has suggested high levels of Scottish participation in these wars.[94] While the English may have discerned little support from north of the border, it was reported from Edinburgh in August 1666 that 'people want peace with Holland and war with France. The King might have 20,000 volunteers from Scotland'.[95] There are specific cases of Scots actively pursuing the French, not only in Europe but further afield, and not simply in terms of privateers' captures of ships or cargo. Scots under the authority of Sir William Alexander of Menstrie (later Earl of Stirling), Admiral of Nova Scotia, captured Quebec in 1629, a prize not returned to the French until 1632 despite the Peace of Susa in April 1629.[96]

Scotland did participate in these conflicts, but it is important to note that the country maintained a level of independence, rather than being subject solely to pressure from the south. During conflict with the French as part of the Second Anglo-Dutch War, Scotland entered the war as an independent nation, under different rules of engagement and separate legal jurisdiction, despite sharing a crown with England.[97] Scotland's independent participation in these conflicts was noted throughout Europe. As stated by Thomas Cunningham, Conservator of the Scottish nation in the Dutch Republic, 'the States of Zeland were very willing to contribute towards the protecting and exempting of our Staple shipps, so as our Staple trade might still be continued notwithstanding of the warre with England'.[98] The Second Anglo-Dutch War was seen explicitly as England's conflict, but as an inconvenience rather than as entirely detrimental to Scotland's own commerce. The survival of Franco-Scottish trade throughout both the Anglo-French and Second Anglo-Dutch Wars owed much to the continued accord between the two nations. The release of Scottish, but not English, ships by the Governor of Guyenne in 1626 was explicitly 'in respecte of the ancient league'.[99] This accord would stand Scottish merchants in good stead through the rest of the seventeenth and into the eighteenth century, as the 'ancient league' between Scotland and France was again tested, this time by broader, European-wide conflicts.

6 'FOR THE SECURITY AND ENCOURAGEMENT OF THE FREE TRADE OF SCOTLAND': THE NINE YEARS' WAR AND THE WAR OF THE SPANISH SUCCESSION, 1688–1713

From 1688 British relations with the continent took on a new dimension that was precipitated by events in Europe in the preceding decades. In allying himself with Louis XIV in the Third Anglo-Dutch War (1672–4) Charles II had increased fears across Europe that a papist and arbitrary government would be imposed on Britain with the help of the French King.[1] These fears were exacerbated further when the Treaty of Nijmegen concluded the Franco-Dutch War in 1678.[2] Concerns shifted with the Glorious Revolution of 1688–9 and the rise of Jacobitism – the Franco-Dutch War had established William of Orange as the chief opponent of France's ambitions in Europe,[3] and on acquiring the British thrones William immediately became embroiled in war against France. Though the Glorious Revolution was an internal conflict, 'in a wide historical perspective it is arbitrary to make any separation of the Revolution of 1688–9 from the war which followed'.[4] William's antagonism towards France manifested itself first in the Nine Years' War, lasting until the Treaty of Ryswick in 1697, and then in preparations for the War of the Spanish Succession. In 1702 Queen Anne completed these preparations by declaring war on France just two months after succeeding to the British thrones.

As with all early modern conflict, both of these wars comprised open declarations of hostility, embargoes on commerce and domestic pressures on men, ships and finance, and the Franco-Scottish commercial relationship has been seen as particularly vulnerable. Following William's accession to the British thrones any remaining vestige of this historic association allegedly disappeared as a direct consequence of war, which 'undermined relations with France and wiped out the special privileges Scotland had enjoyed a hundred years before, under the Auld Alliance'.[5] Scotland 'suffered acutely under William', as his wars 'had a devastating effect on Scottish overseas trade and shipping'.[6] Such assertions are hard to reconcile with the continuation of the Franco-Scottish association explored in Chapter 1, which saw mutual commercial privileges outlast the 1707 union and the War of the Spanish Succession. This chapter provides a new interpretation of the post-1688 period, in which Franco-Scottish commerce continued in line with enduring Franco-Scottish accord. The persistence of mercantile agents and the influence they exercised on legislation played a large part in this, but once more commercial participants were assisted by authorities who recognized the economic benefits of allowing apparently illicit trade to continue. Though the political events of 1688–1713 may seem commensurate with commercial decline, viable Franco-Scottish trade once again defied an outwardly hostile context.

It is in examining these two conflicts, even more so than those already investigated, that we see the benefit of a methodological approach that considers not only the political climate but also the realities of continuing trade. Franco-Scottish commerce between 1688 and 1713 does not mirror a political context in which Britain and France were enemies and Scotland's overseas commerce was damaged. In addition to telling us a great deal about the particular Franco-Scottish association, patterns of trade during these wars reveal much about the relationship between the British nations themselves. William's declarations of war on France have been described as 'the untimely upset that wrecked the fine balance of Anglo-Scottish rivalries that had been held in check by their common allegiance to the Stuart monarchy'. Scotland's interests, which had been accommodated within 'the existing framework of independent nations ruled by the divinely appointed James VII, a sovereign informed in Scottish maritime affairs and benevolent towards his northern subjects', were now allegedly subsumed into the wider interests of Britain, dominated by England. Scottish concerns were arguably of secondary importance for the House of Orange, as the domination of the English Parliament 'guaranteed the supremacy of the English mercantilist interest in British maritime affairs'.[7] As a result the Nine Years' War, 'so damaging to Scottish shipping and markets', was 'undertaken purely in the interests of the King and of his southern kingdom'.[8]

As has been mooted in preceding chapters, continuing Franco-Scottish trade in the later seventeenth and early eighteenth centuries suggests alternative conclusions. Scottish, English and indeed Irish merchants had diverse experiences of trading with France between 1688 and 1713, being held to different standards and varying codes of conduct. Scottish merchants in particular, and Irish merchants to a lesser extent, received preferential treatment that was offered in spite of, not because of, Scotland's closer political association with England. These experiences are compared in practical terms here, before explanations for these discrepancies are discussed in the following chapter.

I.

It is not difficult to see why scholars have asserted that direct trade between France and Scotland was virtually ruined as a result of William III's foreign policy.[9] William and Mary declared war on France with the support of the English Parliament on 17 May 1689, immediately authorizing British government officials to

> stay and arreast all ... ships and vessels ... conveying any goods or merchandize in them belonging to the French King or to his subjects and inhabitants or belonging to any persone within ... this kingdome [Scotland].[10]

When the Scottish Privy Council declared war on France on 6 August restrictions on commerce, communication and emigration were imposed, as the declaration 'discharg[ed] all the leidges of his Majesties antient kingdom of Scotland to trade, corospond or have any intercourse or medling with the said French king or any of his subjects'.[11] The French Trade Bill, passed in November 1690, along with the 1693 Trade with France Prohibition Act, consolidated these restrictions.[12] Freedom of movement, in addition to exchange of goods, was curtailed: 'we have thought fitt to require ... all persones during this tyme of warr who intend to goe out of [Scotland] to apply themselves for passes'.[13] Practically this was inconvenient for merchants, as mobility was the crux of their success. There were consequences for those who disregarded such restrictions – in October 1689 the Earl of Shrewsbury wrote to the Mayor of Dover,

> I hope the example of Joyce, who is sent for in custody, will be a warning to all others concerned to be more faithful and diligent in securing the best course to be taken with those who pursue a trade in carrying persons to France, who have no allowance to go, from several of the adjacent ports and creeks.[14]

Prohibitions returned when war broke out between Britain and France in 1702, some being laid before the official declaration of war. In January 1701 the Scottish Parliament issued an 'Act Dischargeing Wine Brandie and all other Liquors of the growth of France', declaring an embargo on 'the importation of all French wines, Brandie and other strong waters and vinegar made in France from any place whatsomever'. This proclamation was largely retaliatory, expressly to remain in force until 'the same liberties and immunities be granted to herrings and all other goods exported from this Kingdom into France and the same freedom and immunities granted to Scots ships sailing thither that any other Nation enjoy in that Kingdom'.[15] In September of the same year the French issued an arrêt preventing the importation of alcohol, textiles and metal from Great Britain,[16] and placed greater impositions on goods 'of the growth and manufacture of England, Scotland, Ireland and dependent countries'.[17] On 11 April 1702, a month before war was declared, the French reiterated their ban on the entry of any manufactures from England, Scotland or Ireland.[18] In May the British crown imposed an additional duty on French goods, which was reported in London in June, and shortly afterwards all trade with France was prohibited.[19] The French Council of Commerce consolidated their position in August by issuing an arrêt prohibiting trade with all enemy powers – England, its dependencies, Holland and Germany.[20] As was the case during the Nine Years' War, those who did not abide by these regulations were punished. In March 1712 Edward Northey, the Attorney-General, reported to the Secretary of State, Lord Dartmouth, that an Irish vessel had been taken by an English privateer at Bordeaux. Northey stated that this ship was a legitimate prize, before noting that 'as to her Majesties subjects who were in the same & are now in Custody if they went voluntarily into France without her Majesties Pass, the same is high Treason and they may be prosecuted therefore if her Majesty shall think fit'.[21] Even after the Treaty of Utrecht had been signed on 11 April 1713 reports circulated in London of ships encountering problems in renewing trade with France:

> A great many of our Merchant Ships are arrived at Rochel, Bourdeaux, Nantz, and other Harbours of France; but being ordered to keep at a certain Distance from the Harbour for 30 or 40 Days, the Chamber of Commerce have writ to the Intendants, representing the Prejudice which will thereby accrue to Trade.[22]

Outbreak of war with France of course played a significant role in precipitating the implementation of stoppages on exchange and movement. As considered at length in Chapter 3, however, even when warfare may appear to have dominated the minds of monarchs and governments, a great deal of legislation continued to be influenced by domestic concerns. From 1688 the danger of a Jacobite rebellion against a fledgling monarchy was one felt very keenly by William and Mary. It was perhaps this, coupled with the outbreak of the Jacobite War in Ireland in March, rather than the impending Nine Years' War that broke out two months later that fuelled the embargo implemented on 23 April 1689 against 'all shipes and Barkes within this Kingdome ... no shipes or Barkes aforesaid be allowed to sail abroad till they first find cautione to the respective collectors that they shall not goe to France or Ireland'.[23] Throughout the Nine Years' War concern regarding Jacobitism continued to shape regulations. A proclamation for apprehending people who remained in France illegally after 1694 was published in 1696, listing many suspected Jacobites.[24] The weight of domestic, as well as international, concerns was demonstrated a year following the Treaty of Ryswick. The 'Act anent Persons going to and returning from France' specifically concerned

> severall disaffected persons who did go into or remain in the Kingdom of France during the late war contrary to the late Act of Parliament ... We hereby Command and

Appoint all Masters of Ships who shall bring home any passengers from any forraigne Countreyes after the date hereof that they do detain them and take security of them'.[25]

In addition to direct prohibitions, whatever motivation lay behind them, merchants had to contend with logistical interruptions to their activities following both 1689 and 1702. The inevitably higher taxation rates imposed during war allegedly disrupted Franco-Scottish trade following the Glorious Revolution.[26] The need to recruit men for the war effort was damaging as it led to unseasonable patterns of sailing – during the Nine Years' War all trading ships were prevented from leaving port between February and May, and were required to have returned by February the following year. As ships were appropriated for naval operations there was a decline in protective convoys, meaning that there was little protection against privateering available for those merchant ships that did venture out.[27] In logistical terms the impact of Anne's French war was similar to William's, particularly in the problems it created for merchants through unseasonal sailings, delays and insufficient protection for shipping.[28] Using merchants and their ships to furnish the armed forces remained standard policy for all participants – an anonymous correspondent informed Charles Hedges, the English Secretary of State, in 1705 that France was restricting sailings of merchant vessels in order to impress the sailors they required for the Navy during the War of the Spanish Succession.[29] News of the perceived impact on trade of prohibitions and impressment travelled throughout Scotland. Charles Lord Yester wrote to his father John, second Marquess of Tweeddale, on 23 September 1701, stating his belief that 'the project you write off, about our trade with France ... it wil come to nothing; for, by the accounts we have in the last publick news, the King of France seems to have discharged all trade with Brittain'.[30]

II.

The lack of convoys, coupled with a rise in antagonistic naval operations, once again placed privateering high on the list of concerns for merchants. In some cases this was with good reason. David and John Williamson, father and son from Kirkcaldy, were taken to Amiens as prisoners in May 1689 after being captured by a French privateer while bound for Holland.[31] Less than a month after this was reported the Grangepans skipper Thomas Smith and his seamen were captured by a Dunkirk privateer and taken to Rochefort while on a voyage from Bo'ness to Rotterdam.[32] Some merchants suffered severe material loss – George Lockhart of Glasgow claimed that he lost his share on twenty-two ships between 1690 and 1698, and on two more in 1699 and 1700.[33] That Lockhart lost ships during the five-year lull between the Treaty of Ryswick and the outbreak of war with France in 1702 suggests that the 1688–1713 period was one in which

Franco-British tensions remained consistent. Ryswick was, after all, a peace of exhaustion rather than a lasting solution to continuing tensions.

During the War of the Spanish Succession too, Scottish shipping suffered at the hands of the French. James Cuming had been granted a convoy in 1709 to trade to France, but was left by this convoy and subsequently taken by French privateers.[34] St Malo privateers took the *Eagle Galley* of Aberdeen in 1706 on its return voyage from Liborne.[35] The *Anna* of Pittenweem was taken off the coast of Aberdeen by *l'Amazon* of Calais and ransomed for 5,123 livres 14 sous; payment of the ransom was facilitated by Scottish factors in France.[36] Scottish ships taken by French privateers during this conflict were not always those engaged in specific Franco-Scottish trade. The *Helen* of Dunbar, skippered by John Ferguson, was taken by a French privateer in 1704 while returning from Stavanger with timber, and the *Henrietta* of Bo'ness, skippered by Duncan Finlayson, was captured by a French privateer in 1710 and taken to Calais while en route from Holland.[37] Though French privateers apparently targeted the Baltic convoy, Scots continued to engage Scandinavian shipping.[38] English merchants employed this tactic with more limited success. In June 1707 *The Little Jacob*, 'of and for Stockholm' with Jacob Gentleman master, arrived in Falmouth laden with salt from La Rochelle, facilitating trade to London in a ship that was at least claimed to be of Swedish origin. On 6 June, the *Daily Courant* reported that the ship had been 'plounder'd by 4 French Privateers of 26, 18, 14 and 12 guns'.[39]

As shown in other contexts above, however, recent claims that the effect of the infamous French privateers was not as disastrous as previously assumed, particularly for Scottish shipping, are once again justified.[40] Following the battle of La Hogue in 1692 the French corsairs faced a crisis of recruitment that continued throughout the period.[41] Significantly, the impact that the French privateering fleet had on British shipping was not uniform and there were discrepancies in the numbers of Scottish, English and Irish prizes seized by the French during the Nine Years' War. Prizes taken into Nantes by French corsairs between 1689 and 1691 include several English ships but no Scottish or Irish vessels.[42] Similarly, prize lists kept by the port of Le Havre between 1692 and 1697 register no Scottish or Irish ships but do include several English, one Portuguese, two Dutch and one Danish ship which was released (Appendix C).[43] Daniel Defoe focused on losses of English ships, claiming in 1701 that

> they know very little of Trade, who are ignorant that the greatest advantage the French gain of us in a War, is in their Privateers surprising so many of our Merchant Ships, which can never be avoided in a War, because of the great quantity of Shipping we employ in every corner of the Seas, and the Impossibility of assigning Convoys to every Part of the World. Some have affirm'd, how true I know not, that during the last War they took Three Thousand Sail of our Ships, and the loss to the English has been Computed at Twenty Million.[44]

In 1704 Defoe's *Review of the Affairs of France* reported even greater losses during the first years of the War of the Spanish Succession, though he noted that trade was not curtailed: 'in general, our Trade has thriven upon the War, notwithstand-ing I compute above 30 Millions Sterling lost at Sea, by French Privateers'.[45] How accurate such estimates were is open to debate, but in any case damages were not shared equally by the British nations – it was again the English who suffered the greatest losses. During the 1700s the Admiralty of Le Havre took receipt of a high percentage of captured English and Irish ships, but no Scots.[46] Similarly, prizes recorded by the Admiralty of Dieppe from 1702 to 1705 included many English ships, but only one Irish (in 1705) and no Scots.[47] These patterns were reciprocated. In 1702 the French closed ports between Dunkirk and Bayonne because of 'a large number of frigates and other vessels of the ports of England and Holland, who cruise off the coast of France and remove merchants' vessels, boats, and other boats who sail'.[48] No comparable Scottish activity was reported.

Ominously, though, it was not only French privateers with whom Scottish merchants had to contend. A report from the Captain of the *Pembroke*, commis-sioned by the Lords of the English Admiralty in 1691, noted that

> the Scots had a free trade with France, which I now confirm ... I heard of one Francis Duncombe, master of the *John*, pink, whom I followed to this place, intending to have examined him, but about twenty of his men presented their arms at me ... and farther they told me that free trading was allowed in these parts with France.[49]

In response, the English Admiralty deployed privateers and men-of-war to cruise around the Scottish coasts and arrest ships suspected of trading with France and the American colonies.[50] England targeted Scottish shipping in other ways; in 1695 the Navigation Acts were made more stringent and the penalties for infringement more severe.[51] During the War of the Spanish Succession com-plaints of Scottish merchants were more commonly directed at the behaviour of English ships than French. A group of Edinburgh merchants petitioned Queen Anne, complaining that Scottish vessels were being stopped and seized by English ships under fabricated claims that they were bound for France – even though the Scots could prove that they had in fact been freighted for Lisbon.[52] It has been suggested that 'as far as the Scots were concerned, the worst offenders in terms of piracy were the English', with routes to France and the Netherlands being particularly liable to attack.[53] Further, Scotland was forced to retaliate against these practices, exhausting her resources through fitting out planned expeditions against the English.[54] If France permitted and protected Scottish trade, and the actions of England deliberately damaged it, this suggests a contradictory state of affairs to one where England was Scotland's partner and France Scotland's enemy.

III.

Just as they had earlier in the century British merchants employed evasive meth-ods in order to pursue contraband trade during both the Nine Years' War and the War of the Spanish Succession. This included the use of neutral ships, registering ships as belonging to a neutral country, carrying falsified documents and passes, or adjusting the places or commodities they traded in. The *Maria* was registered as a Swedish ship in 1694, despite being owned by a Scot and skippered by Jasper Stewart, a Scottish burgess of Stockholm; Swedish neutrality allowed the ship to sail from Aberdeen to La Rochelle and then on to Sweden.[55] As later discovered by *The Little Jacob*, however, neutrality did not translate to immunity from dangers at sea, mirroring experiences in the Franco-Stuart Wars. In May 1695 the *London Gazette* reported that 'a Flushing Privateer brought last Tuesday into Leith Road 4 Suedes and Danes laden with Wine, Salt, Brandy and Mollosses from France'.[56] While not always successful, the same familiar tactics were prevalent during the War of the Spanish Succession. In 1704 it was reported in the English Parliament that the Irish 'sometimes freight Deanish vessels and load them with Beeffe and Butter enter them for portingall but ship them in to nants or Rochell'.[57] The testimony of the Liverpool merchant Daniel Collett, indicted for participating in illegal trade in 1704, included a statement that he witnessed illegal Franco-Scottish and -Irish trade while in Bordeaux.

> Several Irish and Scottish vessels come thither to trade, one whereof he particularly knew called the *Mary Ann* belonging to Dublin which ship brought thither butter and other provisions, and was loading back wines etc onboard which ship the said informant called and desired the master (whence he knew but cannot positively call by name) to afford him passage for Ireland or elsewhere, which the said Master refused alledging he was bound to Norway.

Following his return to Liverpool, Collett embarked on a voyage for Bridgewater with a loading of rocksalt, and had occasion to dock at Waterford. There, he saw the *Mary Ann* unloading a cargo of her wines and being fitted for another voyage, having sailed to Ireland despite protesting her destination to be Norway.[58] These practices were utilized throughout the conflict. In 1712, a Jersey Privateer near Bordeaux captured two Dublin ships with Irish crews. It was reported that 'both masters had passes for Bilbow, the owners of the privateer made no doubt of having them condemd, believing they have sufficient proof they lodeth at burdux'.[59]

On other occasions the use of clandestine tactics was deliberately ignored or even assisted. In 1702 a paper was submitted to the English Treasury concerning French wine being brought over from St Sebastian:

> It was taken there from Bordeaux, a Spanish name given to it, and reshipped in Spanish casks. Sufficient number of hogskins were kept in every cellar, and mules were also kept that it might be supposed the wines were brought from Navarre on mules' backs in hogskins. Mr Manly and Mr Cooke, who were sent over to inspect the trade were blinded with this device.[60]

In January 1703 it was recognized that there was a 'clandestine trade carried on from Bourdeaux and other parts of France by way of St Sebastian and other ports of Spain, whereby great quantities of French wine were imported, paying only the Spanish duty'. The complicity of the port officials was noted: 'this management seemed to be carried on in concert between the consuls in foreign parts and some officers in the Customs ... who for private gratuities undertook for and passed such wines as were of the growth of Spain'.[61] A House of Lords enquiry in 1704 reported fifteen ships in Bordeaux loading brandies and wines, mostly from the West Country, Scotland and Ireland – but suggested that the government discouraged informers and was inclined to hush the matter up rather than pursue the offenders.[62]

One of the tactics used by merchants to circumvent prohibitive legislation, as discussed in Chapter 2, was to turn to alternative locations or commodities.[63] While Spanish wine was a viable alternative it was more profitable to import French wine, which explains why the rigmarole of transporting French wine to St Sebastian and disguising it as Spanish was undertaken. Re-export figures for wine taken to England in the twelve months from November 1669 show French wines outnumbering those of Spanish by a ratio of more than three to one.[64] The Leith customs records for wine imports throughout the 1680s reflect the continuing popularity of French as opposed to Spanish wines (see Figure 6.1).[65]

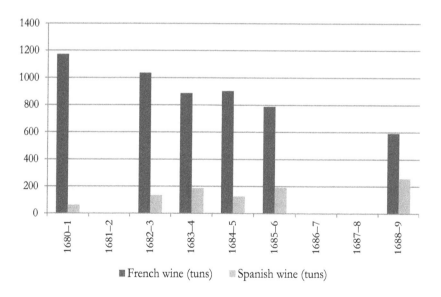

Figure 6.1 French and Spanish wine imported into Leith, 1680–9.

While merchants did increasingly take advantage of alternative routes – particularly following the outbreak of war in 1688 – on the whole French wine remained favoured, and the upward spiral in the use of Spanish ports by Scottish merchants is reflective of their burgeoning transatlantic trade in the Restoration era.[66] Prevailing financial motivations are clear, as the excise on French wine in the 1680s was set at £36 per tun, compared to £54 per tun on Spanish wine.[67] The potential for profit was higher as consumers, 'tired of inferior and unfamiliar wines from Portugal, Spain and Italy', were happy to pay higher prices for the French product.[68] Though wine was available from alternative locations, Scottish merchants continued to favour French wines; hence they pursued commerce along familiar trading routes, drawing on the retention of their trading privileges in France.

Despite the continued popularity of French wine in Scotland, by 1700 the deputies of the French Council of Commerce lamented that French ports were being bypassed and wines bought in Spain and Portugal, a phenomenon blamed on excessive taxes on wine and brandy exports that were decreasing foreign sales.[69] Certainly debate concerning French and Portuguese goods was rife in Britain in the early eighteenth century, with taste, fashion and demand being additional factors that led merchants to favour one destination over another.[70] The London newspaper the *Mercator* claimed in 1713 that 'to take these People then at their own Words ... They had rather drink Port Wine, if the French Wines and the Port Wines were all at a Price'.[71] In typically satirical vein, the editors of the *Tatler* had reported much the same fashion three years earlier: 'He went on, Do you love French Wine? I believe you may; I did once my self: But let me tell you, that White Port is not only the cheapest, but the best Wine now about Town'.[72] Such assertions may reflect outward Francophobia, as well as the availability of alternative avenues of trade, but the market for French wines defied such propaganda and remained buoyant.

Neither evasive methods nor alternative routes were always necessary, however, and merchants – both Scottish and English – chose blatantly to disregard prohibitive legislation during both of these conflicts. In 1689 the Commissaries of Customs told the Lords of the Treasury that they

> daily received advice of ships, by art and violence, getting out of port and going to France, without giving security, according to the King's late order not to go to France, and that there was a great number of English shipping then at Bourdeaux.[73]

Though it has been asserted that between 1689 and 1713 normal supplies of French and Spanish salt were cut off by conflict,[74] it was reported in London in the summer of 1695 that the *Rupert* brought in a vessel to London 'laden with salt from France', with no indication given that this was contrary to any legislation or an unusual occurrence in the prevailing political climate.[75] Scottish port records corroborate the continuation of trade with France during the Nine Years' War. Edward Burd, bringing the *George* of Edinburgh into Leith in May 1689, was not accused of being in contravention of the April 1689 embargo. While he may have been in a position to prove that he began his voyage before the implementation of the embargo, such testimony was not required of him.

Following 1691 restrictions were tightened – the embargo issued in Britain in April 1689 only prohibited trade exports to France, whereas the 1691 embargo was much more emphatic in also banning the importation of French goods.[76] As noted by the collectors of Customs and Foreign Excise many ships continued to bring in merchandise from France between 1689 and the implementation of the more stringent embargo in 1691.[77] Further privateering commissions were issued which threatened continuing trade – at the same time as the 1691 embargo was issued in May Ninian Gibsone, Glasgow merchant and captain of the *Lamb*, was granted a commission to 'arreast all other ships and vessels of whatsoever other kingdome, country, nation or people, conveying any goods or merchandize in them belonging to the French King or to his subjects'.[78] Nevertheless, following 1691 open trade continued. In December, Robert Watson brought the *Constantina* of Copenhagen into Leith from Bilbao, carrying 110 tuns and two hogsheads of French wine; another shipment carried through Spain. William Wemyss, in the *Pearle* of London, brought twenty-six tuns of French wine into Leith 'conforme to the Lords of Thesirii ther order', and in September several merchants are recorded bringing in French wine to the same port – one of these being George Clark in the *Golden Flight* of Stockholm, with eighty-eight tuns.[79] Again there is no suggestion that these events were in contravention of wartime embargoes – quite the opposite, with Wemyss fulfilling a commission brought by the Lords of the Treasury. Neutral Scandinavian shipping was widely utilized, but Wemyss's choice of a London vessel is perplexing. It is possible that in receiving his commission from the Lords of the Treasury he was granted permission to circumvent prohibitions, but an English ship would presumably have been a more likely target for French corsairs. Perhaps his successful completion of this voyage confirms the decline in effectiveness of French privateering.

Reports of continuing trade with France circulated during the War of the Spanish Succession. In January 1705 it was reported in London that the *Prince* of Flushing, which had come into Falmouth from Bordeaux with a Dutch ship as prize, had 'left in that Port several sail of Dutch, Irish and Scotch ships, which were taking in their lading'.[80] The same anonymous correspondent cited above informed Sir Charles Hedges of the ramifications of this trade, but concern was with the potential damage caused to other trading relationships rather than the issue of contravention of wartime embargoes on the French. It was stated that the liberty that the Scots[,] Irish & Dutch have to trade with France, doth very much prejudice our Swedish trade, there is at present about 50 saile Scots & Irish at Bourdeaux who have brought butter & beef from thence as also great many here, at Rochelle & Nantes.[81]

Later that year, reports reached London that 'the Franchises of the Fair of Bordeaux have been extended to the last day of Novemb., a month more than they used to be, in favour of the Dutch and Scotch Ships that shall come there to lade Goods of the Growth or Manufacture of this Kingdom'.[82] In all three of these examples it was explicitly Scottish and Irish trade with France that continued, with no mention of any Anglo-French exchange.

As the conflict continued, so too did Franco-Scottish trade. In February 1706, Captain Archibald Cockburn of Edinburgh, along with Daniel Masson and Alexander Young of St Martin, brought a case to the Admiralty Court of Scotland against the Bordeaux merchant Samuel Martin and Peter Lawson, master of the *St Anne* of Bergen, who were represented by George Gordon in Leith, formerly of Bordeaux. Cockburn, Masson and Young claimed £13,026 Scots for 'tonnage for fourty tuns claret wyne from Bordeaux to Leith'.[83] Presumably if this voyage had been seen as illegal, they would not have risked trying to claim this debt in a public court. In February 1706 Robert Arbuthnot wrote to Henri François d'Aguesseau, the procurator fiscal in France, concerning the continuation of Franco-Scottish commerce, and one month later his kinsman Thomas was registered entering the port of Dieppe.[84] In 1712 a transaction for the sale of salmon and grilse from James Menzies of Pitfodels, merchant in Aberdeen, was performed in Dieppe through James Arbuthnot, confirming the integration of the Arbuthnots in Franco-Scottish affairs as well as the retention of French markets for Scottish goods.[85] By the beginning of 1713 reports were coming from England of ships from France entering British ports, these occurrences being reported in strikingly blunt terms with no indication of obstacles presented by persistent conflict.[86]

Though Scottish merchants did report experiencing difficulties trading in France following the agreement of the Treaty of Utrecht, this was attributed to market conditions rather than the political climate. On 16 May 1713 Robert Arbuthnot wrote to James Menzies of the 'miserable market' for salmon in Rouen, but ascribed this to 'the bad condition your salmond came to france in', not to the conflict of the preceding decade.[87] The account books of William Russell & Company, merchants in Wigtown, denote trading with various destinations in Holland, Norway, England and Scotland, but also with Nantes and Rouen throughout the 1700s, with no mention of disruption caused by war.[88] Certainly there was some impact on Franco-Scottish commerce, including the misfortune of some merchants who were taken by privateers or who lost their cargoes in other ways. Yet the charge that the leading Scottish factors left Bordeaux eighteen months after the War of the Spanish Succession broke out in 1702 because they no longer had any business in France must be reconsidered in light of the realities of continuing Franco-Scottish trade during this conflict.[89]

IV.

Some merchants did not have to turn to falsified passes or neutral shipping in order to continue to trade, but were able to trade legitimately with the conniv-ance of civil authorities on either side of the Channel. In addition to turning a blind eye to evasive tactics, and despite the continuing war effort, passes were granted that allowed Franco-Scottish trade to continue; providing an additional layer of bureaucracy for merchants to contend with but preserving commercial links. In January 1692 six passes were issued by the Scottish Privy Council for five Glasgow ships and one Leith ship to travel to Bordeaux on a commercial ven-ture, though permission was only granted to transport unspecified 'authorised goods'.[90] In May 1693 an official decree was passed allowing Scots to correspond with and travel to France with 'express leave' of the Monarchs or Privy Council – a loophole that allowed merchants to continue their trade while simultaneously allowing the government to guard against insurgency.[91]

In France, too, Scottish merchants were frequently granted passes to allow them to trade during the Nine Years' War. In November 1691 a French mer-chant in La Rochelle, Abraham Duport, petitioned the Admiralty of that town for a passport for John Broune, commander of the Scottish ship the *Jean* of Pittenweem, to travel from La Rochelle to Scotland. The pass was granted on 22 November, opening the floodgates for a slew of such passes throughout the 1690s.[92] These included documentation to allow Edmond Gould to pass through La Rochelle on his way to Norway in May 1692,[93] and a number of passes for Charles Cahell and Robert Mackarel to pass from La Rochelle to Scot-land in the same year.[94] Irish merchants were also successful in acquiring passes in La Rochelle – in 1695, fifteen passports were granted to British ships, with twelve of those being Scottish and the remaining three Irish (Appendix D).[95] In addition, the records of these passes further corroborate some of the trading methods explored in Chapter 2. Several individuals had shares in more than one of the ships being granted passports in this year – Daniel Masson, Jean Mackarel and Abraham Duport being particularly prolific – supporting the notion that those involved in commerce were practised in spreading their interest as insur-ance against loss.

The Admiralty of La Rochelle was not anomalous. The records of other west coast French ports corroborate these patterns of British trade in France and the records for Bordeaux are particularly revealing. Throughout the 1690s numer-ous Scottish ships were granted permission by the Admiralty of Guyenne to pass through this port (Appendix E). As in La Rochelle there was significant Irish activity and passes were granted to Irish vessels throughout the 1690s.[96] The available sources permit direct comparison between the commercial activities of Scottish and English merchants in Bordeaux during the Nine Years' War, and reveal that during the course of this conflict ninety-nine English ships were granted passports by the Admiralty of Guyenne, compared to fifty-four Scottish (Appendix F).[97] This data, however, despite suggesting almost twice as much English as Scottish activity across the conflict, is somewhat misleading. Greater insight can be gleaned through examination of the patterns of this trading activity across the period, as the times at which passes were granted belie England's apparent advantage (see Figure 6.2).

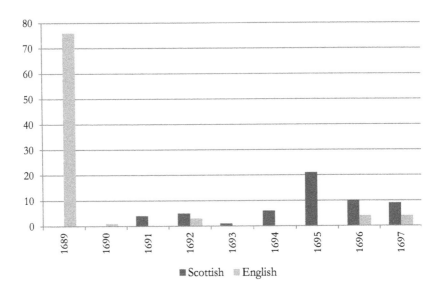

Figure 6.2 Passports granted to British ships by the Admiralty of Guyenne, 1689–97.

The vast majority of passes granted to English merchant vessels to enter the port of Bordeaux fall during the year 1689, with no passports being granted to English ships between July 1692 and April 1696. That many passports were granted at the beginning of the conflict is unsurprising – as explored in earlier chapters, if merchants could demonstrate that they had begun their voyage before legislation was implemented they were usually allowed to complete it. Furthermore, as explored above, the 1691 embargo was much more emphatic than that issued in Britain in April 1689.[98] Conversely, the majority of passports granted to Scottish ships were issued at the height of war. The lack of passes granted to Scots in 1689 and 1690 attests not to a lack of activity, but is instead indicative of the continuing commercial and naturalization privileges enjoyed by Scots in France. Scottish merchants, being naturalized French subjects, did not ordinarily require passes in French law to enter the country or to participate in commercial activities. When Scotland and France were at war and trade explicitly prohibited, however, passes were required to allow Scottish vessels to bypass these sanctions. Scottish merchants were thus inconvenienced by warfare, but only by the need to acquire passes that were surplus to requirements in peacetime. Patterns of passes granted to British vessels by the Admiralty of Guyenne attest that authorities consciously held Scottish and English merchants to different rules, undoubtedly in recognition of the long held and deeply felt association between Scotland and France.

There were similarities in Queen Anne's approach to commerce with France during the War of the Spanish Succession, and as we saw in Chapter 3 restrictions on the importation of French wine during this conflict were not absolute. In addition, Anne earned a reputation amongst Scottish authorities for granting passes that allowed trade with France to continue, though this contravened her own wartime embargoes. In August 1705 James Ogilvy, the Earl of Seafield, wrote that

> ther is a letter from the Councel too her Majestie sent to Sir David Nairn, advising the granting of passes to Scots ships for ther securitie in ther tread with France and Spain, this being agreable too the treatie with the States of Holand. Without wee had done this, the merchants wer to have applyed to the Parlament, so wee thought it better to send this letter, which, wee hope, will be granted.[99]

It was perhaps this precedent for passes being granted that encouraged a group of Edinburgh merchants to petition Parliament in September 'in relation to passes from her Majestie dureing the time of war of carrieing on their trade', and to

> request that passes be granted by her Majestie to the subjects of this Kingdome trading to France and Spain and that her Majesty may be pleased to give such orders as shall protect them in their said trade as well against her Majesties ships of war and privateers as those of her allies.[100]

Restrictions on trade during both the Nine Years' War and the War of the Spanish Succession were thus flouted legally and illegally, openly and covertly. Furthermore, Scotland's merchants benefited from unbalanced enforcement of legislation and prohibitions. The Admiralty of La Rochelle issued an ordinance in 1690 concerning the opening and closing of ports, 'prohibiting English and Dutch vessels and vessels of Spanish Flanders leaving the ports of France unless they are loaded with the food or goods of France', but placing no similar stipulation on the Scots or the Irish.[101] During the War of the Spanish Succession too, restrictions were relaxed or revoked during the course of the war. Contrary to the arrêt they had issued on 28 August 1703, the French Council of Commerce announced the following month that they were reopening trade with Scotland and Ireland. The Council was soon flooded with requests for passports from Frenchmen to go to Scotland and Ireland and from Irish and Scottish merchants residing in French ports who wished to trade with or travel back to their homeland.[102] Scotland again demonstrated a degree of independence, with the Scottish Wine Act of 1703 rescinding all previous legislation concerning the importation of French wine – in direct contravention of the economic blockade that was a key strategy in the Crown's war effort against the French.[103]

As war progressed, compromises were struck that permitted economic exchange between Britain and France to continue. In 1708 and 1710 the Lord High Admiral of Great Britain ordered all 'captains and commanders of her Majesty's ships and vessels, as also all persons who now have, or shall have private commissions or letters of Marque, not to molest any of the fishing vessels belonging to the subjects of France' – part of a reciprocal agreement with the French.[104] On 15 March 1711, two years before the Treaty of Utrecht was enacted, the British Parliament formally allowed the importation of French wine in neutral vessels. Though restrictions on other commodities remained in place, this did not prevent their exchange. Items including stockings, herring and various cloth continued to appear in merchant transactions between Scotland and France, as the account book of an anonymous Edinburgh merchant testifies.[105] By 1713, prior to the agreement reached at Utrecht, it was being suggested in London that 'all laws made in Great Britain since the year 1664 prohibiting the importation of any goods from France [should] be repealed'.[106] Franco-British trade was once again fully open, but it had been Scotland, and to a lesser extent Ireland, who received the most assistance in pursuing trade at the height of war.

V.

This brings us once more to the question of Scotland's independence, and whether or not her participation in both of these conflicts was indeed a manifestation of the dominance of the English Parliament within Britain. Scotland's declaration of war on her auld ally at the start of the Nine Years' War came only after a direct order from the Crown. On 10 July 1689, having declared war in England's name in May, William wrote to the Privy Council of Scotland that 'wee have thought fit to authorize and requyre yow to isue furth a declairatione of warr in our name against the said king and his subjects'.[107] This request was duly fulfilled in August, despite Scotland being poorly prepared, in some respects, for warfare. Following the Glorious Revolution she had been left with no Lord High Admiral of the Navy, leaving her Privy Council to issue commissions for individuals to contribute to Scotland's war effort. There were willing volunteers.

In May 1689 a commission had been issued to Captaine William Burnsyde to man the *Dogarwyne* of Edinburgh and

> to take and apprehend, and incaise of resistance to fyre, burne, sink and destroy the ships and goods of the French or Irishes in rebellione against their Majesties ... and alsoe to stay and areist all other ships and vessells of whatsomever other kingdome, countrey, natione of people conveying any goods or merchandise in them belonging to the French king or to his subjects and inhabitants.[108]

The following February the Privy Council granted 'letters of marque and generall reprizall' to John Boswell 'for apprehending ships or goods belonging to the French or Irish'.[109] Of course, at this juncture Scotland retained both her Parliament and Privy Council, affording her some legislative autonomy; and again the influence of concerns for domestic security can be seen.

The extent to which Scotland only participated in this war as a result of English wishes is, however, debatable. Despite England's apparent superiority Scotland was not overwhelmed by English interests. The Privy Council of Scotland acted to prevent Scottish merchantmen being pressed into service, in 1690 granting protection to David Wood, a Montrose skipper, and his entire crew, as 'Scots trading ships shall have protectione on board for preventing their mens being pressed'.[110] Indeed, despite claims that William 'regarded Scotland solely as a source of troops ... for his endless European wars',[111] like Cromwell before him William demonstrated active concern for the effect of the conflict on his northern kingdom. When implementing a press for the Navy in February 1693 he stated that 'for the security and encouragement of the free trade of Scotland we have ordered that no pressmen seize any seaman on board any ship belonging to Scotland',[112] explicitly protecting Scotland's overseas trade during the Nine Years' War. Despite some inconveniences, Scottish merchants continued to enjoy a flourishing trade with France during this conflict, in several ways being explicitly protected from its effects and receiving favourable treatment on both sides of the Channel.

It is clear that Scotland was not governed solely by English policies during the War of the Spanish Succession; indeed, Scotland voiced its disgust over perceived English domination of foreign policy in the Act anent Peace and War of 1703. Scotland's declaration of war had been its own, coming over a week after England's,[113] and once officially involved the Scottish Parliament refused to augment the tariffs on merchandise imported from France despite urgent requests from Queen Anne to do so.[114] By declaring war one week after England, Scotland not only asserted its independence but used this time to preserve its relationship with France. During this week a renewed Franco-Scottish alliance was actively considered, presumably as an alternative to warfare. On 5 May 1702 one J. G. wrote from Paris to Caspar Frederick Henning, keeper of the Privy

Purse, that 'since Wednesday the Court is at Marly where it is deliberating on the alliance between France and Scotland, and how to engage the Scots in the interest of France'.[115] Though inevitably considering their own interests, action on the part of both the French and the Scots during a time of ostensible conflict highlights the desire to prolong their reciprocal commercial relationship, as well as suggesting that Scotland actively considered alternatives to entering the war as France's enemy. Louis XIV's 1703 assertion that 'the whole French nation had their hearts unfeignedly Scottish' indicates continued recognition of the Auld Alliance, as well as a desire that conflict should not be allowed to damage this ancient confederation.[116]

Once involved in the War of the Spanish Succession, Scottish participation was not viewed as one with England's. It has already been noted that in 1703 the French Council of Commerce authorized the granting of passports to Scottish and Irish vessels. In 1706, the Council also permitted direct trade with England.[117] Although France thus allowed trade to all of the British nations while war continued to rage, English merchants had to wait three years longer than the Scots for this prohibition to be relaxed, suggesting both Scotland's continued commercial independence from England and the special favour she received from France. It is worth emphasizing that these revocations were not reciprocated by Great Britain – only the French saw post-1703 trade as legal and Scottish institutions supported continuing trade that was, strictly speaking, illicit. Again, both the attitudes of England and Scotland towards participation in the conflict and how they were viewed on the continent is strikingly different – the following chapter explores the reasons why.

The Anglo-Scottish union of 1707 was, of course, implemented almost exactly at the mid-way point of the War of the Spanish Succession, even if contemporaries were not to be aware of that. Discussion of the effect of union on Franco-Scottish trade deserves its own monograph, but in the context of the War of the Spanish Succession there are several pertinent points to be made. The behaviour of Scottish merchants in the months preceding union demonstrates both that Franco-Scottish trade continued and that English government officials were perfectly aware of this, despite apparently maintaining sanctions on the importation of French wine into Britain. In preparation for union huge quantities of wine were imported into Scotland, as merchants aimed to take advantage of the impending freedom of movement between the British nations that would allow them to re-export this wine into England customs free.[118] Such a possibility was firmly recognized – wine that was imported into Scotland before 1 May was specifically prohibited from being re-exported to England; this prohibition in itself conceded that the continuation of the Franco-Scottish wine trade had become accepted practice, even if the illegality of this trade continued to be professed. This behaviour was condemned publicly, prompting the *Review of the State of the British Nation* to comment that there were

> immediate effects of the Union, particularly in Trade ... While in the Interval, to the 1ˢᵗ of May, the Scots are crowding the whole nation with French goods, wine and Brandy, &c, which paying but a Trifle of Custom there, will be imported upon us here; while we having paid high Duties, and imported from other Countries, feel the loss already in a general stop of Trade.[119]

In July 1707, perhaps buoyed by previous success in obtaining passes to trade with France during the War of the Spanish Succession, a group of Scottish merchants appealed to Queen Anne to be allowed to move their goods freely around Great Britain. They stated that they,

> with a due regard to the welfare of this Island ... have now at this time with sufficient permits and clearances granted by your majesties officers, for coasting from one part of Great Britain to the other, brought into the Port of London and other Ports of this Kingdom such a quantity of effect in wine etc as we found necessary.

These merchants maintained that the fourth article of the treaty allowed for 'freedom and intercourse of trade to and from any Port or Place within the United Kingdom', and argued that if the English were able to import freely into Scotland the reverse should also be true.[120] Yet Scottish merchants were not left unmolested even when they had contravened no legislation. Alexander Naughtie, a skipper in Leith, lodged a complaint against the Surveyors and Warehouse-keeper in Berwick-upon-Tweed that his ship, the *Ann of Wech* of Aberdeen, contained a lading of tar and a parcel of fish that was imported before the 1 May. The officers who 'hazarded and damaged the ship', and who were allegedly violent towards Naughtie and his men, were charged and the ship and goods returned, suggesting that the vessel and its lading were unlawfully arrested.[121] Once more, Scottish vessels suffered at the hands of English vessels rather than French privateers.

Despite various appeals and complaints port officials in London stood their ground against this practice. When Scottish merchants imported French wine into London after 1 May, 'to their unspeakable astonishment & great griefe, your Majesties Board of Customs has not only refused to Grant the peticioners any Warrant for unloading the Goods above mention'd, but have actually seized such Goods as were landed'.[122] The Port Officials explained upon being questioned that

> the goods of the growth, product or manufacture of France, or any other goods which by the Law of England before the Act of Union were under an absolute prohibition of being Brought into England upon any termes, or in any manner howsoever, such goods being in Scotland before the 1 of May 1707, cannot after the 1 of May, be brought thence into England, without being liable to Seizure. That notice of these

opinions was transmitted to Scotland, to prevent the petitioners and other being surprised if they had any thought of bringing such goods hither.[123]

The ability of Scottish merchants to import French wine into Scotland despite persistent European conflict is clear, with no mention that the presence of this wine in Scotland in the first place contravened any wartime embargoes. Further, this consolidates the argument presented in Chapter 3 that although certain regulations may have been implemented during wartime, primary motivation for legislation was just as often domestic and economic as it was international and political.

VI.

Both Scottish and Irish merchants continued to pursue trade with France throughout the international conflicts of the long seventeenth century, whether under a Stuart, Orange or Hanoverian regime. Though some clandestine tactics were adopted many merchants traded openly with their 'enemy' and this frequently with explicit governmental and monarchical encouragement. During the international wars of the seventeenth century the monarchy and government of both France and Britain were complicit in what were essentially contraband trading ventures. While some rogue Scottish merchants employed clandestine methods to pursue trade that they knew to be illegal, during these conflicts many asked permission of authorities, ensuring that they obtained the correct paperwork.

There were, of course, broad agendas that contributed to the support offered by authorities to ongoing 'illegal' trade and as they had in earlier periods both the French and British governments recognized the benefits of allowing commerce to continue. The Scottish Wine Act of 1703, as well as legalizing practices merchants were already pursuing, benefited the Treasury through increased import duties.[124] In January 1709 a petition was brought to the Lord High Treasurer by merchants trading to Portugal, Spain and Italy, complaining of a proposal brought by merchants in Virginia and Maryland asking for liberty to export tobacco, plantation goods and British manufactures to France in neutral ships and in return to import wine from France. The petition had initially gone to the Commissaries of Customs, who

> were of opinion that though the trade of Portugal, Spain and the Straits was very beneficial to Great Britain, and ought by all means to be encouraged, yet that the enlarging the vent of the plantation goods and British manufactures, would be a further advantage to the nation; even on the supposition that some French wines might be imported in return for such goods.

The Treasury concluded that they were not qualified to determine 'whether this advantage were of importance enough to open any trade with France at this time', which 'was a subject for much higher consideration than for this Board'.[125] However, the pronouncement of the commissaries does reflect the prevailing opinion that the entry of French wine into Britain was a reasonable price to pay for the expansion of the Plantation Trade. Specific wartime regulations were superseded by concerns for the expansion of the British economy as a whole.

On the part of France, it has been argued that it was only once the French Council of Commerce realized that total commercial warfare was damaging to their interests that they relaxed their arrêt to allow the importation of goods from Scotland, both because France had come to rely on Scotland and Ireland for various foodstuffs, and because she wished to foment divisions within Queen Anne's kingdoms.[126] That the latter was one of the objectives of the French government was recognized by contemporaries, and when Robert Arbuthnot wrote to d'Aguesseau in February 1706 he claimed that France granted favours to Scotland precisely because of this political aim.[127] The leniency shown to the Scots, moreover, was not consistent. In October 1705 the French Board of Trade granted an extension of time to the passports of Dutch traders, who were technically the direct enemies of France, but did not formally grant the same to Scots. Once again, contemporary perception of the relationship between France and Scotland overrode such a technicality as Scotsmen, believing that these decrees were also applicable to them, set sail for Le Havre in December.[128]

While concessions granted by the French may not always have been consistent, the extent to which Scotland, and to a lesser extent Ireland, was offered favoured-nation status over England during these conflicts is remarkable, as is the level of government knowledge of and consent for the continuation of commerce. As discussed in the Introduction, this is less surprising when the nature of early modern relationships is considered, and the application of modern notions of 'total war' to this period again appears anachronistic. 'The early modern national economies of Europe were interdependent, leading to adjustments rather than momentous change', and those involved in commerce were well prepared for dealing with the issues warfare gave rise to.[129] The desire of merchants themselves to continue to trade despite the political climate was echoed by governments and monarchs, who appreciated the necessity of maintaining an economic balance whatever the political context. Thus it was possible, even expected, to pursue actively a conflict against a sworn enemy but simultaneously allow commerce to persist. The Auld Alliance itself continued to play a central role – in addition to individual passes or exemptions from prohibitions being granted, the specific perpetuation of the commercial privileges enjoyed by Scottish merchants in France were reiterated during the Nine Years' War. In 1690 Sir John Hall of Dunglass, Lord Provost of Edinburgh, petitioned on behalf of the royal burghs of Scotland for the return of several charters of the Great Council of France and decreets of the Parliament of Rouen, containing exemptions and privileges in favour of Scottish merchants in the kingdome of France and duchy of Normandy, which have been allwayes keeped in a particular shuttle of the chartor chist of the town of Edinburgh and were taken out to be advised in order to the borrowes sending one in their name to the king's ambassador at Paris for continueing and renewing these privileidges.[130]

The House of Lords returned these charters to the petitioner, knowing that they would be used to facilitate French trade and to cement further exclusive Scottish trading privileges in France. The return of these charters, in addition to passes granted in Britain, demonstrates that despite William's political and religious grievances with France he recognized the importance of the continuation of Franco-Scottish trade.

The realities of continuing Franco-Scottish commerce during both of these conflicts suggest that Scotland did not become an English satellite state during the course of the seventeenth century, and instead maintained an independent overseas agenda even after 1707, at least where France was concerned. Continuing desire for commerce, as well as further reiterations of the historic alliance, consolidated the Franco-Scottish relationship during periods ostensibly hostile to trade. Merchants themselves wanted to continue to pursue their business, and as one merchant stated during the height of the Nine Years' War, 'I will trade to France, in spite of anybody'.[131] Certainly, the assertion that 'Franco-Scottish trade … was decisively brought to an end in 1689 by the Glorious Revolution'[132] now requires qualification, but the reasons behind the contrasting treatment of the British nations during these conflicts merit further consideration. Not only do these trading realities have implications for the specific Franco-Scottish – and Anglo-French – relationship, they raise additional questions regarding the comparative roles played in European affairs by the three kingdoms of Britain. This broader agenda is the focus of the following and final chapter.

7 BEYOND 1707: FRANCO-'BRITISH' RELATIONS?

In 1650 James Mowat wrote in a letter to a business associate in Edinburgh that 'if you werre hier you could gaine what you please, for theris many english and severall Scots that you might deall with'.[1] The recipient of this letter was none other than John Clerk of Penicuik. As has been made apparent throughout this volume, Clerk was at the heart of a wide-ranging network of Scottish individuals and, along with other prolific Scots including Michel Mel in Dieppe and William Popple in Bordeaux, he not only pursued Franco-Scottish commerce but encouraged the participation of other Scots in these endeavours despite the inclement political climate. He was able to do this because of his own skills and knowledge, but he also drew on a wide range of networks and associations fostered over a long period.

Though the primary purpose of this book has been to explore the specific Franco-Scottish relationship, limiting focus to the Scottish experience leaves a great deal unsaid about the wider British agenda. As suggested by Mowat the networks fostered by Scottish mercantile agents in France during the long seventeenth century were not exclusively Scottish. English as well as Irish individuals participated in French commerce, if in different circumstances and with varying levels of success. The British perspective is one that is particularly pertinent in a period when the domestic political status of the three kingdoms of Britain was changing. As already discussed, the events of 1560 have been heralded not only as the moment the Auld Alliance ended, but as the beginning of closer relations between Scotland and England, apparently cemented by the 1603 and 1707 unions. As the century progressed, Scotland's loss of status as an autonomous nation was apparently confirmed, as was its inability to govern its own foreign, diplomatic, economic or military policies independently.

The preceding chapters have shown that in the country's relationship with France, Scotland – and particularly Scottish merchants – defied this state of political affairs. In fact, Scotland remained in control of these commercial links, and its agents outperformed their English counterparts who, as we saw in Chapter 2, relied on 'the greater affability of the French towards the Scots' in employing Scottish merchants in Anglo-French trade.[2] Irish merchants also provided a route for English merchants into France; in 1713 the owners of the *Henry* of Hull exploited their business relationship with Thomas and Daniel Macnemara, Irish merchants in Nantes, to ship grain into France.[3] Although this attempt failed, with the cargo seized at Konigsberg in Prussia, it emphasizes the awareness among English merchants that Irish ships were more likely to succeed in French commercial ventures. Pertinently, in many arenas it was Scottish and Irish agents, not English, who dominated British overseas commerce. The work of other scholars has highlighted the importance and strength of Scotland's relations with several European nations in the early modern period, and this volume corroborates these findings for the case of Catholic France.[4] In the post-1688 conflicts discussed in the previous chapter, records from the west coast ports of France show that while Scottish and Irish merchants were left largely unmolested by French privateers (the former more so than the latter), English ships were targeted as part of the French war effort. Irish as well as Scottish merchants were assisted by exemptions from prohibitions and restrictions on trade. The 1690 ordinance that prevented English ships leaving the port of La Rochelle unless carrying French goods did not extend to Scotland or to Ireland.[5] When the French Council of Commerce reopened trade with Scotland in September 1703, they also reopened trade with Ireland. Though not protected by the same privileges or status as Scottish merchants, the Irish were nonetheless treated more leniently than their English counterparts as they pursued their business in French ports. Further, despite Scotland's political relationship with England, it was England's actions, rather than the actions of her supposed 'enemy' France, that were most damaging to her commerce during the Nine Years' War and the War of the Spanish Succession.

In addition to these broad, national variances in fortunes there were regional discrepancies that require closer investigation. In the previous chapter I suggested that during the Nine Years' War Scottish merchants dominated British trade with the port of Bordeaux, and throughout this book it has become clear that a large number of Scottish merchants and factors were active in this port, despite previous assertions that they were 'few in number'.[6] Patterns of Irish trade were different. Though Irish agents can be found participating in trade throughout France, they dominated in Nantes, particularly during the War of the Spanish Succession. Surviving records in this port for the period between April 1707 and February 1710 highlight a level of commercial activity far greater than either Scottish or English, albeit in a part of France in which it was the Dutch who undertook the majority of trading activity (see Table 7.1).[7]

Table 7.1: Nationality of foreign ships departing the port of Nantes, 1707–10.

Year	Dutch	Irish	Scottish	Other (excl. English)	Total
1707 (April–Dec.)	83	11	0	65	159
1708 (Jan.–Dec.)	182	27	1	60	270
1709 (Jan.–Dec.)	87	28	1	49	165
1710 (Jan.–Feb.)	4	4	0	3	11

Source: *Repertoir des conges par l'éstranger*, Archives départementales de la Loire-Atlantique, Nantes, B4725.

No English ship is present in these records – entries in the 'other' category comprise vessels primarily of Scandinavian and Spanish origin. That this trade was recorded in official port records suggests that Franco-Irish trade continued with the knowledge and consent of authorities in Nantes. This consent was consolidated by the numbers of Irish merchants granted passes to trade with France throughout the War of the Spanish Succession. According to Captain Masterton's 1704 report to the English Parliament, in France 'passes are att all times granted, to those who will undertake to bring [comb'd wooll] to France'. Masterton noted that at

> about the begening of September next passes will be granted to ships to bring over beefe and butter amongst wooll being prest into Barrells is frequently sent and by this means of tradeing they have constent intelligence what they are adoeing here.[8]

This final chapter is concerned with providing explanations for these discrepancies. Reasons why Scottish and Irish merchants were, on the whole, more successful in France than English will be suggested, but crucially particular attention is paid to regional patterns of trade. As argued in the Introduction, bi-lateral, national trading patterns tell us only part of the story of international exchange. Here, focus is on the comparison between Scottish dominance in Bordeaux and Irish dominance in Nantes, particularly in the post-1688 period. Traditionally, common political or religious adherence has been heralded as central to successful integration in foreign countries. Irish émigrés' adherence to Catholicism, for example, has been seen as a decisive factor determining successful integration, based on the acceptance that religious affiliation was a pre-requisite for integration into any host community.[9] This has been assumed to have been particularly important at a time when religion remained such a contested issue throughout Europe. Support for Jacobitism in France following the Glorious Revolution, too, seems an obvious explanation for French complicity in continuing Franco-Scottish and -Irish trade. This chapter suggests some problems with these conventional explanations in light of regional patterns of British trade in France, offering alternative suggestions that, it is argued, provide much more compelling justifications for the patterns of trade that emerged throughout the long seventeenth century.

I.

There are obvious political explanations for Scottish commercial success in France, as the historic alliance cultivated since 1295 remained the cornerstone of the Franco-Scottish relationship up to and beyond the 1707 union (Chapter 1). The reciprocal political, social and commercial benefits that Scots enjoyed continued throughout the long seventeenth century, allowing merchants to undertake lucrative trade in France despite the inclement political context. As is explored below, however, this was only one element that contributed to Scottish commercial success. Though the Irish received some political support from the French, there were no comparable official privileges for them to take advantage of. In fact, the Irish were in a position to exploit historic ties elsewhere in Europe, holding privileges of citizenship in Spain as a result of a tradition of economic links going back to the later middle ages that encouraged Irish migration and commercial activity.[10] That the Irish enjoyed their own political protection in lucrative markets elsewhere raises further the question not only of how they came to be so successful in French markets, but why they chose to pursue contentious avenues of trade during war when commerce elsewhere might have been more easily practised.

There are other convenient explanations for both Scottish and Irish commercial success in France in this period. Religious adherence has customarily been key to explaining the apparent shift in Scotland's primary European allegiance from France to England, with the Scottish Reformation of 1560 placing a religious barrier between the auld allies and bringing Scotland in line with England's Protestantism (Chapter 1). Religion allegedly dictated future patterns of Scottish migration to France, as the division of France into regions of Catholic and Protestant influence played into the hands of the Scots as their traditional haunts (including La Rochelle and Dieppe) became strongholds of Protestantism.[11] Political events governed religious changes, which in turn governed patterns of settlement – following the Siege of La Rochelle in 1627–8, this port and particularly its trading links to New France slowly became Catholicized,[12] thus creating an arena in which Protestant Scots should no longer have found integration or business easy. Scholars of the post-1688 period, too, have seen a common religion as key to settlement, arguing that 'those who were Catholics found financial and moral support from the religious orders on the continent'.[13]

Religion seems central to continuing Irish links with France, as the nations were linked by their common Catholicism.[14] It has been argued that Irish clerics chose France because of this shared religion, as home-based seminary education was being made impossible by anti-Catholic repression.[15] It is true that for some their Catholicism may have been a factor in decisions to emigrate to France. Irish births, marriages and deaths occurred with consistent frequency in Catholic parishes in Nantes,[16] and local support for Irish immigrants has been deemed to have been strongest in Brittany because Catholicism was so strong there.[17] Similarly, some French individuals chose to settle in Ireland apparently because of shared religious views – the French merchant François Roux declared himself 'native of St Malo, at the present resident in Limerick, Ireland, professing the Catholic, Apostolic and Roman [faith]'.[18] Political events, also, have previously been relied upon to explain patterns of Irish migration and settlement abroad. During the Cromwellian Protectorate hundreds of Catholic religious, many from Ireland, were forced into exile on the continent to escape persecution. Most sought refuge in countries loyal to the Catholic faith – including France, Spain and the Spanish Low Countries.[19] This period has been seen as marking 'a new phenomenon in the migration of Irish Catholics to France', including soldiers as well as clerics, who arrived in large numbers through the late 1630s and again from 1651 onwards, as Ireland was cleared of regiments connected with the Confederation of Kilkenny.[20]

Support in France for the Stuart cause and Jacobitism has similarly taken centre stage in accounting for ongoing Scottish and Irish ties after 1688.[21] There were of course those who took advantage of Jacobite support in the belief that it might increase their chances of success in the commercial sphere. Professing allegiance to the Jacobite movement was one route through which Irish migrants could guarantee a level of institutional support, both in the military and intellectually through the Irish College that had been established in Bordeaux in 1603.[22] Irish merchants contributed to French and Jacobite privateering efforts throughout the period, adding to tensions between the British nations – we have already seen examples of Scottish ships being targeted by Irish frigates, particularly during the British Civil Wars. Participation in French privateering offered a lifeline to some Irish immigrants, with those in need being advised to approach the local *commissaire de marine*, who could put them in touch with a corsair captain who might give them a place on their ship.[23] The Walshes of Ballynacooley in County Kilkenny, a prominent Irish merchant family in France, were involved in French and Jacobite privateering.[24] In 1691 a charter party was entered into by Henry Duguay, commissioner of the Navy in St Malo, with Patrick Lambert, captain of the *Providence*, Jacques Walsh, captain of the *Saint-Arroze* and Jean Jordan, captain of the *Thomas*, to go to Nantes and Ireland for the 'king's service'.[25] Although Jacques was executed in March 1694 for treason, having being condemned by the Admiralty Court in England the previous year, future generations of the Walsh family continued to support the Stuarts.[26] As Charles Edward Stuart was preparing for the 1745 uprising, Lord Moreton wrote that the Young Pretender's expedition had been financed with £2,000,000 provided by an heirless Irish merchant named Walsh, a member of the same family that had contributed to Jacobite privateering in the Nine Years' War.[27]

The contribution of Irish soldiers to France's military operations – and vice-versa – reflected an established reciprocal arrangement, providing another political basis for later Irish success. During the British Civil Wars the French ambassador Pompone de Bellièvre confirmed that he had 'the verbal assurance of the leaders of Parliament and of this Committee ... that the ships in the service of Parliament on the coast of Ireland [would] allow the ships sent there from France to convey the soldiers to pass and repass'.[28] During the Nine Years' War and the War of the Spanish Succession this military relationship was consolidated through Irish soldiers who fought in French service. The deaths of thirty-nine Irish soldiers were officially recognized in Nantes in October 1690.[29] Supplies were transferred from France to Ireland during the Nine Years' War – in January 1691 'French letters' reported that 'Tirconnell [governor of Ireland] ... laden with ammunition, arms, provision, cloths, shoes, sayled on the 9th out of Brest for Ireland, and a 2d convoye is preparing and shall consist of 18 vesels [*sic*] with wine, brandy and other necessaryes for Ireland'. Later in the month 'a Barke arrived on the 19th at Brest from Limerick with advice, that Tirconnell was arrived at Galloway on the 14th with the Ammunition [and] cloth'.[30] After the culmination of the War of the Spanish Succession Irish merchants continued to be recruited into French service. In 1714 James Pollock of Portaferry, Patrick Boyde, William Clarke and Robert Drake, mariners of the *William and Mary*, were examined regarding the arrival of troops in Nantes from Ireland – with links to the Pretender's possible movements, plans and the support he might receive.[31] These military ties provided an official avenue of support for Irish merchants to draw on. Indeed, the role of merchants in transporting goods, victual and soldiers during these conflicts placed them at the centre of ongoing ties. A long precedent of military cooperation and the participation of Irish soldiers in the French military – including against Britain – suggests the extent to which the Irish were welcomed in France despite the lack of an official political agreement. Parallel career opportunities in military service, in education and in the church all encouraged the integration of the Irish in French coastal regions and, therefore, the enduring success of commercial activity.[32]

Both the religious and political context contributed to continuing Scottish and Irish success in France, in commercial as well as in other spheres. It perhaps stands to reason that immigrants would choose to settle in areas where they could continue to practice their religion, or where they might be welcomed on account of their political adherence. It is clear that for some, this was indeed the case, and ethnicity and religion have been seen as key components of successful business relationships.[33] Some individuals saw religious adherence as so vital to commercial success that they converted, lending support to this notion. John Lauder recorded the conversion of Alexander Strachan to Catholicism in 1665; 'for Mr Alexr its some 17 years since he came to France: he had nothing imaginable. Seing he could make no fortune unless he turned his coat, he turned Papist.[34] In Scotland, too, there were regulations surrounding naturalizations that compelled Frenchmen to adhere to the Protestant religion. Both Abrahame Turrin, a hatmaker from Rouen, and the feltmaker Francis Shammo had to testify to the Privy Council of Scotland that they were 'of the Protestant reformed religion' before naturalization.[35] Despite these instances (and public statements of adherence tell us little about private belief), there are problems with relying solely on religious or political explanations for commercial success.

II.

Continuing Franco-Scottish and -Irish associations have been seen as direct products of the European political and religious context, but the notion that religious adherence was the decisive factor in successful (or unsuccessful) integration in this period is only partially valid. A detailed understanding of the people who participated in commercial exchanges suggests that many were not led by their religious or political beliefs and that the importance of religious fellowship tends to be over-emphasized.[36] Despite the context, merchants did not necessarily adhere to the religious or political policies of the area in which they worked or the people they worked with. For many if not most Scots, religious considerations were a much weaker motivation than previously assumed – as indicated in Chapter 1's discussion of the limited influence of religion on choices of where to study in sixteenth- and seventeenth-century France.[37] Indeed, although Turrin and Shammo adhered to the naturalization requirement that they profess support for Protestantism, there were instances in which this was not upheld. In spite of official rules, Dutchmen in Nantes were not refused naturalization based on religious affiliation, and for those operating in the Netherlands 'mercantile success did not hinge on being a Protestant'.[38]

In the case of the Irish in France, common religion may be a neat justification for success, but closer examination of Irish settlement highlights too many discrepancies for this explanation to be exhaustive. While there were many Irish births, marriages and deaths registered in Catholic parishes in Nantes, the same are found in the records of Protestant Civil Registration, with Irish baptisms being recorded in the reformed churches of Pont-Hus, Sucé-sur-Erdre and Vieil-levigne prior to the Revocation of the Edict of Nantes in 1685.[39] Following the Revocation French Protestants successfully sought sanctuary in Catholic Ireland, with a group of them being 'granted the house they desire' in Cork in March 1696.[40] Studies in other European contexts in the early modern period have argued convincingly that too much emphasis has been placed on religion as a factor in economic success. Pauline Croft, in her study of ongoing Anglo-Spanish commerce during the Armada Wars, demonstrates that many English merchants simply tried to maintain a working relationship regardless of religious differences. Most 'kept their mouths shut ... few merchants saw their Protestantism as an insuperable barrier to contact with Spain', opting to stay out of trouble and conform to local religious practices where necessary. Croft argues that despite emphasis on the explicitly Protestant nature of the Elizabethan regime, 'there were also many who had consistently opposed provocation and tried to maintain a working commercial relationship regardless of religious differences'.[41] In the case of the Irish, Louis Cullen has noted that 'political or religious ties with a foreign power' were secondary considerations in the expansion of smuggling in the eighteenth century, which was governed primarily by the fiscal motivations of those involved.[42] On the Iberian peninsula Catholicism 'was never an impediment to doing business with Protestants' for Irish merchants,[43] and in Protestant Sweden – not an immediately obvious destination for Irish settlement – many Irishmen 'remained aloof from [Jacobite] plotting', with the majority adopting 'a pragmatic position', prioritizing economic opportunities and keeping personal allegiances to themselves.[44]

It was not uncommon for merchants throughout Europe to choose to hide or divulge their religious beliefs when it might help them to turn a profit, but nor was it uncommon to forge business relationships with individuals who held contrasting beliefs if these ties would be of financial benefit.[45] Having won release from prison, where he was being held on suspicion of participating in illegal trade during the War of the Spanish Succession, Captain Masterton honoured his word to report to the English government on continuing Franco-Irish exchanges. In his 'account of the arts and methods used by those who in times of peace, and now in Warr, carry a clandestine trade with France from Ireland', one of the first points made concerned religion.

> As this trade is generallie carred on by papists so when they feare to be suspected they make use of there [sic] protestant frends to enter there [sic] ships butter and beeffe, either for Holland or Lisbon butt the wooll is always in small creks or carred in to little illands and from thence carred of on bord the ship at sea.[46]

Masterton acknowledges that Irish merchants were willing to make use of Protestant 'frends' when it became economically expedient, suggesting that consideration of financial success was more important than religious conscience. His belief that it was Catholics who generally carried on Franco-Irish trade is a point worthy of debate in itself; in Cork, foreign trade was 'overwhelmingly in the hands of Protestant traders'.[47] Irish merchants 'were not all of a kind', and it has been argued that the Catholic merchant element was exaggerated by contemporaries for political reasons.[48] Jean Mackarel – the Irish owner of a number of the fifteen ships granted passes in La Rochelle in 1695, as seen in Chapter 6 – came under investigation during the War of the Spanish Succession for transporting

Protestants, suggesting either that he held Protestant beliefs himself, or that he did not discriminate on the grounds of religion.[49] Just as a common religion was not invariably necessary for a successful working partnership, corresponding religious beliefs were not always enough to foster positive relationships.[50] Even where bonds of religion existed, rivalry was present among merchants and seamen.[51] In the commercial sphere religious affiliation was not a prerequisite for successful trade – Irish associations with both established and reformed churches provided institutional support for those pursuing trade in Nantes, with merchants largely choosing to place financial concerns above religious dedication.

There are similar problems with relying on the broad political context as an indicator of potential commercial success abroad. Despite assertions that 'political affiliations were significant for the trading classes',[52] Scottish merchants chose to prioritize 'their commercial affairs, and for many their primary concern was to make money, to restore their fortunes'.[53] The post-1688 period provided a clear source of institutional support for those of Jacobite persuasion in the Stuart exile court, but though it has been suggested that all Scots present in France during this period were necessarily affiliated to St Germain, this was not the case.[54] In Jacobite haunts including Bordeaux and La Rochelle Hanoverians were also present, and those of both Whig and Tory persuasion settled in France during the Jacobite period.[55] Not even those commercial agents who openly held Jacobite sympathies took advantage of their political status. The Irish White family, based in Nantes, ran one of France's largest tea firms and managed a bustling trade with Ireland, but there is no evidence of their taking advantage of any institutional Jacobite support.[56] The Whites, like many others, chose to concentrate on their business – an approach the Irish in Sweden and countless other mercantile agents elsewhere adopted. The Jacobites 'were only one possible network' that the Irish (and Scots) could integrate within.[57]

Business dealings of several Jacobite commercial agents suggest that even those invested in politics cared more for personal gain than political affiliation. The Earl of Mar – 'Bobbing John' Erskine – dealt with both Robert Arbuthnot and Robert Gordon after beginning to act for the Stuart cause.[58] However, while Mar was still working for the British government – and well before the calamitous moment when he offered his allegiance to George I – he had been trading with the Jacobite Arbuthnot. In March 1716 Mar wrote to Arbuthnot from Paris that

> I wish I had been to drink the wine you were sending me on the other side ... the thin wines here do not agree with my stomach for constant drinking, so I want some good old claret very much, which is not to be got here, and I wish you could find me a way of sending me some soon.[59]

The Arbuthnot family was prolific in Franco-Scottish exchanges; in Chapter 6 we saw both Thomas and James active during the War of the Spanish Succession. Their half-brother George, baptized in 1688, was a career officer in Queen Anne's army. After Anne's death, however, he remained in France and worked as a wine merchant, before later returning to Hanoverian Britain and trading on London East India Company ships to China.[60] For this family, despite their prominence in British politics, fiscal success was prioritized.

Ultimately, neither merchants nor authorities appear to have discriminated widely based on political affiliation, and on the whole Scottish commercial migrants simply wished to continue their business undisturbed. This included Moses Corbett, who declared in 1691 that 'he would trade to France in spite of anybody'; commercial priority outweighing national concerns.[61] Others simply wanted no part in political strife, such as James Axton, described in 1700 as 'a loyal subject to [King James], and a good Catholic', who sought permission from the Stuart Court 'to continue to work at his trade of weaver at Paris, where he has already worked for several years, without giving cause of complaint to anybody'. The Jacobite Court did not object, granting permission that Axton 'might continue his trade in Paris without molestation'.[62] Individuals such as Andrew Russell, deeply engrained in Scottish commerce with France, evidently preferred to concentrate on their commercial interests, rather than turning their efforts towards politics.[63] Even those who were tied to the Stuart exile court did not prioritize these connections over personal gain and many looked to improve their own position regardless of the political issues surrounding them.[64]

Chronologically, there are problems in citing Jacobitism as a central premise for either Scottish or Irish commercial success in France. Robert Gordon, William Gordon and Robert Arbuthnot all acted as Jacobite financiers, but their participation stemmed from careers as successful merchants already established in Rouen and Bordeaux.[65] Irish communities in all spheres were well established on the continent before the 'waves' of migration caused by political events at home;[66] before the 1690s Irish and French mercantile families had forged numerous domestic and business links with each other.[67] As Ó Ciosáin compellingly argues, all of the Irish dynamics operating in France after the Glorious Revolution had begun much earlier and those who made the journey from Ireland post-1688 relied on those already established for support. Perhaps, in his words, it is indeed only Jacobite memory that sees 1688 as the 'année zero'.[68] Following the end of the War of the Spanish Succession, the failed 1715 Jacobite uprising and the pro-British policy shift in France under the Duc d'Orléans, productive Franco-Irish ties may be assumed to have come to an end. Indeed, after the terms of the Treaty of Rastatt were agreed in March 1714, Louis XIV promised to prevent Irish officers in the

French army from recruiting in Ireland for the Pretender. Matthew Prior wrote to Bolingbroke that

> The Duke of Shrewsbury sent me from Dublin, a complaint against me one Tobie Butler a Lieutenant in the Regiment of the Lord Galmoy, who had inlisted [*sic*] people in Ireland, telling them it was to serve the Pretender ... He will acquaint Monsieur Voysin with the complaint, who will give the most effectual admonition to the Irish Officers in this service that such Traiterous practices may for the future be prevented.[69]

Following this policy shift, however, neither settlement nor commercial activity appears to have suffered unduly, and Irish commercial activity in France remained robust throughout the eighteenth century.[70] It was not until the late 1720s that Irish commercial activity in Nantes peaked; Irish trade with Bordeaux continued to flourish until the later decades of the eighteenth century, and at the beginning of the nineteenth century Irishmen were involved in the cotton industry in Rouen, following a century of continuous settlement in the region.[71]

III.

The political or religious contexts within which international commerce took place in the early modern period have rightfully been seen as important. Their dominance of discussions of migration patterns or commerce, however, has neglected full consideration of the social context which goes much further in explaining both the extent of Scottish and Irish commercial success in France and the regional variations in these trade links. In recent years there has been an upsurge in research examining communities formed by groups of migrants abroad, as studies of international commerce have increasingly focused on the role played by mercantile networks in maintaining and developing trade routes.[72] Some of these British communities have already been studied in depth, and in many of these cases the institutional or social support available to them in their host societies has been seen as vital to their success. As discussed in Chapter 2, this includes the Scottish trading staple in the Netherlands, as well as Scottish integration in Stockholm and Gothenburg.[73] In these locations the attention paid by scholars to the social context and the institutional support that this made available has added vital new dimensions to our understanding of these European relationships that cannot be gleaned from the broader political context alone. Also previously noted is that the Scottish merchant community in France operated slightly differently in practical terms, being more transient, utilizing widespread networks, and relying less on organized or distinctly Scottish institutional support. Thus rather than being found operating within discrete Scottish communities, the individuals involved in Franco-Scottish trade were more adept at integrating fully into the civic and commercial life of their host country, in a number of different locations. In Dieppe, for example, it has been suggested that Scotsmen were so at home that they 'seem to have been absorbed by the indigenous population'.[74] As the remainder of this chapter will suggest, one of the attributes key to their success in France was that they did not confine their dealings to fellow Scots or to family members.

Rather than doing business within a self-contained national group, commercial Scots in France integrated fully with the indigenous population. John Clerk provides a good example of this behaviour, explicitly contributing to Scottish success in France by consistently recommending Frenchmen to the Scots in his network. Clerk recommended the Frenchman Monsieur Poncet multiple times, acting as an intermediary for business between Poncet and Henry Hope.[75] Other Scots in Clerk's network followed suit. In 1654 Alexander Charteris thanked Clerk from Paris

> most hartily for your good advise in reference to my livin and tradeing in this place ... and for your sake shall recommend such of my acquaintance as hav neede of draperi to Monsieur Poncet who is my neare neighbor for I am now lodged *a la pomme d'or* the next shop.[76]

Such recommendations reflect a history of integrated commercial ventures. In some spheres, formal partnerships between merchants of different nationalities were rare, but in the Franco-Scottish context these appear to have been more commonplace.[77] In 1603 a contract was drawn up between George Christie of St Andrews, master of the ship the *St Michael*, and the merchant brothers Jean and Jean Dorath from Bordeaux, for a joint return venture from Bordeaux to London. Although there is no mention of the nature of the cargo, the Dorath brothers financed 586 livres 11 sols – presumably Christie's contribution was the use of his ship.[78] Scotsmen continued to embark on transnational ventures despite government attempts to dissuade them; in 1665 Michel Mel made a successful application to the Privy Council for a voyage to France in the *Margret of Diep* with salmon and herring, 'of which vessel the master skipper and whole company (except three Scotsmen) are Frenchmen'.[79]

By delving further into the social context within which Scottish merchants operated in France, the regional differences highlighted at the outset of this chapter begin to be explained. Though Scottish merchants were active and successful throughout France they particularly dominated in Bordeaux, and it is not coincidental that the Scottish commercial community in this port was exceptionally buoyant and well integrated into society. Generations of merchant families became engrained in Bordeaux culture, including the Lavie family, one of the most prominent Scottish merchant families in France in this period. As noted in Chapter 2, Henry Lavie senior undertook commissions from, among other people, the wife of the Scottish Lord Lothian, and acted as factor for a cartel of Glasgow wine merchants seeking to control the Bordeaux vintage of

1674.[80] Several generations of his family were later active in Bordeaux. The death of 'Samuel Lavie, natural and legitimate son to Sir Henry Lavie, merchant in Bordeaux' was recorded in June 1676.[81] Less than two years later another son, Henry Lavie junior, was born, and at the beginning of the eighteenth century Pierre Lavie is recorded in the records of ships' captains for this city.[82] The latter example suggests the extent to which this family had become assimilated into French society, with Pierre keeping the family name but adopting – or being given – a Francophied version of his given name. Well into the eighteenth century, branches of this family remained in Bordeaux; François Lavy married a Frenchwoman, Marie Judith François, in Bordeaux in 1758 and twenty-five years later a Jeanne Elisabeth Lavie is included on the death registers.[83]

In addition to the longevity of merchants' ties with Bordeaux (and the Lavies are only one example among many), Scots held positions in civic government in this port, thus assisting countrymen in pursuing their business interests. One of the most prominent was Robert Gordon, who held office in the Admiralty of Guyenne, the institution that controlled Bordeaux trade. He used his position to offer support to a number of his countrymen. In October 1717 Gordon testified on behalf of William Ramsay, stating that 'I certify to the Gentlemen officers of the Admiralty and all those called that the said William Ramsay is Scottish, and he desires to return to his home in Bordeaux'.[84] In addition to facilitating entry to Bordeaux – and one postulates that the emphasis on Ramsay's Scottish nationality is significant – Gordon testified on behalf of those who wished to leave Bordeaux and return home. This included Jacques Strachen in 1718, who 'is Scottish and wishes to return to his country'.[85] When George Gordon's application to the Admiralty in April 1717, supported by a J. Albertson, was unsuccessful, he turned to the support of his kinsman, who duly testified on his behalf on 4 May the following year.[86] The presence of Scots within society and within institutions in Bordeaux helped to facilitate a healthy commercial relationship, providing support within indigenous French institutions rather than as part of distinct expatriate Scottish enclaves as seen elsewhere in Europe. In Bordeaux, both the extent of settlement and integration and the ongoing development of British trading patterns were dominated by Scots, with success in society directly reflected by success in commerce.

The same patterns can be observed in the case of the dominance of the Irish in Nantes, a city where Irish immigrants were well accepted.[87] Irish merchants integrated successfully within both civic and maritime society in this port, and like their Scottish counterparts participated in multi-national commercial ventures. In 1702, crews including both Frenchmen and Irishmen can be found facilitating commercial exchanges. The frigate the *Biche* of Nantes was commanded by Jean Saupin and principally owned by François Burguerie Gayac and Louis Lamandé of Nantes. In addition to Nantais and Breton partners were 'a

Swede, two Irishmen of Rochelle, and men of Agen, Bruges, Ostend, Hendaye, Verdun [and] Bordeaux'.[88] On the *Vigilent* of Bordeaux, captained by the Bordeaux Scotsman Robert Kay on a voyage to the port of Plaisance in the New World, 'the crew is made up of foreigners (Scots, Irish, Swedes)'. The *St Jacques* of Rouen had in 1711 '8 persons of the nation Irish' in its crew.[89] The following year, a Jersey privateer 'went in to Bordux River where he took two ships belonging to Dublin the masters and men found on board, are all her majestys subjecks of ierland, exept the pylots who are French men'.[90]

These commercial activities were supported by Irish integration into society in Nantes. There were large numbers of registered Irish and Franco-Irish births, marriages and deaths, which as explored above occurred in both Catholic and Protestant parishes. At these occasions protection was frequently offered by nobles, members of the judiciary and those in the legal professions, who acted as godparents, as well as by local clergy who sponsored those with no support.[91] The acceptance and assimilation created by this behaviour was reflected in the relatively high rate of Irish naturalization among those who sought permanent settlement in France. In Nantes this included Cornelius O'Driscoll in March 1619 and Thomas Kirwan in March 1621.[92] Peter Sahlins has suggested that more Irish were naturalized under the ancien régime than English and Scots combined, with Irish immigrants comprising 14 per cent of all naturalized foreign merchants in France in this period. This does speak to a particularly high level of Irish integration when compared to English, though Sahlins's figures for the Scots must be treated with some caution. He has calculated that between 1660 and 1789, 978 Britons were naturalized in France; 678 of whom were of Irish origin (69 per cent), 270 English (28 per cent), and the remaining thirty Scottish (3 per cent). Given the extent of Scottish activity in France in this period that recent research in several spheres has revealed, the figure of 3 per cent seems extraordinarily low. However, under the terms of the Auld Alliance Scots were recognized as being French citizens, meaning that formal naturalizations were not necessary.[93] As we saw in Chapter 1 this was explicit, as Scots were entitled to their rights 'without taking any letter of naturalization'.[94] Naturalization rates differed between social groups; members of the clergy seldom sought naturalization as they usually intended to return home, rather than coveting the church benefices in France that naturalization would have opened up for them.[95] Data from elsewhere demonstrates that merchants were extremely active in seeking naturalization, and successful in being granted it. Françoise Bayard's study of Lyon corroborates that in this city it was merchants, when compared to other professions including priests, artists, doctors and soldiers, who were the most frequently naturalized class.[96] This pattern is unsurprising, given that those individuals with assets had the greatest vested interest in becoming naturalized. These included the Irishman Nicholas Lee, of the prolific Lee merchant dynasty, who achieved this status in Nantes in 1673.[97] That Irish migrants, and particularly merchants, were able to integrate so well with the indigenous population throughout France contributed in large part to the commercial success they enjoyed. Though Irish settlement is most noticeable in Nantes there were merchant families who settled elsewhere, including the Black family who operated in Bordeaux.[98]

In both Bordeaux and Nantes trading patterns with a distinct correlation to settlement and integration can be identified. Such delineation along national lines was not so evident everywhere, however. In La Rochelle a much more recognizably British dynamic was apparent, with the successful integration of those of different British nationality being reflected in commercial transactions in which Scottish, Irish and English merchants more commonly worked together.[99] There is much less evidence within this port of distinctions between British national groups, presenting a different state of affairs altogether in which common nationality was not a driving force in forging business links or demonstrating loyalty. In March 1662 a Scot based in Bordeaux, William Robertson, brought a case to the admiralty court of La Rochelle on behalf of Anthoine Hal, an English merchant based in Ireland. Hal was owed 800 livres by Daniell Smythe, a native Scot based in La Rochelle.[100] In this case, for reasons that are not documented, loyalty between Robertson and Hal appears stronger than that between Robertson and Smythe, despite the common nationality of the latter pair, loyalty presumably being governed by financial expediency rather than ethnic ties. In La Rochelle, rather than an exclusive national identity being the guiding force in commercial transactions and success, English, Scottish and Irish merchants displayed shared interests, and worked together in developing these interests. In some places there were recognizably 'British' networks in operation before 1707, raising the question of whether a British commercial identity was formed by agents at ground level before being politically formalized in the parliaments of Westminster and Edinburgh. This phenomenon opens up significant grounds for future research.

Differences in Scottish, Irish and English commercial activity in France bears a direct correlation to patterns of settlement, despite previous arguments that there is little evidence of different patterns of socialization or of specific customs setting the Irish apart in France.[101] Focus on politics at the national level does not take such variances into account, yet much can be learned through closer examination of the link between social context and trading patterns. As geographical comparison within France suggests, understanding of international associations in any context benefits from prioritizing local customs and societal realities, rather than the perceived European – or global – political climate.

IV.

Consideration of the wider picture of British trade with France in this period consolidates many of the conclusions drawn in preceding chapters regarding the specific Franco-Scottish relationship, but additionally suggests a number of indicative conclusions regarding the relative contribution of the three British kingdoms to overseas trade in the pre- and post-union periods. There were clear discrepancies in the experiences of British merchants trading with France, particularly during periods of conflict. Broadly speaking Scottish merchants, and to a lesser extent Irish, were able to continue their business despite the inclement political context, being left largely unmolested by French privateers and being held to more flexible legislation by the French authorities. Significantly, inconsistencies in the commercial experiences of the three British kingdoms went beyond the broad, national picture, varying from port to port. In Bordeaux Scottish merchants dominated, in Nantes it was the Irish, and in La Rochelle a more fully integrated British commercial community acted towards common goals, suggesting that despite domestic political tensions national allegiance was less important to mercantile agents than personal relationships and profit. This contrast in British trading patterns has significant implications for our understanding of 'British' trade in the years before and after 1707, highlighting the importance of drawing distinctions between the activities and relationships of the three kingdoms and acknowledging Scotland's continued autonomy in at least some of her international affairs.

In breaking down British commercial activity in France by port, a clear relationship emerges between migration, settlement, society and the development and maintenance of commercial markets and trade routes. The varying political relationships enjoyed by Scotland, Ireland and England with France certainly contributed to these inconsistencies – that facets of the Auld Alliance in both commercial and social spheres remained in force throughout the long seventeenth century inevitably helped Scottish merchants to pursue their business in France. For others, finding common ground with the business network in which they operated – notably political or religious values – may well have fostered integration and profit. These routes, though, were not the only ones leading to commercial success; the Nine Years' War and the War of the Spanish Succession may well have 'contained a strong confessional and denominational angle' but not necessarily for all those participating in the conflict or affected by it.[102] The Scottish and Irish networks operating in France were supported by Protestants, Catholics, Jacobites and Hanoverians, with neither nation's success being governed principally by any one of these causes. Further, successful Scottish and Irish commercial communities in France pre-dated the Glorious Revolution, as well as remaining successful – and continuing to expand – in the period following 1715. Although some Irish did 'predictably ... use religious and Jacobite causes to gain the sympathy and trust' of authorities and maritime communities,[103] they integrated across the social spectrum, and established Catholic or Jacobite communities in France did not monopolize later arrivals.

If political and religious justifications for the success of Scottish and Irish merchants in France at the expense of their English counterparts are inadequate, alternative explanations must be offered. Along France's Atlantic coast settlement and integration was directly reflected in the volume and success of commercial endeavours. Business and personal links were forged with the indigenous population, as well as with agents of any nationality who proved themselves worthy of this level of trust. The integration of some individuals into civic institutions in French ports, including Robert Gordon in the Admiralty of Guyenne, played a vital role in ensuring ease of settlement and integration and thus the health of commerce. The commercial success – or failure – of British merchants in France more accurately reflected their social and commercial environment than the wider European political context. Crucially, commercial agents judged the worth of business associations not by beliefs, nationality, or political affiliation, but by the trustworthiness of that particular individual in the transaction they were interested in pursuing. Although it has been said that Catholics and Huguenots only did business with each other out of necessity and 'the pressure of economic circumstance',[104] the most successful merchants took advantage of the best opportunities rather than limiting themselves in ways that were, economically speaking, arbitrary. This approach to their business allowed them to continue to pursue active commerce at a time when this activity was under threat from policies brought about by international conflict. In Pauline Croft's words, merchants 'cared more for their livelihoods than for any consideration of foreign policy. Profit and old business links proved stronger than war fervour'.[105]

CONCLUSION: 'THE SAID PRIVILEGES ARE STILL IN VIGOUR'

Sanjay Subrahmanyam suggests that 'once one leaves behind the antiseptic realm of theoretical economic models, and enters into an historical world of flesh and blood, merchants appear not as faceless facilitators, but as a social reality'.[1] The merchants active in Franco-Scottish commerce during the long seventeenth century certainly were not faceless facilitators, but were individuals who participated in networks and communities whose actions influenced economic policy and shaped early modern trading patterns. Deeper understanding of the actions of these commercial agents forces a reconsideration of the specific Franco-Scottish relationship, but the conclusions drawn within each of the preceding chapters contribute to wider debates regarding warfare, legislation, and British and European dynamics in the early modern period. Crucially, modern responses to conflict cannot be applied to the seventeenth-century experience. The early modern world was indeed a 'multi-cogged machine of interconnected national and local economies that performed well despite frequent political realignments'.[2] The wars of the seventeenth century may have shaped the arena in which commerce took place, but they did not dictate merchants' activities.

Fundamental to all of the issues discussed in this book is the continuation of the Auld Alliance. Contrary to accepted historiography, the Auld Alliance was not 'shattered' in 1560,[3] nor did the events of 1603, 1654 or 1707 extinguish this historic association. Throughout the early modern period Scotland and Scottish commercial agents continued to enjoy their 'special relationship' with France, which was continually confirmed by overtures from both sides seeking its formal re-establishment. Inevitably, the nature of this association evolved from its initial incarnation in the middle ages as a military alliance against England. By the early modern period the alliance was invoked most commonly as a means of establishing trading privileges and the reciprocal naturalization rights that remained key to Scottish settlement and thus to commercial success. It has proved difficult, if not impossible, to ascertain the precise terms of any continuing formal alliance; contemporaries themselves were unsure of them, despite making 'diligent searches' of the Edinburgh charterhouse.[4] Nonetheless, the perception that a special commercial accord continued to exist was as important in many contexts as legally binding documents. We have seen numerous examples of merchants and institutions inherently believing in the continuation of reciprocal Franco-Scottish trading rights regardless of whether these were legislatively confirmed. In the hearts and minds of merchants the Auld Alliance remained intact, and at the highest political levels too there was a conviction that the Franco-Scottish relationship endured up to and beyond the 1707 union. Lewis Innes underlined this conviction when, in this year, he informed Nathaniel Hooke that 'the said privileges' the Scots enjoyed in France were 'still in vigour'.[5]

The continuation of the Franco-Scottish alliance into the early modern period has significant ramifications for how we view both the British and European political and economic dynamic. Whiggish accounts may view the events of 1560 and 1603 as part of a natural progression from Scotland's medieval accord with France to her early modern association with England, but analysis of the commercial realities of the Franco-Scottish relationship tells a very different story. Significantly for our understanding of early modern Britain, it should now be clear that not all facets of 'an independent foreign policy disappeared over the border with James after the regal union'.[6] Scotland entered the conflicts of the long seventeenth century with different agendas and under different rules of engagement to England, maintaining autonomous commercial links that worked directly against the apparent intentions of the British monarchy. Significantly, this was fully recognized on the other side of the Channel. French authorities continued to treat their auld ally as an independent nation, and by holding Scottish merchants to different regulations they guaranteed diverse British experiences of trade with France in this period. While England continues to be seen as the 'senior partner' in the British alliance in all spheres, English merchants relied on 'the greater affability of the French towards the Scots' to employ Scottish vessels in French trade.[7] Additionally, as we have seen during the Nine Years' War and the War of the Spanish Succession, Scottish merchants had more to fear from the aggression of English vessels than they did from French privateers, contradicting accepted notions of who Scotland's allies and enemies were in this period. This state of affairs fundamentally contradicts Linda Colley's influential thesis that

> Great Britain ... was an invention forged above all by war. Time and time again, war with France brought Britons, whether they hailed from Wales or Scotland or England, into confrontation with an obviously hostile Other and encouraged them to define themselves collectively against it.[8]

Conversely, the present study has uncovered no evidence that a 'collective' approach to war with France existed up to 1713. This realization might now be usefully tested for later Franco-British conflicts.

It is understandable that warfare, bringing with it trade embargoes, prohibitive customs rates, impressment and active privateering, has been assumed to have had a negative effect on commerce and shipping. In the Franco-Scottish context this has been stated more emphatically than in most, with the Franco-Stuart war of 1627–9 described as 'the last straw on the back of the Auld Alliance',[9] and the Nine Years' War as 'so damaging to Scottish shipping and markets' that 'by 1700 the continental trade was declining or stagnant; war had undermined relations with France and wiped out the special privileges Scotland had enjoyed a hundred years before, under the Auld Alliance'.[10] No doubt George Lockhart, James Cuming and John Ferguson, who lost ships and cargoes to French privateers between 1688 and 1713, would agree with these assessments. Individual grievances aside, however, the strength of the Franco-Scottish relationship manifested itself in continuing commerce throughout the supposed 'crisis' of the long seventeenth century. Crucially, in continuing their activities commercial agents did not have to resort to smuggling or to other means of illicit trade, though some saw this as their only option. Many sought – and received – sanctions from both British and French governments and admiralties that allowed them to trade with the correct paperwork and permissions. Although the primary concern of some customs officials was inevitably to line their own pockets with 'private gratuities',[11] at higher political levels the foremost intention was to maintain trade routes in spite of political policy.

It has been empirically proven here that Franco-Scottish commerce continued throughout specific conflicts, but this evidence additionally suggests that a reassessment of early modern warfare more generally is required. Acting within the 'multi-cogged machine' of the early modern world demanded successful commerce and economic growth whatever the political context.[12] That the necessity of continued commerce was fully recognized in local and national government begins to explain the generosity with which passes were granted that allowed trade to continue, even when they seem to have fundamentally contradicted political agendas. Attitudes towards politics and commerce were not inextricably linked; not all economic sanctions were politically motivated and not all political actions necessarily had an economic effect. The conception and implementation of legislation in this period was complicated, not least for the merchants who had to negotiate the 'maze of customs duties' before them.[13] Regulations that appeared on the surface to be directed towards a political enemy often had domestic concerns at their heart, emphasizing the danger of relying on such sources for an unequivocal evaluation of commercial relationships. Moreover, merchants were not passive bystanders of legislation imposed indiscriminately from above. Though merchant groups allegedly 'had no direct control over the state or policy',[14] we have seen them involved at every level in the formation and implementation of economic regulations. Certainly the mercantile community should no longer be seen as 'mere victim, passively experiencing the vagaries of administrative centralization, political exclusion, economic deprivation and cultural marginalization', but as 'active, autonomous agents operating within and through communities'.[15]

Once these autonomous agents are recognized, and their activities prioritized, it becomes clear that evaluation of international trade cannot accurately take place at a national level. Explanations of patterns of trade along bi-lateral lines are unsatisfactory, and as Henriette de Bruyn Kops suggests 'a two-dimensional representation of early modern connections misses the reason why those networks functioned as well as they did'.[16] Though the continuation of facets of the formal Franco-Scottish alliance and the complicity of authorities played their part, international commerce continued to flourish because of the contributions of the people at the heart of trade. The sophisticated commercial understanding exhibited by merchants meant that 'official bans on trade diminished neither supply nor demand for import/export commodities'.[17] Instead, merchants created 'new routes, new destinations and new commercial connections'.[18] The ability of merchant groups to adapt swiftly was fundamental in being able to navigate a changing political context, as well as in circumventing prohibitive legislation such as the Navigation Acts. The expansion of their commercial horizons when necessary made a distinct contribution to the globalization of trade.

The early modern merchant was demonstrably proficient, operating within traditional frameworks and recording transactions – even those involving family members – in a professional manner. Though merchants' actions influenced the development of international relationships both directly and indirectly, their primary concern was their own success rather than national foreign policy. While the English government lamented the 'scandal to the nation' caused in 1704 by 'ships arriv[ing] every day with wooll, and provisions from Ireland' while the same was under embargo,[19] merchants simply wished to be allowed to continue their work 'without giving cause of complaint to anybody'.[20] This reflects merchants' attitudes across early modern Europe. Jan Parmentier, examining Irish mercantile networks in the Netherlands, recognizes that even following the Williamite War and the introduction of anti-Catholic legislation in the Irish Parliament 'economic considerations still prevailed over political and religious motivations for Irish emigration'.[21] Jean Agnew notes that 'political restrictions on trade did not impose any kind of moral obligation on merchants and trading with the enemy was not seen as unpatriotic'.[22] This attitude continued later into the eighteenth century, as demonstrated by Thomas Truxes, who has found that 'New York's Irish merchants were ideally situated to take a leading part in trade with the enemy' during the Seven Years' War, further emphasizing the need to reconsider the wars of the later eighteenth century.[23] Despite acting primarily in their own interests, these networks and communities did not 'bring a general calamity upon trade',[24] instead making impressive contributions to the development of international associations. Though it is tempting to assess early modern commerce based on broad notions of political relationships, it is not possible to attain an accurate picture of commercial activity through a national lens. Patterns of trade differed regionally and locally, as has been seen here through comparison of the experiences of Scottish, Irish and English commercial agents on the west coast of France.

These regional patterns may have been informed in part by decentralized government or local policy, but this study has demonstrated the significance of the social and cultural contexts within which merchants operated; contexts that do not support accepted understandings of either the British or the European political framework of the long seventeenth century. In Bordeaux and Nantes Scottish and Irish merchants functioned within communities and networks that were both Catholic and Protestant, Jacobite and non-Jacobite, all of which were conducive to successful commercial activity. Analysis of political or economic legislation or notions of common religion cannot fully explain commercial success; instead, the social and cultural environment within which trade links were developed shaped the picture of Franco-Scottish and -British trade throughout this inclement period, with patterns of migration and settlement fundamentally influencing patterns of trade. Such conclusions emphasize the importance of an inclusive approach to any form of historical study. Commercial historians are increasingly shaking off the shackles of statistical economic history, and the results for the field thus far have been compelling.[25] It should not be surprising that merchants were most comfortable acting within groups of people they trusted, or that they acted primarily for their own financial interests with little recourse to the political or religious context within which they operated. What remains surprising is the lack of previous focus on the people involved in Franco-Scottish commerce, which is responsible in large part for the continuation of historiographical traditions that misrepresent this specific association, as well as suggesting why the realities of Scotland's position within Great Britain have not been more deeply probed. Evaluating international commercial associations along political lines – gauged on the terms of treaties or conflicts, or on our understanding of a broad international political context – has encouraged simplistic accounts of international associations, based on the notion that commercial success or failure can be assessed accurately from trade agreements, trade embargoes or the general inconveniences to commerce inherent during times of international warfare. Instead, the conclusions reached here suggest the importance of understanding the people involved in international exchange, validating a micro-historical approach to commercial history.

The merchant James Battie, operating during the British Civil Wars, believed that there was 'no greater enemy to trade than war, be in what country it will'.[26]

Other merchants we have encountered in this study would not have agreed, and by recovering their experiences of wartime trade an alternative assessment can be offered. During times of war adjustments had to be made by both merchants and governments in order to reconcile political relationships and economic necessity, but it was in nobody's interest to destroy established trading routes. Merchants were involved at every stage of this process, in both practical and legislative capacities, playing an active role in shaping the regulations that controlled trade as well as establishing communities and networks that ensured the continued success of economic exchange in the early modern period. In the Franco-Scottish relationship, conflict and commerce were not mutually exclusive.

APPENDICES

Appendix A: Consumers of wine imported in the *Rowland* of Hambrough by John Harmonson Lepman, 22 January 1673

Merchant	Consumers
John Hall (5 tuns)	John Bowes, Widow Livingston, Alexander Brusson, James Allison, Widow Garvine, William Cunningham, George Braithwitt, William Davidson
Robert Learmonth (16 tuns)	Isabell Rae, James Cleghorn, James Angus, James Tompson, Mrs Campbell, Widow Caddell, James Alson, Alexander Abercromby, Adam Darling, Richard Wilkie, John Browne, James Geines, John Bining, William Ewing, Henry Gourlay, John Murray, James Hamilton, Herr Gourlay, Captain Cockburne, George Blyth, William Davidson, Widow Livingston, Widow Caldwell, James Hary, Sam Cranston, Duke Hamilton, James Geines, Thomas Speirs, Stephen Douglas
Andrew Stevinson (11 tuns 2 hogsheads)	Alexander Bryson, Andrew Wardlaw's relict, James Menteith, James Steith, William Cunningham, Alexander Pearson, Thomas Fisher, John Anderson, James Penterer, William Cunningham, Andrew Smart, William Seaton, Patrick Young, Widow Herrick, James Monteath, Widow Murray, William Cunningham, Alexander Pearson, John Anderson, Widow Pollock
William Hay (11 tuns 2 hogsheads)	David Seaton, Hugh Blair, Robert Stark, Patrick Sheill, George Hutson, George Hutson, Widow Caldwall, James Cleghorne, Widow Garvin, Thomas Speirs, John Braice, William Davidson, Widow Watt, Robert Montgomery, Mary Pears, Adam Cunningham, Robert Meine
John Govan (4 tuns 3 hogsheads)	William Sinclair, Widow Greer, Widow Gillis, Mary Pears, John Penston, Widow Greer, Andrew Young, Widow Murray
Thomas Wilson (4 tuns 3 hogsheads)	Alexander Fliskin, William Aickman, Robert Wilson, Francis Tompson, James Ker, Alexander Crumbie, James Clarke, William Aickman

Henry Bourne (4 tuns 3 hogsheads)	William Nicoll, Thomas Fisher, William Aickman, Patrick Steel, James Deane, William Nicoll
David Calderwood (4 tuns 3 hogsheads 1 tearce)	James Campbell, James Robertson, Henry Cunningham, Widow Tompson, Alexander Brysson, Widow Caddell, Walter Baird, William Muirhead, Robert Semple
Patrick Ffyf (8 tuns)	John Anderson, Alexander Pearson, Alexander Hay, George Farquhar, Robert Meince, Adam Cunningham, Alexander Pearson, John Anderson, Widow Hamilton, Alexander Brysson, Widow Wardlaw, Alexander Hay, Hellen Elphingston, Alexander Montgomery, Alexander Hay, Widow Wardlaw, Patrick Steill, Hugh Blair, Widow Fulton, John Bruce, Alexander Pearson
Patrick Andrew (10 tuns)	Andrew Callice, Widow Tompson, Widow Cowan, Adam Cunningham, Widow Gib, John Rotherford, Widow Gibb, Andrew Steir, Peter Coinster, Widow Tompson, James Deane, Widow Masterton, James Cleghorne
Alexander Sympson (5 tuns)	George Hutson, Widow Livingston, Robert Strachan, Widow Steir, Janet Gray, Adam Cunningham, George Strachan, David Livingston, Patrcik Steill, William Aickman
George Reid (12 tuns)	Mary Peirs, Andrew Cassie, Widow Sickeson, Widow Wardlaw, Widow Caddell, Henry Cunningham, David Govan, Mary Pears, James Halliburton, William Ewing, John Rotherford, John Farquson, Patrick Steill, Widow Dickson, James Geines, James Halliburton, Widow Caddell
William Murehead(3 tuns)	For himself
Sir Alexander Hope (20 tuns)	Thomas Tait, Hugh Blair, John Galloway, Widow Garvan, James Deane, Laird Ava
James Law (1 hogshead)	For himself
Andrew Johnston (2 hogsheads)	For himself
John Trotter (2 hogsheads)	For himself

Source: Data compiled from the entry books of Leith, November 1672–November 1673, NAS E74/15/13; E74/15/15. This is one example of several in these sources where the destination of wine can be traced as far as the consumer.

Appendix B: Customs rates, France, 1664 and 1667

Goods	Unit	1664 rate (livres, sous)	1667 rate (livres, sous)
Woollen Stockings	Dozen Pairs	3 10	8 0
Silk Stockings	Pair	0 15	2 0
Cotton Stockings	Dozen Paris	2 0	4 0
English bays	Piece of 25 ells	5 0	10 0
Double bays	Piece of 50 ells	15 0	30 0
Burails (single)	Piece of 25 ells	4 0	8 0
Spanish woollens (fine)	Piece of 30 els	70 0	100 0
English and Dutch woollens (fine)	Piece of 215 ells	40 0	80 0
English cloth called douzaines	Piece of 9–10 ells	4 10	10 0
Woollen hats	Hundredweight	8 0	20 0
Gilt leather	Hundredweight	15 0	30 0
Tanned ox leather	Dozen hides	12 0	14 0
Coal	Barrel	0 8	1 4
Chamois style leather	Dozen hides	1 10	3 0
Lace and embroidery of Linen	Pound	25 0	50 0
Tin plate	Barrel	15 0	30 0
Frizes (Spanish and Flemish)	Piece of 20 ells	8 0	16 0
Frizes (English)	Piece of 18 ells	3 0	7 0
Molletons	Piece of 26 ells	6 0	12 0
Soap	Hundredweight	3 10	7 0
Serges de seigneur et d'Ascot, and so forth	Piece of 20 ells	6 0	12 0
Milled serges	Piece of 15 ells	10 0	15 0
Scotch serges	Piece of 25 ells	2 0	4 0
Tapestries (old or new, Flemish but not from Brussels or Antwerp)	Hundredweight	60 0	100 0
Tapestries (old or new from Brussels or Antwerp)	Hundredweight	120	200

Source: C. Cole, *Colbert and a Century of French Mercantilism*, 2 vols (London: Frank Cass, 1964), vol. 1, pp. 430–1.

Appendix C: Prizes brought into Le Havre, 1692– 7

Date	Ship Taken	Nationality	Ship Taken By
1692	Le Thomas et Marie	English	La Marguerite and Le Granadan of St Malo and La Paix of Granville
1692	La Roue de Fortune	English	Francois le Fer, captain of Le Marquis (avec traduction d'instructions anglaises pour la guerre de course)
24 December 1692	Le Dauphin	English	Failly and Carrion (King's ship)
1693	Le Saint Sacrament	Portuguese	'La Favourite' (King's ship)
1693	L'Ange Tutélaire	Dutch	
1694	Le Renard	Dutch	La Palme Couronnée, Louis Bommelard de Dunkerque
1695	Le Diligent	English	
	Robert et Anne	English	Le Chasseur Royal of Dunkirk, Jean Simon
1697	Le Saint-André	Danish (released)	Le Marie, Gabriel de Jonnaute

Source: Archives départementales de Seine-Maritime, Rouen, 216 BP 316.

Appendix D: Passports granted to British ships in La Rochelle, 1695

Entry No.	Ship Name	Of	Owner	Master	Date
58–9	Hélène	Glasgow	Daniel Masson	Archibald Murchye	15 January
60–1	Daniel	Dublin	Daniel Masson	Edward Taylor	15 January
62	Succèz	Cork (registered as a Scottish ship)	Joseph Comershard		17 January
63	Fortune	Glasgow	Daniel Masson for Galbraith		5 February
67–8	Chester	Irish	Jean Mackerel		16 April
72–73bis	Jean et Jacques	Leith	Abraham Duport	Edward Burd	9 May
74–75	Elisabeth	Scottish	Alexander Lait		19 May
79	Elisabeth	Glasgow	Jean Mackarel	Robert Buckle	12 August
80	Catherine	Leith	Abraham Duport	Jean Lait	3 September
81	Jacques	Leith	Abraham Duport	George Hil	15 September
82	Christine	Glasgow	Jean Mackarel	Hugh Campbell	24 September
84–5	Hélène	Glasgow	Daniel Masson	Jacques Sinclair	5 October
87	Guillaume et Georges	Scottish	Abraham Duport	Robert Kew	22 October
88–89	Jean	Dublin	Daniel Masson	Jacques Moor	5 November
90	Jean et Samuel	Aberdeen	Abraham Duport	David Houisson	3 December

Source: Archives départementales de la Charente-Maritime, La Rochelle, B5691/57-90.

Appendix E: Scottish ships granted permission by the Admiralty of Guyenne to pass through the port of Bordeaux, 1691–7

Document Ref (ADG)	Date	Master of Ship	Name of Ship	Tonnage
6B 75 25v-26	1691	John Bartown	le Holy Island	60
6B 75 53-53v	1691	Thomas Ridle	le Hopeful	102
6B 75 67-67v	1691	François Duncan	la Marguerite	
6B 75 81-81v	1691	Thomas Ridell	le Hopeful Marquet	112
6B 75 124v-125	1692	Alexandre Eroudey	The Hope and Confidence	60
6B 75 129v-130	1692	Danis Fargisson	l'Ami de Glasgow	
6B 75 130v-131	1692	Jean Miller	le Guillaume	60
6B 75 160v-161	1692	Robert Holmes	l'Anne de Belfast (entered as Scottish)	50
6B 75 161-161v	1692	John Watson	la Jeanette	80
6B 75 141v-142v	1693	Hughe Dyat	Jean et Anne	40
6B 76 2v-3	1694	John Barr	The George of Leith	50
6B 76 3v-4	1694	George Still	The James of Leith	50
6B 76 5-5v	1694	Leonard Robertson	le Jacques	30
6B 76 39v-40	1694	Robert Arthur	l'Elisabeth	60
6B 76 40-40v	1694	Jacques Raé	la Marguerite	60
6B 76 147-147v	1695	Jean Marchand	le Grissel	65
6B 76 154-154v	1695	Jean-Jacques Fervier	le George	70
6B 76 154v-155v	1695	Jean Jasson	le Dragon	100
6B 76 159v-160v	1695	Jacques Cook	le George	50
6B 76 160v-161v	1695	Jean Kewe	le Thomas	50
6B 76 161v-162v	1695	Jean Dauling	l'Elisabeth	50
6B 76 162v-163v	1695	Robert Arthur	l'Elisabeth	60
6B 76 163v-164v	1695	Alexandre Stuart	l'Aventure	100
6B 76 164v-165v	1695	Jacques Rail	écossais la Marguerite	60
6B 76 165v-166v	1695	Edouard Burd	le Jean et Jacques	
6B 76 167v-168v	1695	Jean Tist	la Catherine	200
6B 76 169-169v	1695	Robert Alizon	le Henry	60
6B 76 169v-170v	1695	George Hil	le Jacques	50
6B 76 173-174	1695	Charles Ramsri	l'Ange de Glasgow	40
6B 76 174-175	1695	Patrick Higgens	la Madelaine	110
6B 76 175-176	1695	Thomas Gourlay	la Marguerite	90
6B 76 176-177	1695	Adam Tod	la Concordia	50
6B 77 6v-7v	1695	George Beevorick	l'Ami de Kirkaldy	50
6B 77 59v-60	1695	Eric Kruskenk	The Speedwell	90
6B 77 71-71v	1695	Guillaume Ponton	le Lion Rouge	125
6B 77 105v-106v	1695	Jean Jounge	Jacques	30
6B 77 121v-122v	1696	Jacques Simson	la Catherine	50
6B 77 133v-134v	1696	George Hill	Jean et Jacques de Leith	80
6B 77 138-139	1696	Georges Weir	le Christian	100
6B 77 139-140	1696	Edward Hill	le Jacques	45

Document Ref (ADG)	Date	Master of Ship	Name of Ship	Tonnage
6B 77 172v-173v	1696	David Houissan	le Jean et Samuel	90
6B 77 173v-174v	1696	Jean Houisson	l'Elisabeth	
6B 77 174v-175v	1696	Charles Ramsey	James	42
6B 77 190v-191v	1696	George Lay	le Faucon	70
6B 77 211-212	1696	Jacques Gabraith	l'aiguron	80
6B 77 217-217v	1696	William Ponton	le Lion Rouge	120
6B 77 228-229	1697	Charles Ramsey	l'Amitié de Glasgow	60
6B 77 265-266	1697	Jean Honison	le Robert	30
6B 77 285-286v	1697	William Ponthon	le Lion Rouge	120
6B 77 291-292	1697	Alexandre Young	l'Anne	20
6B 77 292 bis-293	1697	Charles Ramezay	l'Unité	55
6B 77 293-294	1697	John Noir	le Jacques	45
6B 77 294-295	1697	Edouard Hic	le Jacques	50
6B 77 295-296	1697	Jacques Wilson	le Bewer	86
6B 77 301v-302v	1697	John Young	la Providence	50

Source: Archives départementales de la Gironde, Bordeaux, 6 B 75-7.

Appendix F: English Ships Granted Permission by the Admiralty of Guyenne to Pass through the Port of Bordeaux, 1689–97

Document Ref (ADG)	Date	Master of Ship	Name of Ship	Tonnage
6B 73 149-149v	13 January 1689	Robert Thurkettol	la Marie	36
6B 73 156-156v	13 January 1689	William Holman	l'Amitié	120
6B 73 74-74v	13 January 1689	Guillaume Gattas	la Bonne Aventure	80
6B 73 146v-147	16 January 1689	Manasses Paine	le Dauphin	80
6B 73 148v	16 January 1689	John Errington	la Bonne-Vivante	45
6B 73 91-91v	16 January 1689	Edouard Smith	le Facteur de Bordeaux	160
6B 73 96v-97	16 January 1689	James Modden	le Lucas	120
6B 73 89v-90v	22 January 1689	Daniel Wisilaw	le Thomas	60
6B 73 79v-80	23 January 1689	Nicolas Flagg	les Deux Frères	44
6B 73 86-87	23 January 1689	Robert Michal	la Tourterelle	60
6B 73 102-102v	24 January 1689	Thomas Knowles	la Dextroite	100
6B 73 104-104v	24 January 1689	William England	le Marigold	120
6B 73 105-105v	24 January 1689	Thomas Wood	le Gladre	300
6B 73 109-109v	24 January 1689	Joseph Brandell	la Bonne Volonté	90
6B 73 126	24 January 1689	John Hirris	le Scedive	60
6B 73 90v-91	24 January 1689	Robert Bristoll	le Félix	60
6B 73 105v-106	27 January 1689	Jean Godrling	le Marie	120
6B 73 145v	27 January 1689	William Henderson	la Recontre	50
6B 73 75v-76	27 January 1689	Roger Grassingham	le Thomas et Elisabeth	140
6B 73 82-82v	27 January 1689	Jean Pilton	la Prospérité	50
6B 73 88v-89	27 January 1689	John Dyx	le Hopewell	80
6B 73 94	27 January 1689	Samuel Castent	la Sacrade	100
6B 73 83	30 January 1689	Henry Moon	le Désiré	70
6B 73 102v-103	31 January 1689	Richard Miles	le Bon Plaisir	100
6B 73 104v-105	31 January 1689	Richard Dany	l'Amitié	90
6B 73 121-121v	31 January 1689	Jean Fuller	le Lys	200
6B 73 124-124v	31 January 1689	Jean Miquitsil	le Bachelier	200
6B 73 140v-141	31 January 1689	John Roch	le Saint-Patrice	100
6B 73 59-59v	31 January 1689	Guillaume Alington	le Guillaume et Jeanne	50
6B 73 92-92v	31 January 1689	William Godleg	l'Estoille	100
6B 73 99-99v	31 January 1689	Thomas Hercher	la Catherine	120
6B 73 91v-92	6 February 1689	Nicolas Willy	le Heron	200
6B 73 151v	8 February 1689	Allan Scott	l'Aventurier	150
6B 73 100v-101	16 February 1689	Ambroise Lorrain	le Loyal Jacques	75
6B 73 101v-102	16 February 1689	Jean Beale	le Marchand de Golchester	130
6B 73 112v	16 February 1689	William LeRoy	l'Edouard	160
6B 73 147v-148	16 February 1689	Thomas Weir	l'Hélène	100
6B 73 155-155v	16 February 1689	François Pety	la Prospérité	50

Document Ref (ADG)	Date	Master of Ship	Name of Ship	Tonnage
6B 73 58-58v	16 February 1689	Thimothé Tourson	le Bourgeois Aven-turier	100
6B 73 74v-75v	16 February 1689	Michel Williams	l'Anne et Marie	160
6B 73 92v-93	16 February 1689	Conry Cobb	le Robert	60
6B 73 76-76v	16 February 1689	Thomas Bealle	la Rebecca	30
6B 73 107	20 February 1689	William Lanes	le Vilain	32
6B 73 108v-109	20 February 1689	Edouard Tomlin	l'amitié	75
6B 73 126v-127v	20 February 1689	William Chipman	le Marchand	100
6B 73 165-165v	20 February 1689	Joseph Goodrrin	la Rébecca	52
6B 73 59v-60	20 February 1689	Jacob Farland	les Armes de Bis-caye de Londres	150
6B 73 60-60v	20 February 1689	William Shower	le David Jacson	70
6B 73 85v-86	20 February 1689	Henry Pay	la Suzane	34
6B 73 89v	20 February 1689	Leonard Mocher	l'Anne	60
6B 73 93v	20 February 1689	George Linhorn	l'Anne	65
6B 73 97v-98v	20 February 1689	Henry Olding	l'Avanture des Amis de Londres	150
6B 73 98v-99	20 February 1689	Roger Clame	le Devoir	80
6B 73 99v-100v	20 February 1689	Abraham Downton	le Francois de Londres	140
6B 73 103-103v	21 February 1689	Edouard Tibfort	le Scort	110
6B 73 114-114v	26 February 1689	Richard Robin	la Contrintude	75
6B 73 108-108v	19 March 1689	Robert Addelses	le Robert	66
6B 73 130-130v	21 March 1689	Thomas Jackson	la Marie et Sarra de Hull	60
6B 73 126v	23 March 1689	Georges Hephens	l'Industrie	65
6B 73 97-97v	23 March 1689	Joseph Chapprott	le Joseph	90
6B 73 150-150v	30 March 1689	Thomas Burton	le Jean	150
6B 73 106-106v	31 March 1689	Daniel Clark	la Bretagne	60
6B 73 107v	31 March 1689	John Ross	le Henri	50
6B 73 109v-110	31 March 1689	William Receng	le Retour	175
6B 73 130v-131	31 March 1689	Peter Thornson	la Marie et Anne	70
6B 73 131v	31 March 1689	Thomas Grimston	la Providence	120
6B 73 149v-150	31 March 1689	Joseph Ould	La Bonne Volonté	64
6B 73 152-152v	31 March 1689	Philips Smith	le Succès	40
6B 73 150v-151		Thomas Allan	l'Anne	110
6B 73 155v-156	07 April 1689	William Tronnard	le Saint-Mathieu	200
6B 73 122v-123v	12 April 1689	Joseph Fray	le Sprituel	44
6B 73 123v-124	29 April 1689	Daniel Janneran	la Judith	80
6B 73 127v-128	29 April 1689	Jacob Maczten	le Saint-Pierre	75
6B 73 154-154v	31 April 1689	Thomas Petit Jean	la Marie	100
6B 73 165v-166	07 May 1689	Thomas Sutton	John Canton	26
6B 73 166-166v	30 June 1689	John Canton	le Thomas et Anne	26
6B 74 55-55v	12 July 1690	William Wilson	le Blessing	30

Document Ref (ADG)	Date	Master of Ship	Name of Ship	Tonnage
6B 75 83-84	12 January 1692	Jean Cain	le Thomas de Londres	50
6B 75 84-84v	11 February 1692	Jacob Seale	le Guillaume et Pierre de Londres	150
6B 75 128-128v	30 July 1692	Henry Bichet	le Lion	50
6B 77 101-102v	05 April 1696	Jean Baroe	La Princesse de Lancaster	30
6B 77 103-104	06 May 1696	Jean Wellon	la Fortune	25
6B 77 130v-131v	21 July 1696	Patrick Willson	le Henri	60
6B 77 132-132v	31 July 1696	Robert Ballandin	la Catherine	60
6B 77 240-241	10 February 1697	Jean Baron	la Princesse de Lancaster	30
6B 77 231-232	18 February 1697	Jean Young	la Providence	60
6B 77 284-285	17 July 1697	Johan Swift	La Ville de Bristol	45
6B 77 300v-301v	03 August 1697	Wil Kinson	la Loyalité	50

Source: Archives départementales de la Gironde, Bordeaux, 6 B 73-7.

NOTES

The following abbreviations have been used throughout the notes:

ACA Aberdeen City Archives.

ACL Taylor, L. (ed.), *Aberdeen Council Letters*, 6 vols (Oxford: Oxford University Press, 1942–61).

ADC Archives diplomatiques de la Corneuve, Paris.

ADCM Archives départementales de la Charente-Maritime, La Rochelle.

ADG Archives départementales de la Gironde, Bordeaux.

ADLA Archives départementales de la Loire-Atlantique, Nantes.

ADSM Archives départementales de Seine-Maritime, Rouen.

AMB Archives municipales de Bordeaux.

AMN Archives municipales de Nantes.

AN Archives nationales, Paris.

APCE Lyle, J. (ed.), *Acts of the Privy Council of England: New Series*, 45 vols (London: H. M. S. O., 1890–1964).

APS *Acts of the Parliament of Scotland, 1124–1707*, 12 vols (Edinburgh, 1814–44).

ASWA Taylor, L. (ed.), *Aberdeen Shore Work Accounts, 1596–1670* (Aberdeen: Aberdeen University Press, 1972).

AUSC University of Aberdeen Special Collections.

BnF *Bibliothèque nationale* de France, Paris.

CLPS *Calendar of Letters, Dispatches and State Papers relating to the Negotiations between England and Spain: Preserved in the Archives at Simancas and Elsewhere*, 13 vols (London: H. M. S. O., 1862–1954).

CRB Marwick, J. (ed.), *Records of the Convention of the Royal Burghs of Scotland: With Extracts from Other Records relating to the Affairs of the Burghs of Scotland, 1295–1711*, 5 vols (Edinburgh: William Paterson, 1866–80).

CSP Mackie, J. (ed.), *Calendar of State Papers relating to Scotland and Mary Queen of Scots, 1547–1603*, 9 vols (Edinburgh: H. M. S. O., 1898–1969).

CSPD *Calendar of State Papers, Domestic Series* (London: H. M. S. O., 1856–1927).

DRA Rigsarkivet (Danish National Archives), Copenhagen.

GCA Glasgow City Archives, The Mitchell Library.

HL Huntington Library, San Marino, California.

NLS National Library of Scotland, Edinburgh.

NRS National Records of Scotland, Edinburgh.

ODNB *Oxford Dictionary of National Biography*.

RPCS	*Register of the Privy Council of Scotland*, 38 vols (Edinburgh: Oliver & Boyd, 1877–1970).
RPS	*Records of the Parliaments of Scotland to 1707*, online at http://www.rps.ac.uk.
SAUL	University of St Andrews Library, Special Collections.
SRA	Riksarkivet (Swedish National Archives), Stockholm.
TNA	The National Archives at Kew, London.

Introduction

1.   Contract, John Smith and John Clerk, 16 August 1634, Edinburgh, NRS GD18/2359. Clerk returned to Scotland in the autumn of 1646: in August he was still styling himself 'John Clerk, marchant [*sic*] in Paris', whereas in September this changes to 'merchant in Edinburgh': John Clerk to William Gray of Pittendrum, 16 August 1646, NRS GD18/2381/7; Account, same to same, September 1646, NRS GD18/2381/5. See S. Talbott, 'The Letter-Book of John Clerk, 1644–45', *Scottish History Society Miscellany*, 15 (forthcoming, 2014).

2.   See *ODNB* entries for Sir John Clerk of Penicuik, first baronet (1649/50–1722) and Sir John Clerk of Penicuik, second baronet (1676–1755).

3.   Notably E. Hobsbawm, 'The Crisis of the Seventeenth Century', *Past and Present*, 6 (1954), pp. 44–65; H. Trevor-Roper, 'The General Crisis of the Seventeenth Century', *Past and Present*, 16 (1959), pp. 31–64; G. Parker and L. Smith (eds), *The General Crisis of the Seventeenth Century* (London: Routledge, 1978).

4.   J. Roberts, *The Military Revolution* (Belfast: M. Boyd, 1956). There has been vociferous debate surrounding this concept: G. Parker, *The Military Revolution, 1500–1800* (Cambridge: Cambridge University Press, 1996); J. Black, 'Was there a Military Revolution in Early Modern Europe?', *History Today*, 58:7 (2008), pp. 34–41.

5.   T. C. Smout, 'The Road to Union', in G. Holmes (ed.), *Britain After the Glorious Revolution* (London: Macmillan, 1969), pp. 176–96, on p. 187.

6.   E. Charters, E. Rosenhaft and H. Smith (eds), 'Introduction', to *Civilians and War in Europe, 1618–1815* (Liverpool: Liverpool University Press, 2012), pp. 1–21, on p. 6.

7.   H. Trevor-Roper, *The Crisis of the Seventeenth Century* (Indianapolis: Liberty Fund, 2001; original essays 1954–67), preface, p. 1. Contributions to debate on the general crisis can be found in T. Aston (ed.), *Crisis in Europe 1560–1660: Essays from Past and Present* (London: Routledge, 1965); Parker and Smith (eds), *The General Crisis of the Seventeenth Century*. See also discussion in S. Ogilvie, 'Germany and the Seventeenth-Century Crisis', *Historical Journal*, 35:2 (1992), pp. 417–41, on pp. 418–21.

8.   Ogilvie, 'Germany and the Seventeenth-Century Crisis', pp. 440–1.

9.   P. Wilson, 'Was the Thirty Years' War a "Total War"?', in Charters, Rosenhaft and Smith (eds), *Civilians and War in Europe*, pp. 21–35, on p. 35.

10. H. de Bruyn Kops, *A Spirited Exchange: The Wine and Brandy Trade between France and the Dutch Republic in its Atlantic Framework, 1600–1650* (Leiden: Brill, 2007), p. 7; S. Haggerty, *The British-Atlantic Trading Community, 1760–1810: Men, Women and the Distribution of Goods* (Leiden: Brill, 2006), pp. 8–9.

11. R. Mousnier, J. Elliott, L. Stone, H. Trevor-Roper, E. Kossman, E. Hobsbawm, and J. Hexter, Discussion of H. Trevor-Roper: 'The General Crisis of the Seventeenth Century', *Past & Present*, 18 (1960), pp. 8–42, R. Mousnier, on p. 23.

12. De Bruyn Kops, *A Spirited Exchange*, p. 7.

13. J. Takeda, *Between Crown and Commerce: Marseille and the Early Modern Mediterranean* (Baltimore, MD: Johns Hopkins University Press, 2011), p. 1.

14. J. Ball, *Merchants and Merchandise: The Expansion of Trade in Europe, 1500–1630* (London: Croon Helm, 1977), p. 45.

15. K. Barclay and S. Talbott, 'New Perspectives on Seventeenth- and Eighteenth-Century Scotland', *Journal of Scottish Historical Studies*, 31:1 (2011), pp. 119–33, on pp. 128–30.

16. De Bruyn Kops, *A Spirited Exchange*; Haggerty, *The British-Atlantic Trading Community*; X. Lamikiz, *Trade and Trust in the Eighteenth-Century Atlantic World: Spanish Merchants and their Overseas Networks* (Suffolk: Boydell & Brewer, 2010). See also A. Macinnes, *Union and Empire: The Making of the United Kingdom in 1707* (Cambridge: Cambridge University Press, 2007), p. 11; S. Murdoch, *Network North: Scottish Kin, Commercial and Covert Association in Northern Europe, 1603–1746* (Leiden: Brill, 2006), pp. 127–248.

17. There are notable exceptions, for example T. C. Smout's examination of Andrew Russell's trading networks (the Russell Papers can be found at NRS, RH15/106): T. C. Smout, *Scottish Trade on the Eve of Union, 1660–1707* (London: Oliver & Boyd, 1963), pp. 99–115.

18. De Bruyn Kops, *A Spirited Exchange*, p. 7.

19. For one of the exceptions to this rule see S. Talbott, 'Beyond "The Antiseptic Realm of Theoretical Economic Models": New Perspectives on Franco-Scottish Commerce and the Auld Alliance in the Long Seventeenth Century', *Journal of Scottish Historical Studies*, 31:2 (2011), pp. 149–68, on pp. 160, 167–8; also Appendix A.

20. *RPCS*, 1st series, vol. 9, p. lxix.

21. *ACL*, vol. 1, pp. xxii–xxxiii.

22. Murdoch, *Network North*, p. 207.

23. C. and P. Martin, 'Introduction' to the Watson Papers, SAUL ms38527, p. 2.

24. Talbott, 'The Letter-Book of John Clerk'.

25. 2 May 1675, NRS GD29/1474.

26. See Barclay and Talbott, 'New Perspectives on Seventeenth- and Eighteenth-Century Scotland', pp. 128–9.

27. There are many examples, but see J. Laidlaw (ed.), *The Auld Alliance; France and Scotland over 700 Years* (Edinburgh: Edinburgh University Press, 2011); H. Fenwick, *The Auld Alliance* (Kineton: Roundwood Press, 1971); N. MacDougall, *An Antidote to the English: The Auld Alliance, 1295–1560* (East Linton: Tuckwell Press, 1988); A. Broadie, *Agreeable Connexions: Scottish Enlightenment Links with France* (Edinburgh: John Donald, 2013); D. Dawson and P. Morère (eds), *Scotland and France in the Enlightenment* (Lewisburg: Bucknell University Press, 2004).

28. T. Pagan, *The Convention of the Royal Burghs of Scotland* (Glasgow: Glasgow University Press, 1926), p. 199.

29. M. Glozier, *Scottish Soldiers in France in the Reign of the Sun King* (Leiden: Brill, 2004); M. Glozier, 'Scots in the French and Dutch Armies during the Thirty Years' War', in S. Murdoch (ed.), *Scotland and the Thirty Years' War* (Leiden: Brill, 2001), pp. 117–42; M. Tucker, *Maîtres et étudiants ecossais à la Faculté de Droit de l'Université de Bourges 1480–1703* (Paris: Champion, 2001); M. Tucker, 'Scottish Students and Masters at the

Faculty of Law of the University of Bourges in the Sixteenth and Seventeenth Centuries', in T. van Heijnsbergen and N. Royan (eds), *Literature, Letters and the Canonical in Early Modern Scotland* (East Linton: Tuckwell Press, 2002), pp. 111–20.

30. There is a long historiographical tradition of focus on the Scottish trading staple: J. Davidson and A. Gray, *The Scottish Staple at Veere: A Study in the Economic History of Scotland* (London: Longmans, 1905), pp. 190, 202–10; M. Rooseboom, *The Scottish Staple in the Netherlands* (The Hague: M. Nijhoff, 1910), pp. 146–94. The Scottish staple continues to attract scholarly attention: V. Enthoven, 'Thomas Cunningham (1604–1669): Conservator of the Scottish Court at Veere', in D. Dickson, J. Parmentier and J. Ohlmeyer (eds), *Irish and Scottish Mercantile Networks in Europe and Overseas in the Seventeenth and Eighteenth Centuries* (Gent: Academia Press, 2007), pp. 39–66.

31. Scottish merchants continued to take staple goods to other ports, to the consternation of the Convention. *CRB, passim.*

32. I. Guy, 'The Scottish Export Trade, 1460–1599', in T. C. Smout (ed.), *Scotland and Europe, 1200–1850* (Edinburgh: John Donald, 1986), pp. 62–81, on p. 67; Pagan, *Convention of the Royal Burghs of Scotland*, p. 151.

33. *CRB*, vol. 1, pp. 143, 272–3, 284, 287, 483, 494, 531–2, 557; vol. 2, p. 39.

34. *Articles Concluded at Paris the xxiiij of February 1605, stylo Angliae, by Commissioners of the High and Mightie Kings, James by the Grace of God King of Great Britaine, France, and Ireland, Defender of the Faith, &c. and Henrie the Fourth Most Christian French King, and King of Navar, for the More Commodious Entercourse in Traffique Betweene their Subjects* (London, 1606). The fact that this treaty is entitled 'Articles Concluded betweene Great Britain and France' has led to the assumption that Scotland was not a major part of it: B. Dietz, 'England's Overseas Trade in the Reign of James I', in A. Smith (ed.), *The Reign of James VI and I* (New York: St Martin's Press, 1973), pp. 106–23, on p. 107. See Chapter 1, p. 28.

35. Primarily: S. G. E. Lythe, *The Economy of Scotland in its European Setting, 1550–1625* (London: Oliver & Boyd, 1960); Smout, *Scottish Trade on the Eve of Union*. More recent works expanding our knowledge of Scotland's commerce and economy include I. Whyte, *Scotland before the Industrial Revolution: An Economic and Social History* (London: Longman, 1995); E. Graham, *A Maritime History of Scotland, 1650–1790* (East Linton: Tuckwell Press, 2002); P. Rössner, *Scottish Trade in the Wake of Union (1700–1760)* (Stuttgart: Franz Steiner Verlag, 2008).

36. Murdoch, *Network North*, pp. 240–1.

37. I. Whyte, *Scotland's Society and Economy in Transition, c. 1500–c. 1760* (London: Palgrave Macmillan, 1997), p. 157; T. Devine, 'The Spoils of Empire', in T. Devine (ed.), *Scotland and the Union, 1707–2007* (Edinburgh: Edinburgh University Press, 2008), pp. 91–108, on p. 93.

38. Murdoch, *Network North*, p. 423; D. Dickson, 'Introduction', to Dickson, Parmentier and Ohlmeyer (eds), *Irish and Scottish Mercantile Networks in Europe*, pp. 2–3.

39. T. Keith, 'The Economic Causes for the Scottish Union', *English Historical Review*, 24:93 (1909), pp. 44–60, on p. 44; T. Keith, 'The Economic Condition of Scotland under the Commonwealth and Protectorate', *Scottish Historical Review*, 5:19 (1908), pp. 273–84, on p. 276.

40. D. Catterall, *Community Without Borders: Scots Migrants and the Changing Face of Power in the Dutch Republic, c. 1600–1700* (Leiden: Brill, 2002); A. Grosjean and S. Murdoch, *Scottish Communities Abroad in the Early Modern Period* (Leiden: Brill, 2005); E. Mijers, 'News from the Republick of Letters': Scottish Students, Charles Mackie and the United

Provinces, 1650–1750 (Leiden: Brill, 2012); Murdoch, *Network North*; K. Zickermann, *Across the German Sea: Early Modern Scottish Connections with the Wider Elbe-Weser Region* (Leiden: Brill, 2013).

41. A. Grosjean, *An Unofficial Alliance: Scotland and Sweden, 1569–1654* (Leiden: Brill, 2003), pp. 189, 205.
42. Including D. Worthington, *Scots in Habsburg Service, 1618–1648* (Leiden: Brill, 2004).
43. E. Corp, 'The Jacobite Presence in Toulouse during the Eighteenth Century', *Diasporas, Histoire et Sociétés*, 5 (2004), pp. 124–45. This work recognizes the commercial importance of the Jacobite community in France, but does not discuss the many commercial individuals not tied to these institutions: p. 128; S. Talbott, 'Commerce and the Jacobite Court: Scottish Migrants in France, 1688–1718', in K. German, L. Graham and A. Macinnes (eds), *Living with Jacobitism* (London: Pickering & Chatto, forthcoming 2014).
44. D. Allan, 'The Enlightenment and the Book' (review), *Library*, 8:4 (2007), pp. 456–8, on p. 457.
45. J. G. A. Pocock, 'British History: A Plea for a New Subject', *Journal of Modern History*, 47:4 (1975), pp. 601–21; J. G. A. Pocock, 'The Limits and Divisions of British History: In Search of an Unknown Subject', *American Historical Review*, 87:2 (1982), pp. 311–36.
46. N. Canny, 'Writing Early Modern History: Ireland, Britain and the Wider World', *Historical Journal*, 46:3 (2003), pp. 723–47, on p. 738.
47. É. Ó Ciosáin, 'Hidden by 1688 and After: Irish Catholic Migration to France, 1590–1685', in D. Worthington (ed.), *British and Irish Emigrants and Exiles in Europe, 1603–1688* (Leiden: Brill, 2010), pp. 125–38, on p. 138.
48. D. Ditchburn, *Scotland and Europe: the Mediaeval Kingdom and its Contacts with Christendom, 1215–1545, Volume I: 'Religion, Culture and Commerce'* (East Linton: Tuckwell Press, 2001), pp. 146–91.
49. Smout, *Scottish Trade on the Eve of Union*, p. 185.
50. T. Devine, *Scotland's Empire, 1600–1815* (London: Allen Lane, 2003), p. 3.
51. E. Graham, 'In Defence of the Scottish Maritime Interest, 1681–1713', *Scottish Historical Review*, 81 (1992), pp. 88–109, on p. 90.
52. This issue is discussed in Macinnes, *Union and Empire*, p. 5.
53. Devine, 'The Spoils of Empire', pp. 94–5; G. Holmes, 'Introduction' to Holmes (ed.), *Britain After the Glorious Revolution*, pp. 1–38, on p. 26. For an alternative view, see A. Mackillop, 'A Union for Empire? Scotland, the English East India Company and the British Union', in S. Brown and C. Whatley (eds), *Union of 1707: New Dimensions, Scottish Historical Review*, supplementary issue (Edinburgh: Edinburgh University Press, 2008), pp. 116–34, on pp. 116–17.
54. A. Cummings, 'Scotland's Links with Europe, 1600–1800', *History Today*, 35 (1985), pp. 45–9, on p. 46.
55. Macinnes, *Union and Empire*, pp. 137, 150, 157–71, 183.
56. Ibid., *Union and Empire*, pp. 210, 318.
57. H. Sée and A. Cormack, 'Commercial Relations between France and Scotland in 1707', *Scottish Historical Review*, 23 (1926), pp. 275–9, on p. 277.
58. NRS, Andrew Russell Papers, RH15/106; Smout, *Scottish Trade on the Eve of Union*, pp. 99–115; Murdoch, *Network North*, p. 145.
59. *RPCS*, 3rd series, vol. 15, p. 125.
60. Guy, 'The Scottish Export Trade', p. 62.

61. K. Wrightson, *Earthly Necessities: Economic Lives in Early Modern Britain* (London: Yale University Press, 2000), p. 97; see also S. Mowat, *The Port of Leith: Its History and its People* (Edinburgh: Forth Ports & John Donald, 1994).
62. H. Hamilton, *An Economic History of Scotland in the Eighteenth Century* (Oxford: Clarendon Press, 1963), pp. 30, 287.
63. T. C. Smout, 'The Glasgow Merchant Community in the Seventeenth Century', *Scottish Historical Review*, 47:143 (1968), pp. 53–71.

1 Beyond 1560: The Auld Alliance

1. W. Guthrie, *A General History of Scotland from the Earliest Accounts to the Present Time*, 10 vols (London: Robinson & Roberts, 1768), vol. 6, p. 130.
2. The date at which the Auld Alliance was first implemented has enjoyed some vociferous debate, but 1295, the year the Treaty of Paris was signed, is accepted. See E. Bonner, 'Scotland's "Auld Alliance" with France', *History*, 84:273 (1999), pp. 5–30, on pp. 5–7.
3. Original version of the Treaty of Paris, in Latin: AN trésor des chartes, J667/1. A copy in French can be found at TNA C47/22/4/20. See notes to *RPS*, 1296/2/1.
4. *RPS*, A1296/2/1; AN trésor des chartes, reg. v, fos. 132v–135v.
5. Bonner, 'Scotland's 'Auld Alliance' with France', pp. 12–19.
6. Guthrie, *A General History of Scotland*, vol. 6, p. 130; J. Spottiswoode, *The History of the Church of Scotland* (Menston, Yorkshire: Scolar Press, 1972), p. 148; July 1560, *CSP*, vol. 1, pp. 422–4.
7. Bonner, 'Scotland's "Auld Alliance" with France', p. 29; Smout, *Scottish Trade on the Eve of Union*, p. 167.
8. Bonner, 'Scotland's "Auld Alliance" with France', p. 29; see also Macdougall, *An Antidote to the English*, pp. 4, 143.
9. This notion has been applied to the Franco-Irish relationship in the early modern period: P. O'Connor, 'Irish Clerics and Jacobites in Early Eighteenth-century Paris, 1700–30', in T. O'Connor and M. Lyons (eds), *The Irish in Europe 1580–1815* (Dublin: Four Courts Press, 2001), pp. 175–90, on pp. 175–6. This is debated throughout this volume and in detail in Chapter 7, pp. 137–43.
10. Whyte, *Scotland before the Industrial Revolution*, p. 92. This opinion has been espoused by many scholars, including: M. Lynch, *Scotland, A New History* (London: Pimlico, 1992), p. 209; T. Keith, *Commercial Relations of England and Scotland, 1603–1707* (Cambridge: Cambridge University Press, 1910), p. 47; MacDougall, *An Antidote to the English*, p. 3.
11. J. Ohlmeyer, 'Seventeenth-Century Ireland and Scotland and their Wider Worlds', in T. O'Connor, and M. Lyons (eds), *Irish Communities in Early Modern Europe* (Dublin: Four Courts Press, 2006), pp. 457–83, on p. 459.
12. S. Murdoch, 'Scotland and Europe', in B. Harris and A. MacDonald (eds), *Scotland: The Making and Unmaking of the Nation, c. 1100–1707* (Dundee: Dundee University Press, 2007), pp. 126–44, on p. 127.
13. Lythe, *The Economy of Scotland*, p. 167.
14. Bonner, 'Scotland's "Auld Alliance" with France', p. 29.
15. T. Moncrieff (ed.), *Memoires concerning the Ancient Alliance between the French and the Scots and the Privileges of the Scots in France* (Edinburgh: W. Cheyne, 1751), p. 3.

16. Bonner, 'Scotland's "Auld Alliance" with France', p. 6; E. Bonner, 'French Naturalization of the Scots in the Fifteenth and Sixteenth Centuries', *Historical Journal*, 40:4 (1997), pp. 1085–115, on p. 1102.
17. D. Calderwood, *The History of the Kirk of Scotland*, 8 vols (Edinburgh: Wodrow Society, 1842–9), vol. 2, pp. 122–3.
18. Macdougall, *An Antidote to the English*, p. 5.
19. J. Mackie, 'Henry VIII and Scotland', *Transactions of the Royal Historical Society*, 29 (1947), pp. 93–114, on p. 113; see also Lythe, *The Economy of Scotland*, p. 167.
20. I. Grant, *The Economic History of Scotland* (London: Longmans Green, 1934), p. 85; Pagan, *The Convention of the Royal Burghs*, pp. 151, 198–200.
21. *RPCS*, 1st series, vol. 2, p. 654; see also 18 April 1571, *CSP*, vol. 3, p. 550.
22. 20 May 1583, Bernadino de Mendoza to the King, London, *CLPS*, vol. 16, p. 471.
23. January 1588, A. Cameron (ed.), *The Warrender Papers*, 2 vols (Edinburgh: Edinburgh University Press, 1932), vol. 2, pp. 59, 66.
24. M. du Bosc to Cardinal Mazarin, Fontainebleau, 21 October 1644, J. Fotheringham (ed. and trans.), *The Diplomatic Correspondence of Jean de Montereul and the Brothers de Bellièvre: French Ambassadors in England and Scotland, 1645–48*, 2 vols (Edinburgh: Scottish History Society, 1898–9), vol. 1, pp. 564–5.
25. 3 January 1644, *RPS*, 1644/1/2.
26. Fotheringham (ed. and trans.), *Diplomatic Correspondence*, vol. 1, pp. xi–xv.
27. [n.d.] 1570, *RPCS*, 1st series, vol. 14 (addenda), p. 56.
28. 1597, *RPCS*, 1st series, vol. 5, p. 369.
29. 1597, *RPCS*, 1st series, vol. 5, p. 369.
30. Guerau de Spes to the King, 28 November 1570, *CLPS,* vol. 15, 1568–1579, p. 285.
31. Henri III to Monsieur de Castelnau, 9 May 1584, A. Teulet (ed.), *Relations Politiques de la France et de l'Espagne avec l'Écosse au XVIe Siècle (1515–1560)* (State Papers relating to France and Scotland in the 16th Century (1513–1561)), 5 vols (Paris: Renouard, 1862), vol. 2, p. 651.
32. These levies included Irish as well as Scottish troops. Montereul to Cardinal Mazarin, 26 March 1647, Edinburgh, Fotheringham (ed. and trans.), *Diplomatic Correspondence*, vol. 2, pp. 62–4; Montereul to Mazarin, 7 June 1646, Newcastle, Fotheringham (ed. and trans.), *Diplomatic Correspondence*, vol. 1, p. 208; Mazarin to Bellièvre, 12 January 1647, Paris, A. Chéruel (ed.), *Lettres du Cardinal Mazarin pendant son ministère*, 9 vols (Paris: Imprimerie nationale, 1872–1906), vol. 2, pp. 356–7; Mazarin to Harcourt, 1 January 1644, [Paris], Chéruel (ed.), *Lettres du Cardinal Mazarin*, vol. 1, p. 524; Mazarin to Bellièvre, 12 January 1647, Paris, Chéruel (ed.), *Lettres du Cardinal Mazarin*, vol. 2, pp. 356–7. French attempts to levy Scottish troops are documented well before these occurrences. See Richelieu to Bellièvre, 6 October 1638, Paris; 13 November 1638, M. Avenel (ed.), *Lettres, instructions diplomatiques et papiers d'état du Cardinal de Richelieu*, 8 vols (Paris: Imprimerie impériale, 1853–77), vol. 6, pp. 211–13, 238–40.
33. Montereul to Cardinal Mazarin, Newcastle, 30 May 1646, Fotheringham (ed. and trans.), *Diplomatic Correspondence*, vol. 1, pp. 197–201.
34. Bonner, 'French Naturalization of the Scots', p. 1086; Lythe, *The Economy of Scotland*, pp. 167–91.
35. Smout, *Scottish Trade on the Eve of Union*, p. 167.
36. 21 August 1604, Haddington, *CRB*, vol. 2, pp. 189–90.
37. Pagan, *The Convention of the Royal Burghs*, p. 48.
38. Balfour, *Annales*, vol. 2, p. 58, cited in Pagan, *The Convention of the Royal Burghs*, p. 48.

39. *CRB*, vol. 2, pp. 576–7. See examples of such embassies cited in the Introduction, p. 8.
40. Lythe, *The Economy of Scotland*, pp. 211, 172; see also Whyte, *Scotland before the Industrial Revolution*, p. 272.
41. G. Donaldson, *Scotland, James V–James VII* (Edinburgh: Oliver & Boyd, 1965), p. 388.
42. Smout, *Scottish Trade on the Eve of Union*, p. 240; S. Lythe, and J. Butt, *An Economic History of Scotland, 1100–1939* (Glasgow: Blackie, 1975), p. 62.
43. 13 October 1663, Edinburgh, 8 July 1664, Edinburgh, *RPCS*, 3rd series, vol. 1, pp. xxxvi–xxxvii, 445–6, 563.
44. 19 January 1664, Edinburgh, *RPCS*, 3rd series, vol. 1, pp. xxxvi–xxxvii.
45. *RPCS*, 3rd series, vol. 1, pp. xxxvi–xxxvii, 488.
46. Council to the King, June 1684, *RPCS*, 3rd series, vol. 9, p. 43.
47. Supplication by the lord provost and magistrates of Edinburgh, 19 August 1684, Edinburgh, *RPCS*, 3rd series, vol. 9, pp. 115–6.
48. 1 March 1698, *CRB*, vol. 4, p. 260.
49. Macinnes, *Union and Empire*, p. 238.
50. Pagan, *The Convention of the Royal Burghs of Scotland*, p. 199.
51. John Murray, Duke of Atholl, 18 July 1704, P. Hume-Brown (ed.), *James Ogilvy, First Earl of Seafield and Others: Letters relating to Scotland in the Reign of Queen Anne* (Edinburgh: Scottish History Society, 1915), pp. 137–8.
52. HL 89284, G. Ridpath, *Scotland's Grievances, relating to Darien, &c. Humbly Offered to the Consideration of the Parliament* ([Edinburgh], 1700), pp. 34–5.
53. *Mercator*, 7 July–9 July 1713, issue 20.
54. B. Lenman and J. Gibson, *The Jacobite Threat: England, Scotland, Ireland, France: A Source Book* (Edinburgh: Scottish Academic Press, 1990), pp. 85–6, 89, 93.
55. Lewis Innes to Nathanial Hooke, 23–9 January 1707, W. Macray (ed.), *Correspondence of Colonel Hooke*, 2 vols (London: J. B. Nichols and Sons, 1870–1), vol. 2, pp. 109–11.
56. Earl of Errol to Louis XIV, 27 May 1707, Macray (ed.), *Correspondence of Colonel Hooke*, vol. 2, pp. 262–3.
57. HL 89284, Ridpath, *Scotland's Grievances*, pp. 34–5.
58. E. Bonner, 'Continuing the "Auld Alliance" in the Sixteenth Century: Scots in France and French in Scotland', in G. Simpson (ed.), *The Scottish Soldier Abroad, 1247–1967* (Edinburgh: John Donald, 1992), pp. 31–46, on p. 31.
59. See Grosjean, *An Unofficial Alliance*; S. Murdoch, *Britain, Denmark-Norway and the House of Stuart, 1603–1660: A Diplomatic and Military Analysis* (East Linton: Tuckwell Press, 2000); Worthington, *Scots in Habsburg Service*; Murdoch (ed.), *Scotland and the Thirty Years' War*.
60. D. Ditchburn and A. MacDonald, 'Medieval Scotland, 1100–1560', in R. Houston and W. Knox (eds), *The New Penguin History of Scotland: From the Earliest Times to the Present Day* (London: Penguin, 2001), pp. 96–181, on p. 99; P. Contamine, 'Scottish Soldiers in France in the Second Half of the Fifteenth Century: Mercenaries, Immigrants or Frenchmen in the Making?', in Simpson (ed.), *The Scottish Soldier Abroad*, pp. 16–30; S. Murdoch, 'Introduction', to Murdoch (ed.), *Scotland and the Thirty Years' War*, pp. 1–23, on p. 17; G. Parker (ed.), *The Thirty Years' War* (London: Routledge and Kegan Paul, 1984), p. 174.
61. W. Forbes-Leith, *The Scots Men-at-Arms and Life-Guards in France* (Edinburgh: W. Paterson, 1882), pp. 109, 129–33.
62. Glozier, 'Scots in the French and Dutch Armies', p. 118.

63. William Henryson to [the Regent Morton], 16 March 1575, *CSP*, vol. 5, p. 109.
64. 20 January 1584, Robert Bowes to Walsingham, J. Bain (ed.), *The Hamilton Papers*, 2 vols (Edinburgh: H. M. General Register House, 1890–2), vol. 2, p. 14.
65. James VI to the Viscount of Turenne, Holyrood, [26] December 1590, Cameron (ed.), *The Warrender Papers*, vol. 2, pp. 147–8.
66. Robert Bowes to Lord Burghley, 26 December 1590, Edinburgh, *CSP*, vol. 10, p. 441.
67. 14 August 1590, *CSP*, vol. 2, p. 581; proclamation by James VI, 14 August 1590, *CSP*, vol. 10, p. 378.
68. *RPCS*, 1st series, vol. 2, p. 388; *RPCS*, 1st series, vol. 3, p. 614; *RPCS*, 1st series, vol. 4, pp. 19, 216.
69. Charles I's Missive anent the Privileges of the Scots in France, 10 October 1642, cited in A. MacDonald (ed.), *Papers relative to the Royal Guard of Scottish Archers in France* (Edinburgh: Maitland, 1835), p. xiv.
70. Committee of Estates of the Parliament of Scotland to Cardinal Mazarin, 3 August 1648, Edinburgh, NLS mss.98 xiii, fo. 27.
71. B. Kay, *The Scottish World: A Journey into the Scottish Diaspora* (Edinburgh: Mainstream Publishing, 2006), p. 80. Examples of both of these extremes include: A. Cameron, 'Scottish Students at Paris University 1466–1492', *Juridical Review*, 48 (1936), pp. 228–55; V. Montagu, 'The Scottish College in Paris', *Scottish Historical Review*, 4:16 (1907), pp. 399–416; Broadie, *Agreeable Connexions*; Dawson and Morère (eds), *Scotland and France in the Enlightenment*.
72. Tucker, *Maîtres et étudiants écossaise*; Tucker, 'Scottish Students and Masters of the Faculty of Law'.
73. Forbes-Leith, *Scots Men-at-Arms*, pp. 104–6.
74. H. de Ridder-Symoens (ed.), *A History of the University in Europe, Volume II: Universities in Early Modern Europe, 1500–1800* (Cambridge: Cambridge University Press, 2003), p. 300.
75. Ibid., p. 71; J. A. Fleming, *The Medieval Scots Scholar in France* (Glasgow: W. Maclellan, 1952), p. 129.
76. de Ridder-Symoens (ed.), *A History of the University in Europe, Volume II*, p. 419.
77. J. Durkan, 'The French Connection in the Sixteenth and Early Seventeenth Centuries', in Smout (ed.), *Scotland and Europe*, pp. 19–44, on p. 24.
78. J. Cairns, 'Thomas Craig', *ODNB*; J. Riddell, *Remarks Upon Scotch Peerage Law* (Edinburgh: T. Clark, 1833), pp. 164–9.
79. T. Thompson (ed.), *Memoirs of his Own Life by Sir James Melville of Halhill* (Edinburgh: Bannatyne Club, 1827), p. 18; A. Turner, 'James Bassantin', *ODNB*.
80. T. Riis, 'David Cunningham', *ODNB*.
81. Tucker, *Maîtres et étudiants écossaise*, pp. 61, 136, 217–20, 282–4; M. Tucker, 'Henry Scrimgeour', *ODNB*.
82. 11 December 1482, *RPS*, 1482/12/85.
83. Lythe, *The Economy of Scotland*, p. 171.
84. NRS RH9/5/2/1; Moncrieff (ed.), *Memoirs concerning the Ancient Alliance*, pp. 67–8.
85. Moncrieff (ed.), *Memoirs concerning the Ancient Alliance*, pp. 70, 73, 75.
86. Henri III to Monsieur de Castelnau, 9 May 1584, Teulet (ed.), *Relations Politiques de la France*, vol. 2, p. 647.
87. 3 July 1588, Edinburgh, *CRB*, vol. 1, pp. 284–5.
88. *RPCS*, 1st series, vol. 5, p. 369.
89. NRS RH9/5/2/5–10; Moncrieff (ed.), *Memoirs concerning the Ancient Alliance*, p. 75.

90. See articles 8–13 of *Articles concluded at Paris the xxiiij of February 1605, stylo Angliae, by Commissioners of the High and Mightie Kings, James by the Grace of God King of Great Britaine, France, and Ireland, Defender of the Faith, &c. and Henrie the Fourth Most Christian French King, and King of Navar, for the More Commodious Entercourse in Traffique Betweene their Subiects* (London, 1606).

91. Murdoch, *Network North*, pp. 149–50, 155.

92. TNA SP78/53/236; S. Talbott, 'The Auld Alliance: "Still in Vigour?"', *History Scotland* (January/February 2012), pp. 6–7.

93. *RPCS*, 2nd series, vol. 1, pp. lxxii, 479–80, n.

94. General Convention of Burghs, July 1635, Perth, ACA SRO25/3/2, fo. 493v. I would like to thank Dr Alan MacDonald (University of Dundee) for providing me with a transcription of this document.

95. Montereul to Mazarin, 22 October 1647, Edinburgh, Fotheringham (ed. and trans.), *Diplomatic Correspondence*, vol. 2, pp. 283–7.

96. 30 September 1663, Edinburgh, *RPCS*, 3rd series, vol. 1, p. 434; see also 13 September 1663, *CRB*, vol. 3, p. 567.

97. ADC Affaires Étrangères, Mémoires et Documents (Angleterre) 7, fos. 120v–123r: 'Extrait des registres du Conseil d'estat' [1739]. I am grateful to Professor Daniel Szechi (University of Manchester) for providing me with images of this document.

98. P. Sahlins, *Unnaturally French: Foreign Citizens in the Old Regime and After* (London: Cornell University Press, 2004), pp. 159, 172.

99. Bonner, 'Scotland's "Auld Alliance" with France', p. 18.

100. May 1598, NRS GD1/787/1.

101. 21 March 1599, Rouen, *CSP*, vol. 18, i, p. 431; a full copy of this confirmation is recorded as 'confirmation of the privileges of Scottish merchants in France, given by the king Henri IV in 1599', in *Mémoires Touchant l'Ancienne Alliance*, AUSC ms213, pp. 43–9, also at NLS mss.88.

102. J. Macpherson, 'Auld Alliance', *Scottish Field*, 114 (1967), p. 41; Moncrieff (ed.), *Memoirs concerning the Ancient Alliance*, p. 32.

103. A collection held in the AN containing records of 'privileges accordés aux étrangers trafiquant en France' for the period 1295–1652 does not contain a comprehensive record of the Scottish privileges: AN B⁷ 482.

104. Bishop Quadra to the Duchess of Parma, 4 July 1562, *CLPS*, vol. 14, p. 250.

105. 1597, Cameron (ed.), *The Warrender Papers*, vol. 2, p. 350.

106. Supplication by the lord provost and magistrates of Edinburgh, 19 August 1684, Edinburgh, *RPCS*, 3rd series, vol. 9, pp. 115–16.

107. 15 July 1690, *CRB*, vol. 4, p. 121.

108. Macpherson, 'Auld Alliance', p. 41; Talbott, 'The Auld Alliance: "Still in Vigour"?', pp. 6–7.

109. Robert Arbuthnot to the Duke of Hamilton, Rouen, 11 May 1700, NRS GD406/1/4737.

110. 10 and 15 November 1570, *CSP*, vol. 3, p. 423.

111. 19 April 1572, TNA E30/1152.

112. 1577, TNA SP104/163.

113. Monsieur de Mauvissier to Walsingham, 6 April 1583, *CSP*, vol. 6, p. 370.

114. ?1590, *CSPD*, vol. 2, p. 711.

115. [1605], TNA SP78/52/433.

116. [?] to [Henning], 5 May 1702, Paris, TNA SP78/153/72.

2 Markets and Merchants

1. Barclay and Talbott, 'New Perspectives', pp. 128–30.
2. S. Talbott, 'Communities on the Continent: Franco-Scottish Network Building in a Comparative European Context, 1560–1685', in M. Landi (ed.), *L'Écosse et ses doubles: ancien monde, nouveau monde* (Paris: L'Harmattan, 2010), pp. 21–41, on p. 41.
3. S. Subrahmanyam, 'Introduction', to S. Subrahmanyam (ed.), *Merchant Networks in the Early Modern World* (Aldershot: Variorum, 1996), pp. iii–xiv.
4. Murdoch, *Network North*, pp. 240–1, 423.
5. Lythe and Butt, *An Economic History of Scotland*, p. 62; P. McNeill and H. MacQueen (eds), *Atlas of Scottish History to 1707* (Edinburgh: Edinburgh University Press, 1996), p. 266; Guy, 'The Scottish Export Trade', pp. 62–5.
6. 26 February 1628, Holyrood, *RPCS*, 2nd series, vol. 2, p. 243; *ASWA*, p. 68. Examples of trade in commodities such as wine, brandy, vinegar and salt are too numerous to list, but for ubiquitous examples see NRS E71-2.
7. A. Millar (ed.), *The Compt Buik of David Wedderburne, Merchant of Dundee, 1587–1630* (Edinburgh: Scottish History Society, 1989), examples from pp. 221, 242.
8. John Johnstoun to John Clerk, 27 [blank] 1638, NRS GD18/2387.
9. Account between John Clerk and William, Earl of Lothian, 20 January 1645, Edinburgh, NRS GD18/2439; Michel Mel to John Clerk, 30 October 1655, Dieppe, NRS GD18/2542; William, Earl of Lothian to John Clerk, 30 March 1643, Paris, NRS GD18/2425; Account between Clerk and Lothian, 20 January 1645, Edinburgh, NRS GD18/2439; Michel Mel to John Clerk, 30 October 1655, Dieppe, NRS GD18/2542; John, Lord Maitland, to John Clerk, 9 November 1643, NRS GD18/2426; Lothian to Clerk, 1643–44, NRS GD18/2440. See Chapter 4, pp. 85, 93.
10. Letter-book of John Clerk, 1644-5, NRS GD18/2455, for example fos. 13v–14r, 17r–17v, 24r; Account between Lothian and Clerk, 8 March 1650–5 June 1652, NRS GD18/2445; James Mowat to John Clerk, 6 July 1655, Paris, NRS GD18/2505/7; Alexander Charteris to John Clerk, 8 April 1654, Paris, NRS GD18/2528/3. See Talbott, 'The Letter-Book of John Clerk, 1644–45'.
11. Account, Michel Mel and Sir Gilbert Menzies of Pitfodels, NRS GD237/11/95/6, 29 July 1664.
12. Account books of John Clerk, 1646–1659, NRS GD18/2482.
13. Countess of Stair to Sir John Clerk of Penicuik, 3 September 1715, Edinburgh, NRS GD18/5271/4; same to same, 1 October 1715, Edinburgh, NRS GD18/5271/8.
14. Millar (ed.), *Compt Buik of David Wedderburne*, pp. xxxiii, xliv and *passim*.
15. G. Howat, *Stuart and Cromwellian Foreign Policy* (London: A&C Black, 1974), pp. 5–6.
16. ADCM B235.
17. Mungo Mackall to Robert Galbraith, 10 February 1595, Bayonne, NRS JC62/1/31.
18. S. Murdoch, 'The French Connection: Bordeaux's "Scottish" Networks in Context, c. 1670–1720', in G. Leydier, *Scotland and Europe, Scotland in Europe* (Newcastle: Cambridge Scholars Publishing, 2007), pp. 26–55, p. 42.
19. 20 December 1713, NRS RH15/59/5/7/A/4.
20. John Clerk to Lady Pittendrum, 15 April 1645, Paris, NRS GD18/2455, fo. 13v; 20 May 1645, fo. 13r; 20 September 1645, fos. 17r–17v; 3 November 1645 fo. 17v. For more on Clerk, see Talbott, 'The Letter-Book of John Clerk'.
21. A. Hopper, *The World of John Secker (1716–95), Quaker Mariner* (Norfolk: Norfolk Record Society, 2011).

22. J. P. Balfour (ed.), *The Scots Peerage: Founded on Wood's Edition of Sir Robert Douglas's Peerage of Scotland: Containing an Historical and Genealogical Account of the Nobility of that Kingdom*, 9 vols (Edinburgh: David Douglas, 1904–14), vol. 4, p. 289. Mary Gray was the daughter of Sir William Gray, with whom Clerk did business: John Clerk to Michel Mel, 3 February 1645, London; John Clerk to John Dougall elder, 6 February 1645; John Clerk to James Cutler, 1 March 1645, NRS GD18/2455, fos. 7r, 7v, 13v. For correspondence with Mary see NRS GD/18/2455 fos. 14r–15v.

23. John Hutcheson [of Auchingray] to Sir George Maxwell, 14th of Nether Pollok, 1 February 1669, GCA T–PM/113/795/1.

24. Cummings, 'Scotland's Links with Europe', p. 47.

25. A. Grosjean and S. Murdoch, 'The Scottish Community in Seventeenth-Century Gothenburg', in Grosjean and Murdoch (eds), *Scottish Communities Abroad in the Early Modern Period*, pp. 191–223, on p. 191; R. Houston, 'The Scots Kirk, Rotterdam, 1643–1795: A Dutch or Scottish Church?', in J. Roding and L. van Voss (eds), *The North Sea and Culture, 1550–1800* (Hilversum: Verloren, 1996); Catterall, *Community Without Borders*, p. 91.

26. Instructions to Alexander Jaffray, Baillie, January 1630, *ACL*, vol. 1, p. 313; see also 'Instructions to Sir Thomas Mengzes Cultis knicht provest of Aberdeen and George Nicolsoun Commissionaris', July 1619, *ACL*, vol. 1, p. 171; Missive letter for Convention of Royal Burghs to be held at Montrose, 3 July 1632, *ACL*, vol. 1, pp. 347–8; Cummings, 'Scotland's Links with Europe', p. 47. For the decline of this institution see 'A short information of the abuses practised in the Stepell', 1670s, *ACL*, vol. 3, p. 175.

27. 7 July 1669, *CRB*, vol. 3, pp. 675–88.

28. G. Gardner, *The Scottish Exile Community in the Netherlands, 1660–1690* (East Linton: Tuckwell Press, 2004).

29. S. Murdoch, 'Community, Commodity and Commerce: The Stockholm–Scots in the Seventeenth Century', in Worthington (ed.), *British and Irish Emigrants and Exiles in Europe*, pp. 31–66.

30. Grosjean and Murdoch, 'The Scottish Community in Seventeenth-Century Gothenburg', p. 191; Enthoven, 'Thomas Cunningham', p. 45.

31. S. Talbott, '"If it Please God, I Come Home": Scottish Return Migration from France in the Long Seventeenth Century', in M. Varricchio (ed.), *Back to Caledonia: Scottish Return Migration from the Seventeenth Century to the Present* (Edinburgh: John Donald, 2012), pp. 54–72, on p. 62.

32. 9 June 1670, 28 November 1672, Edinburgh, *RPCS*, 3rd series, vol. 3, pp. 173, 607; S. Murdoch, 'Fabricating Nobility?: Genealogy and Social Mobility among Franco-Scottish Families in the Early Modern Period', *Ranam: Recherches Anglaise et Américaines*, 40 (2007), pp. 37–52, on pp. 43–4. Birthbrieves were statements of parentage and ancestry, and thus social status: Glozier, *Scottish Soldiers in France*, pp. 81–2.

33. 1717–8, ADG 6 B 59. See Chapter 7, p. 147.

34. James Mowat to John Clerk, 6 July 1655, Paris, NRS GD18/2505/7.

35. Murdoch, 'The French Connection', pp. 38–9, 41–2.

36. Smout, *Scottish Trade on the Eve of Union*, pp. 96–7; de Bruyn Kops, *A Spirited Exchange*, pp. 44, 60.

37. 5 July 1599, *CRB*, vol. 2, p. 50; Instructions to Alexander Jaffray, Baillie of Aberdeen, July 1624, *ACL*, vol. 1, p. 232; Council of Aberdeen to Convention of Royal Burghs, 7 July 1629, *ACL*, vol. 1, p. 299.

38. Instructions to Alexander Jaffray, Baillie, commissioner of Aberdeen, July 1634, *ACL*, vol. 2, p. 16.
39. Smout, *Scottish Trade on the Eve of Union*, p. 98.
40. Robert Gerard to Robert Stewart and William Popple, 25 June 1681, Aberdeen, AUSC ms3175/Z/156. I would like to thank Professor Allan Macinnes (University of Strathclyde) for bringing this document to my attention.
41. Account book of Archibald Hamilton, 1657–79, NLS Adv.mss.31.3.2, esp. August 1671–February 1674, fos. 51r–87r.
42. Murdoch, *Network North*, esp. pp. 13–48.
43. Discharge, Edward and James MacMath to Robert Galbraith, 21 July 1596, NRS JC62/1 (unnumbered); James MacMath and David Ritchesone to Robert Galbraith, Bloye, 24 March 1596, NRS JC62/1/79.
44. 23 July 1612, Edinburgh, *RPCS*, 1st series, vol. 4, p. 417.
45. 1 September 1652, NRS GD18/2371.
46. Murdoch, *Network North*, pp. 13–48, 49–83; T. Devine, 'The Cromwellian Union and the Scottish Burghs', in J. Butt and J. Ward (eds), *Scottish Themes: Essays in Honour of Professor S. G. E. Lythe* (Edinburgh: Scottish Academic Press, 1976), pp. 1–16, on p. 8; Lamikiz, *Trade and Trust*, p. 10.
47. Millar (ed.), *Compt Buik of David Wedderburne*, pp. xxxv–xxxvi, 79, 83–4.
48. L. Fontaine, 'Antonio and Shylock: Credit and Trust in France, c. 1680–c. 1780', *Economic History Review*, 54:1 (2001), pp. 39–57, on p. 48.
49. Alexander Hope to John Hope, 20 January 1548, Dieppe, NRS RH9/2/126; Letters from James Hope to Anne Hope, 1787–9, Amsterdam, NRS GD253/183/10, particularly nos. 1, 2, 12, 21.
50. John Dougall younger to John Clerk, 6 November 1642, Paris, NRS GD18/2416.
51. John Dougall younger to John Clerk, 10 January 1642, Dieppe, NRS GD18/2416; Dougall expressed his desire to go home and his frustration that his father 'wreatts nothing of my home going' in April of the same year, again in a letter to Clerk: 27 April 1642, Dieppe, NRS GD18/2416.
52. S. Haggerty, *'Merely for Money'?: Business Culture in the British Atlantic, 1750–1815* (Liverpool: Liverpool University Press, 2013), p. 138.
53. Henry Hope to John Clerk (Paris), 10 June 1643, Edinburgh; Henry Hope to John Clerk (Paris), 27 June 1643, Edinburgh; Henry Hope to John Clerk (Paris), Rouen, 11 January 1644; Account between John Clerk and Henry Hope, 26 July 1644, NRS GD18/2437.
54. William Erskine to John Clerk, April 1644, Angers, NRS GD18/2457/5; Selection of letters from William Erskine to John Clerk, regarding money loaned to him whilst on the continent, 1644–52, NRS GD18/2457.
55. Written by Clerk on parchment binding a bundle of twenty letters from William Erskine to John Clerk, 1644–52, 1 January 1669, NRS GD18/2457/1.
56. Account between John Clerk and James Murray younger, Edinburgh, 1636, NRS GD18/2377/77; John Clerk to John Dougall younger, Le Havre, 9 March 1645, Dieppe, NRS GD18/2455, fo. 1v.
57. 17 December 1686, Edinburgh, *RPCS*, 3rd series, vol. 13, p. 93.
58. Y. Ben-Porath, 'The F-Connection: Families, Friends, and Firms and the Organisation of Exchange', *Population and Development Review*, 6:1 (1980), pp. 1–30, cited in S. Haggerty, '"You Promise Well and Perform as Badly": The Failure of the "Implicit Contract of Family" in the Scottish Atlantic', *International Journal of Maritime History*, 33:2 (2011), pp. 267–82, on pp. 267–8.

59. De Bruyn Kops, *A Spirited Exchange*, p. 339.
60. N. Zahedieh, 'Credit, Risk and Reputation in Late Seventeenth-Century Colonial Trade', in O. Janzen (ed.), *Merchant Organization and Maritime Trade in the North Atlantic, 1660–1815* (St Johns, Newfoundland: International Maritime Economic History Association, 1998), pp. 53–74, on pp. 53, 63.
61. De Bruyn Kops, *A Spirited Exchange*, pp. 59–60, 90, 339; Murdoch, *Network North*, pp. 78–83.
62. John Clerk to Michel Mel, 4 October 1644, Edinburgh, NRS GD18/2455, fo. 3v.
63. James Mowat to John Clerk, 8 October 1654, Paris, NRS GD18/2528/4.
64. Swinton to Lavy, 6 November 1673, Letter-book of John Swinton, Merchant (London), 1673–1677, NRS CS96/3264; Henry Lavie to John Anderson, Petter Gemmull, John Walkinshaw, John Cauldwell, Hugh Nisbet and Alexander Knox, 26 October 1674, Bordeaux, NLS Acc.8100/143; Murdoch, 'The French Connection', p. 30.
65. B. Kay and C. Maclean, *Knee Deep in Claret: A Celebration of Wine and Scotland* (Isle of Skye: Auld Alliance Publishing, 1994), p. 190.
66. John Snodgrass to Andrew Russell, 10 March 1678, Leiden, RH15/106/285/5.
67. J. Savary, *Le Parfait Négociant*, 2 vols (Paris: Chez les frères Estienne, 1777 edition) vol. 2, i, ch. 4, cited in Fontaine, 'Antonio and Shylock', p. 54.
68. Fontaine, 'Antonio and Shylock', p. 55.
69. Haggerty, *'Merely for Money'?*, p. 199.
70. Henry Lavie to Lady Lothian, 27 September 1651, Bordeaux, NRS GD40/2/5/13/23.
71. Thomas Smith to Andrew Russell, 4/14 [damaged] 1675, Bordeaux, NRS RH15/106/199/12.
72. Thomas [Dinmuir] to Andrew Russell, 7 May 1677, Nantes, NRS RH15/106/268/11.
73. NRS GD18/2455, fo. 11v.
74. NRS GD18/2455, fos. 12r–v.
75. NRS GD18/2455, fo. 17r.
76. NRS GD18/2455, fos. 18r–v.
77. D. Hancock, 'Combining Success and Failure: Scottish Networks in the Atlantic Wine Trade', in Dickson, Parmentier and Ohlmeyer (eds), *Irish and Scottish Mercantile Networks in Europe*, pp. 5–38, on p. 17.
78. P. Mathias, 'Risk, Credit and Kinship in Early Modern Enterprise', in J. McCusker and K. Morgan (eds), *The Early Modern Atlantic Economy* (Cambridge: Cambridge University Press, 2000), pp. 15–35, on pp. 31–2; Fontaine, 'Antonio and Shylock', pp. 50, 52.
79. Haggerty, *'Merely for Money'?*, pp. 1–2, 174.
80. Ibid., p. 34.
81. Robert, Earl of Lothian to Lady Lothian, 27 January 1680, Montpellier, NRS GD40/2/8/25.
82. Millar (ed.), *Compt Buik of David Wedderburne*, pp. 25–7.
83. 1671–88, NRS CS96/3937; 18 August 1688, ADG 7 B 2581.
84. John Clerk is a prime example: GD18/2455, fos. 3r, 9r, 9v, 13r.
85. Haggerty, *'Merely for Money'?*, pp. 138–9.
86. Ibid., p. 2.
87. Alexander Charteris to John Clerk, 8 April 1654, Paris, NRS GD18/2528/3.
88. De Bruyn Kops, *A Spirited Exchange*, pp. 5, 96; A. Forte, 'Marine Insurance and Risk Distribution in Scotland before 1800', *Law and History Review*, 5:2 (1987), pp. 393–412, on p. 394.
89. A. Francis, *The Wine Trade* (London: A&C Black, 1972), p. 47.

90. Alexander Watson to Ebenezer Watson, Leith, 30 December 1668, SAUL ms38527/1/1/8; two bonds, Alexander Watson for excise on twelve butts and three butts of seck, 1 July 1669, SAUL ms38527/1/2/9.
91. Entry books of Leith, November 1672–November 1673, NRS E74/15/13; E74/15/15. See Talbott, 'Beyond "The Antiseptic Realm of Theoretical Economic Models"', pp. 160, 167–8.
92. Accounts of collectors of H.M. Customs and Foreign Excise, November 1690–November 1691, NRS E73/109/11/9/4; Leith: Entry books (wine), 1 November 1680–1 August 1681, NRS E72/15/22; 1 November 1682–1 November 1683, NRS E72/15/27.
93. Millar (ed.), *Compt Buik of David Wedderburne*, p. 140.
94. Ibid., pp. xxxv, 79. See also the records of Archibald Hamilton of Edinburgh: 4 August 1663, NLS Adv.mss.31.3.2, fo. 31r.
95. NRS GD18/2455, fos. 14r–v.
96. Guy, 'The Scottish Export Trade', p. 67.
97. Pagan, *The Convention of the Royal Burghs of Scotland*, p. 151.
98. D. Defoe, *Essays upon Projects* (1697), cited in H. Roseveare, 'Merchant Organization and Maritime Trade in the North Atlantic, 1660–1815: Some Reflections', in Janzen (ed.), *Merchant Organization and Maritime Trade*, pp. 259–67, on p. 259.
99. NRS GD18/2455, fo. 2r; Talbott, 'The Letter-Book of John Clerk'.
100. NRS GD18/2455, fo. 4v.
101. H. Smith, *Shetland Life and Trade, 1550–1914* (Edinburgh, 1984), p. 38.
102. NRS GD18/2455, fo. 14v.
103. Millar (ed.), *Compt Buik of David Wedderburne*; Account Book of Archibald Hamilton, 1657–79, Edinburgh, NLS Adv.mss.31.3.2.
104. For discussions of 'trust', 'credit' and 'reputation' in commercial relationships, see Haggerty, '*Merely for Money*'?
105. NRS GD18/2455, fo. 1v.
106. Murdoch, 'The French Connection', p. 33. See May 1675, NRS RH15/106/174/6; 9 March 1675, NRS RH15/106/199; 30 November 1675, NRS RH15/106/199/9–11; 4 August 1681, 1 September 1681, Bordeaux, NRS RH15/106/424/23–26; 12 December 1683, NRS RH15/106/163/5; 8 February 1676, Bordeaux, NRS RH15/106/231/30–2.
107. Clerk maintained contacts in Italy, London, Rotterdam, Veere, Middleburgh, and throughout France and Scotland. John Clerk to Robert Inglis, London, 8 February 1645, John Clerk to John Dougall Younger, 9 March 1645, Dieppe; John Clerk to Lady Pittendrum, 20 September 1645; John Clerk to Lady Pittendrum, 3 November 1645; John Clerk to Janet Gray, 3 November 1645, NRS GD18/2455, fos. 7v, 11v, 17r–v.
108. Jacques du Cornet to John Clerk, 9 August 1638, NRS GD18/2375E; same to same, 19 September 1636, and on reverse, Adam Michelsonne to John Clerk, 'with order to remit James de Cornet £1000 and John de Cornet £800', 28 August 1636, Rouen, NRS GD18/2375F. See documents A–I in this bundle.
109. Account between John Clerk and Henry Hope, 15 January, 6 March, 15 March, 26 July 1644, NRS GD18/2437.
110. Defoe, *Essays upon Projects* (1697), cited in Roseveare, 'Merchant Organization', p. 259.
111. 8 July 1630, *CRB*, vol. 3, p. 316.
112. BnF ms8038, fo. 155, cited in W. Scoville, 'The French Economy in 1700–1701: An Appraisal by the Deputies of Trade', *Journal of Economic History*, 22:2 (1962), pp. 231–52, on p. 235.

113. *Flying-Post; or, The Post-Master*, 3384 (4–6 June 1713), p. 2.
114. Meek (ed. and trans.), Quesnay, *L'Analyse*, pp. 164–5, cited in T. Brennan, *Burgundy to Champagne: the Wine Trade in Early Modern France* (Baltimore: Johns Hopkins University Press, 1997), p. xv.
115. A. Smith, *An Inquiry into the Nature and Causes of the Wealth of Nations*, 8 vols (Edinburgh: A&C Black, 1863), vol. 4, pp. 2, 9; Murdoch, *Network North*, p. 127.
116. For example, the case of Dr Alexander Broun of the East India Company who, before setting sail, bequeathed a sum in his will for the establishment of a fishery and linen manufactory in his home town of Kirkcaldy. V. Enthoven, S. Murdoch and E. Williamson (eds), *The Navigator: The Log of John Anderson, VOC Pilot-Major, 1640–1643* (Leiden: Brill, 2010), p. 91.
117. Lythe, *The Economy of Scotland*, p. 230; S. Murdoch, 'The Repatriation of Capital to Scotland: A Case Study of Dutch Testaments and Notarial Instruments 1560–1707', in Varricchio (ed.), *Back to Caledonia*, pp. 34–53.
118. Dickson, 'Introduction', to Dickson, Parmentier and Ohlmeyer (eds), *Irish and Scottish Mercantile Networks in Europe*, p. 4.
119. Robert Gerard to 'RA', 20 January 1701, Aberdeen, AUSC ms3175/Z/156. I would like to thank Professor Allan Macinnes (University of Strathclyde) for bringing this document to my attention.
120. F. Mauro, 'Merchant Communities, 1350–1750', in J. Tracy (ed.), *The Rise of Merchant Empires: Long Distance Trade in the Early Modern World, 1350–1750* (Cambridge: Cambridge University Press, 1990), pp. 255–86, on p. 285; G. Rowlands, 'France 1709: Le Crunch', *History Today*, 59:2 (2009), pp. 42–7, on p. 44.
121. Talbott, '"If it Please God, I Come Home": Scottish Return Migration from France in the Long Seventeenth Century', p. 55.
122. S. Murdoch, *The Terror of the Seas? Scottish Maritime Warfare, 1513–1713* (Leiden: Brill, 2010), p. 311. It was not only Scots who adopted these tactics: E. Graham, 'The Scottish Marine during the Dutch Wars', *Scottish Historical Review*, 61 (1982), pp. 67–74, on p. 72
123. De Bruyn Kops, *A Spirited Exchange*, p. 55.
124. n.d. (1660–1670), 10 April 1667, Anglica VII, DXLII (unfoliated). Thanks to Steve Murdoch (University of St Andrews) for providing images of these documents. See Chapter 5, p. 105.
125. Smith (ed.), *The Reign of James VI and I*, p. 73.
126. Lythe, *The Economy of Scotland*, p. 230.
127. TNA SP78/53/236.

3 'The Custom House Officers are So Agog of Seizing': Legislation and Commercial Policy

1. 6 August 1689, *RPCS*, 3rd series, vol. 14, pp. 17–18.
2. Smout, *Scottish Trade on the Eve of Union*, p. 245.
3. R. C. Nash, 'The Economy', in J. Bergin (ed.), *The Seventeenth Century* (Oxford: Oxford University Press, 2001), pp. 11–49, on pp. 37, 46.
4. T. Schaeper, *The French Council of Commerce, 1700–1715: A Study of Mercantilism after Colbert* (Columbus, OH: Ohio State University Press, 1983), p. 112. See Chapter 6, pp. 115–17.

5. 1691, ADCM B5608
6. 1698, NRS PA7/16/86/1; see also D. Defoe, *The Trade with France, Italy, Spain and Portugal Considered, with Some Observations on the Treaty of Commerce between Great Britain and France* (London, 1713), pp. 22–3.
7. 9 January 1701, *APS*, vol. 10, appendix, p. 82; see also 31 January 1701, *RPS*, 1700/10/239.
8. BnF, *Fonds Français*, ms 8038, fo. 333, cited in Scoville, 'The French Economy', p. 234
9. A. MacDonald, *The Burghs and Parliament in Scotland, c. 1550–1651* (Aldershot: Ashgate, 2007), p. 68; see: 27 February 1581, *APS*, vol. 3, p. 221; 13 May 1597, Dundee, *RPCS*, 1st series, vol. 5, p. 386; 1 November 1597, *RPS*, 1597/11/28.
10. Lythe, *The Economy of Scotland*, p. 106.
11. A. Whatley, *The Scottish Salt Industry, 1570–1850* (Aberdeen: Aberdeen University Press, 1987), p. 2.
12. Lythe, *The Economy of Scotland*, pp. 160, 175–6.
13. 30 April 1573, *RPS* A1573/4/7.
14. Whatley, *The Scottish Salt Industry*, pp. 34, 36–9; Lythe, *The Economy of Scotland*, p. 160.
15. Whatley, *The Scottish Salt Industry*, pp. 40–2.
16. Ibid., p. 3.
17. Additional Instructions to Baillie Cullen, 1652, *ACL*, vol. 3, p. 214; see also Instructions to John Jaffray and Gilbert Gray, 12 October 1657, *ACL*, vol. 3, p. 295; Instructions to Mr Robert Patrie, 3 August 1671, *ACL*, vol. 5, pp. 84, 86; Commission from the provost and baillies to Andrew Skeine, 6 November 1671, *ACL*, vol. 5, p. 101; 6 December 1671, *ACL*, vol. 5, p. 106.
18. Whatley, *The Scottish Salt Industry*, pp. 2, 42–3.
19. Robert Mylne to the Provost and Magistrates, 7 December 1671, Edinburgh, *ACL*, vol. 5, p. 108.
20. 1681, *RPCS*, 3rd series, vol. 7, p. 653.
21. n.d. [early eighteenth century], NRS GD150/3508/38.
22. Instructions from the Council of Aberdeen to Alexander Jaffray, 20 February 1650, Aberdeen, *ACL*, vol. 3, p. 164.
23. Draft Act of Parliament, 1701, NRS PA7/17/1/90iv.
24. October 1579, *APS*, vol. 3, p. 146.
25. 5 September 1649, C. Firth and R. Rait (eds), *Acts and Ordinances of the Interregnum: 1642–1660*, 3 vols (London: H. M. S. O., 1911), vol. 2, pp. 239–40; Instructions to Andrew Cant, Alexander Cant, John Menzies and George Meldrum from the Privy Council, 18 November 1662, Edinburgh, *ACL*, vol. 4, pp. 191–2.
26. 2 November 1625, *RPS*, A1625/10/55; W. Dickenson and G. Donaldson (eds), *A Source Book of Scottish History*, 3 vols (Edinburgh: Nelson, 1958), vol. 3, p. 294.
27. 2 July 1638, W. Cramond (ed.), *The Annals of Banff*, 2 vols (Aberdeen: Spalding Club, 1891–3), vol. 1, p. 88.
28. De Bruyn Kops, *A Spirited Exchange*, pp. 34, 44.
29. 1668, TNA SP117/288.
30. 8 November 1687, ADLA C656.
31. 21 July 1593, *APS*, vol. 4, pp. 29–30.
32. *RPCS*, 2nd series, vol. 1, pp. 479–80, n.
33. Whitehall, 12 December 1626, *RPCS*, 2nd series, vol. 1, pp. 478–9.
34. 16 November 1641, *APS*, vol. 5, p. 421. Similar acts include that 'anent the Exporting of Victual': 12 June 1649, *APS*, series 2, vol. 7, p. 409.

35. 17 December 1629, *RPCS*, 2nd series, vol. 3, p. 386.
36. [Sir George] Downing to [Henry] Bennett [first Earl of Arlington], 14 August 1664, TNA SP84/171/107.
37. 12 September 1712, AMN GG 774.
38. *Universal Dictionary of Trade and Commerce* (1762).
39. 29 July 1644, *APS*, series 1, vol. 4, p. 238; Entry books of wine, Leith, NRS E72/15/22; E72/15/29; E72/15/33, from data available for 1680–1, 1683–4 and 1684–5. See Chapter 6, pp. 121–2.
40. 26 June 1657, Firth and Rait (eds), *Acts and Ordinances of the Interregnum: 1642–1660*, vol. 2, pp. 1186–223.
41. 17 September 1681, *RPS*, 1681/7/51.
42. D. Parker, *La Rochelle and the French Monarchy: Conflict and Order in Seventeenth-Century France* (London: Royal Historical Society, 1980), p. 61.
43. Fontaine, 'Antonio and Shylock', pp. 41–2.
44. *RPCS*, 1st series, vol. 7, pp. xxxv, 472–3; see also 1 July 1601, *CRB*, vol. 2, p. 104.
45. 30 April 1573, *RPS*, A1573/4/3.
46. *CRB*, vol. 1, pp. 493–4.
47. 14 February 1601, Edinburgh, *CRB*, vol. 2, pp. 97–8.
48. 14 January 1612, *CRB*, vol. 2, p. 334.
49. Schedule of Commodities to be taxed, 22 July 1643, Firth and Rait (eds), *Acts and Ordinances*, vol. 1, pp. 208–14.
50. Robert Patrie and Alexander Alexander to the Baillies, 31 August 1672, Edinburgh, *ACL*, vol. 5, p. 192.
51. 9 January 1644, Firth and Rait (eds), *Acts and Ordinances*, vol. 1, p. 365
52. 16 December 1647, Firth and Rait (eds), *Acts and Ordinances*, vol. 1, pp. 1032–42. See also 19 March 1661, *APS*, vol. 7, p. 88.
53. 2 December 1686, Edinburgh, *RPCS*, 3rd series, vol. 13, pp. 7–8, lxiv.
54. Murdoch, 'The French Connection', p. 32.
55. Lord Advocate Stewart to [?], 9 August 1712, Edinburgh, TNA SP54/4/78; Sée and Cormack, 'Commercial Relations between France and Scotland', pp. 276–7.
56. Thomas Inglis against the tacksmen of the customs in the matter of duty on wines, 17 December 1607, Edinburgh, *RPCS*, 1st series, vol. 8, p. 24.
57. Instructions to Master Patrick Sandilands, Treasurer of Aberdeen, commissioner, 4 December 1676, Aberdeen, *ACL*, vol. 6, pp. 58, 60.
58. George Flint to [?], n.d. [early eighteenth century], NRS GD150/3508/38.
59. 20 May 1608, *APS*, vol. 4, p. 408.
60. 18 December 1595, Holyrood, *RPCS*, 1st series, vol. 5, pp. 246–7.
61. 30 January 1627, Holyrood, *RPCS*, 2nd series, vol. 1, p. 506. For the act prohibiting the importation see p. 489. See Chapter 5, pp. 107–8.
62. [The Marquis of Hamilton] to Sir Henry Vane, Yarmouth Road, 16 April 1639, NRS GD406/1/1215.
63. 1672, *ACL*, vol. 5, pp. 120–1.
64. George Skene and David Ardie to the Magistrates, 7 September 1681, Edinburgh, *ACL*, vol. 6, pp. 343–4.
65. *c.* 1681, GCA TD589/972.
66. 9 January 1701, *APS*, vol. 10, appendix, p. 82.
67. February 1685, Edinburgh, *RPCS*, 3rd series, vol. 10, p. 384.

68. Robert Patrie and Alexander Alexander to the Provost and Baillie, 25 July 1672, Edinburgh, *ACL*, vol. 5, p. 172. For similar prohibitions later in the century see 1698, NRS PA7/16/86/2; First Earl of Seafield, 14 July 1705, Edinburgh, in Hume-Brown (ed.), *James Ogilvy, First Earl of Seafield and Others: Letters relating to Scotland in the Reign of Queen Anne*, p. 57.

69. J. Brewer, *The Sinews of Power: War, Money and the English State, 1688–1783* (London: Unwin Hyman, 1989), p. 170.

70. J. Félix, 'The Economy', trans. D. Bell, in W. Doyle (ed.), *Old Regime France* (Oxford: Oxford University Press, 2001), pp. 7–41, on pp. 20, 22; G. Bossenga, 'Society', in Doyle, *Old Regime France*, pp. 43–72, on p. 70; P. Hoffman, 'Rural, Urban and Global Economies', in M. Holt (ed.), *Renaissance and Reformation France, 1500–1648* (Oxford: Oxford University Press, 2002), pp. 62–98, on p. 79.

71. February 1681, *RPCS*, 3rd series, vol. 7, pp. 653ff.

72. Scoville, 'French Economy', p. 231.

73. Nash, 'The Economy', pp. 37, 46.

74. Félix, 'The Economy', p. 23; A. Usher, 'Colbert and Governmental Control of Industry in Seventeenth-Century France', *Review of Economics and Statistics*, 16:11 (1934), pp. 237–40, on p. 237.

75. Ball, *Merchants and Merchandise*, p. 46.

76. AMN HH 194, 237; de Bruyn Kops, *A Spirited Exchange*, p. 124.

77. F. Palm, 'Mercantilism as a Factor in Richelieu's Policy of National Interests', *Political Science Quarterly*, 39:4 (1924), pp. 650–64, on p. 653.

78. H. Hauser, *La Pensée et l'action économiques du Cardinal de Richelieu* (Paris: Presses Universitaires de France, 1944), p. 69; P. Boulle, 'French Mercantilism, Commercial Companies and Colonial Profitability', in P. Emmer and F. Gaastra (eds), *The Organization of Interoceanic Trade in European Expansion, 1450–1800* (Aldershot: Variorum, 1996), pp. 233–54, on p. 238.

79. Boulle, 'French Mercantilism', p. 239; A. Smith, *Creating a World Economy: Merchant Capital, Colonialism and World Trade, 1400–1825* (Boulder, CO: Westview Press, 1991), p. 189. For the debate see: Murdoch, *Network North*, p. 423; Dickson, 'Introduction', to Dickson, Parmentier and Ohlmeyer (eds), *Irish and Scottish Mercantile Networks in Europe*, pp. 2–3.

80. Boulle, 'French Mercantilism', pp. 650, 654, 251–2.

81. C. Cole. *Colbert and a Century of French Mercantilism*, 2 vols (London: Frank Cass, 1964), vol. 1, pp. 360–1.

82. Ibid., vol. 1, p. 415.

83. Voltaire noted that 'the enemy captured fewer French merchant ships because there were fewer to be captured, Colbert's death and the war having greatly reduced trade': Voltaire, *The Age of Louis XIV*, trans. M. Pollock (London: J. M. Dent, 1958), p. 161; Ball, *Merchants and Merchandise*, p. 48 argues that under Colbert France was able to 'direct its economy towards the ideal of self-sufficiency'; while P. Bamford, 'French Shipping in Northern European Trade, 1660–1789', *Journal of Modern History*, 26:3 (1954), pp. 207–19, on p. 209 suggests that Colbert 'damaged French shipping interests and discouraged French efforts to take part in the highly competitive northern branch of shipping enterprise'. J. Scoville, *Persecution of Huguenots and French Economic Development 1680–1720* (Whitefish, Montana: Kessinger Publishing, 2006 edition), pp. 156–9 claims that 'despite persistent and Herculean efforts, Colbert was able to abolish or reform only a few tolls and excises ... local tradition thwarted his attempt to simplify France's hetero-

geneous system of weights and measures'. J. Cornette, *Chronique de Règne de Louis XIV: de la fin de la Fronde à l'aube des Lumières* (Paris: Sedes, 1997), p. 88, asserts that 'the history, personality and the work of Colbert has been distorted by historians'.

84. G. Rowlands, *The Dynastic State and the Army under Louis XIV: Royal Service and Private Interest, 1661–1701* (Cambridge: Cambridge University Press, 2002), p. 111.
85. Bamford, 'French Shipping', p. 208.
86. Ibid., p. 209; Cole, *Colbert*, vol. 1, p. 7.
87. Donaldson, *Scotland, James V–James VII*, p. 388; see Introduction, pp. 21–2.
88. Keith, 'The Economic Causes for the Scottish Union', p. 50.
89. Cole, *Colbert*, vol. 1, pp. 428–30. For comparison with the pre-war duties laid on 18 September 1664 see Anon., *The Tariff Settled by the French King and Council, September 18, 1664: Shewing the Duties Agreed to be Paid upon the Several Sorts of Merchandizes, Goods, Wares etc, being the Growth, Product and Manufactures of Great Britain, which should be Imported from England unto France* (London, 1713).
90. AN Marine B⁷ 499, 118
91. BnF *Fonds Français*, ms 8038, fo. 105, cited in Scoville, 'French Economy', p. 234.
92. Howat, *Stuart and Cromwellian Foreign Policy*, p. 6; Smith, *Creating a World Economy*, pp. 116–17.
93. 27 July 1617, Glasgow, *RPCS*, 1st series, vol. 2, pp. 202–3.
94. 9 February 1619, Edinburgh, *RPCS*, 1st series, vol. 2, p. 511; *RPCS*, 1st series, vol. 11, p. xl; 9 July 1619, Haddington, *CRB*, vol. 3, pp. 87–8; Mowat, *The Port of Leith*, p. 153; Pagan, *The Convention of the Royal Burghs*, p. 156.
95. *RPCS*, 3rd series, vol. 1, p. xxxv.
96. Graham, *A Maritime History of Scotland*, p. 330.
97. 22 February 1681, Edinburgh, *RPCS*, 3rd series, vol. 7, p. 657; Graham, 'The Scottish Marine during the Dutch Wars', pp. 71, 89.
98. Graham, *A Maritime History of Scotland*, pp. 51–2.
99. V. Barbour, 'Dutch and English Merchant Shipping in the Seventeenth Century', in P. Emmer and F. Gaastra (eds), *The Organization of Interoceanic Trade*, pp. 103–32, on pp. 109, 110, 130.
100. 12 July 1626, *CSPD*, 1625–6, p. 374.
101. 14 November 1629, *CSPD*, 1629–31, p. 157; Murdoch, *The Terror of the Seas?*, p. 166 n.72.
102. D. Woodward, 'Anglo-Scottish Trade and English Commercial Policy during the 1660s', *Scottish Historical Review*, 56:162 (1977), pp. 153–74, on pp. 153, 162–4.
103. Hoffman, 'Rural, Urban and Global Economies', pp. 74; R. Knecht, *Richelieu* (Essex: Longman, 1991), p. 150; Parker, *La Rochelle and the French Monarchy*, p. 61.
104. Voltaire, *The Age of Louis XIV*, p. 322; R. Grassby, 'Social Status and Commercial Enterprise under Louis XIV', in R. Kierstead, *State and Society in Seventeenth-Century France* (New York: New Viewpoints, 1975), pp. 200–32, on pp. 200, 202.
105. Scoville, 'French Economy', pp. 246–7; Knecht, *Richelieu*, p. 150.
106. R. Bonney, *The King's Debts: Finance and Politics in France, 1589–1661* (Oxford: Clarendon Press, 1981), pp. 272, 280.
107. Hoffman, 'Rural, Urban and Global Economies', pp. 74, 79–80; P. Benedict, *Rouen during the Wars of Religion* (Cambridge: Cambridge University Press, 1981), p. 17.
108. Bamford, 'French Shipping', p. 2.

109. Hoffman, 'Rural, Urban and Global Economies', pp. 67, 95, 96; R. Mackenney, *Tradesmen and Trades: the World of the Guilds in Venice and Europe, c. 1250–c. 1650* (London: Croon Helm, 1987), p. 177.
110. Hoffman, 'Rural, Urban and Global Economies', p. 68.
111. Macdougall, *An Antidote to the English*, p. 5. See Chapter 1, p. 18.

4 'Fire that's Kindled Within Doores': The British Civil Wars and Interregnum

1. HL 434906, J. Battie, *The Merchants Remonstrance* (London, 1648), p. 2.
2. See Hobsbawm, 'The Crisis of the Seventeenth Century'; Trevor-Roper, 'The General Crisis of the Seventeenth Century'; Parker and Smith (eds), *The General Crisis of the Seventeenth Century*.
3. Ball, *Merchants and Merchandise*, p. 191; J. Condliffe, *The Commerce of Nations* (London: George Allen & Unwin, 1951), p. 59.
4. De Bruyn Kops, *A Spirited Exchange*, p. 49.
5. 4 March 1596, *RPS*, A1597/3/6.
6. Millar (ed.), *Compt Buik of David Wedderburne*, p. x.
7. Ibid., *passim*.
8. Michel Mel to Pitfodels, 16 September 1653, Dieppe, NRS GD237/11/200/8.
9. Michel Mel to Pitfodels, Dieppe and Le Havre, NRS GD237/11/200.
10. M. Holt, *The French Wars of Religion, 1562–1629* (Cambridge: Cambridge University Press, 1995), p. 193.
11. Information from the provost and bailies of Aberdeen, 19 April 1654, *ACL*, vol. 3, p. 228.
12. Tax agreement, 18 August 1675, Aberdeen, AUSC, ms 934.
13. Voltaire, *The Age of Louis XIV*, p. 10.
14. Grant, *The Economic History of Scotland*, p. 185.
15. N. Bund (ed.), *Tabellr Overskibsfart Og Varetranspot Gennem Øresund, 1497–1660* (Copenhagen, 1906). Thanks go to Claire McLoughlin (University of St Andrews) for permission to use her tabulations of this data. The accuracy of the data collected in the Sound Toll Registers has been assessed by James Dow, who concludes that post-1618 less than 10 per cent of cargoes evaded registration: J. Dow, 'A Comparative Note on the Sound Toll Registers, Stockholm Customs Accounts, and Dundee Shipping Lists, 1589, 1613–1622', *Scandinavian Economic History Review*, 12:1 (1964), pp. 79–85, on p. 79.
16. *ASWA, passim*.
17. Data compiled from *ASWA, passim*. S. Talbott, 'British Commercial Interests on the French Atlantic Coast, c. 1560–1713', *Historical Research*, 85:229 (2012), pp. 394–409, on p. 400; Devine, 'The Cromwellian Union', p. 5.
18. J. Ohlmeyer, 'Irish Privateers during the Civil War, 1642–50', *Mariner's Mirror*, 76 (1990), pp. 119–33; E. Murphy, '"No Affair before us of Greater Importance": The War at Sea in Ireland, 1641–1649' (PhD thesis, Trinity College Dublin, 2008).
19. Report for the commission for trying the losses of Aberdeen, 6 December 1648, *ACL*, vol. 3, p. 115; Ohlmeyer, 'Irish Privateers', p. 123.
20. Report for the commission for trying the losses of Aberdeen, 6 December 1648, *ACL*, vol. 3, p. 123; Murdoch, *The Terror of the Seas?*, p. 197 n.32.

21. J Smith, Tho[mas] Bruce, Richard Maxwell, 9 May 1640, Edinburgh, *ACL*, vol. 2, pp. 201–2.

22. E. Courthope, *The Journal of Thomas Cuningham of Campvere, 1640–1654: With his Thrissels-banner and Explication Thereof* (Edinburgh: Scottish History Society, 1928), pp. 242–3.

23. 16 April 1644, *RPS*, 1644/1/124.

24. Report for the commission for trying the losses of Aberdeen, 6 December 1648, *ACL*, vol. 3, pp. 121–2; Murdoch, *The Terror of the Seas?*, Appendix V:2, p. 384.

25. 23 July 1649, *APS*, series 2, vol. 7, p. 494.

26. Robert Petrie, 24 October 1640, Edinburgh, *ACL*, vol. 2, pp. 243–4.

27. Alexander Jaffray to Patrick Leslie, Provost [n.d], 1640, *ACL*, vol. 2, p. 271.

28. J. Spalding, *Memorialls of the Trubles in Scotland and England, AD 1624–AD 1645*, ed. J. Stuart, 2 vols (Aberdeen, 1850–1), vol. 1, p. 267, see also 2 and 27 April 1640, Edinburgh, *ACL*, vol. 2, pp. 191–2, 199.

29. Ordinances appointing the First and Second Committee of Both Kingdoms, 16 February, 22 May 1644, S. Gardiner (ed.), *The Constitutional Documents of the Puritan Revolution, 1625–1660* (Oxford: Clarendon Press, 1899), pp. 271–2.

30. 'An Ordinance to enable the Lord High Admiral to press Mariners, Saylers, and others for the service of the Navy', 21 February 1645, Firth and Rait (eds), *Acts and Ordinances*, vol. 1, pp. 646–7.

31. 10 July 1645, *The Acts Done and Past in the Second, Third, Fourth and Fifth Sessions of the First Triennial Parliament of our Soveraigne Lord Charles* (Edinburgh, 1646), p. 43.

32. Instructions from the Burgh of Aberdeen to Colonel Stein Winthrop, commissioner to the Westminster Parliament, to be held 17 September 1656, *ACL*, vol. 3, p. 272. For more on the impact of domestic conflict on England's home economy see B. Donagan, 'War, Property and the Bonds of Society: England's "Unnatural" Civil Wars', in Charters, Rosenhaft and Smith (eds), *Civilians and War in Europe*, pp. 52–67.

33. Hoffman, 'Rural, Urban and Global Economies', pp. 86–7.

34. 8 September 1643, Firth and Rait (eds), *Acts and Ordinances*, vol. 1, pp. 274–83.

35. 9 January 1644, Firth and Rait (eds), *Acts and Ordinances*, vol. 1, pp. 364–6.

36. 5 January 1644, *APS*, series 1, vol. 6, p. 65.

37. 14 August 1649, Firth and Rait (eds), *Acts and Ordinances*, vol. 2, pp. 213ff.

38. John Clerk to John Murray, 11 November 1640, Paris, NLS Adv.mss.23.3.26, fo. 106.

39. September 1644, NRS GD18/2455, fo. 3r.

40. 20 May 1645, NRS GD18/2455, fo. 14r.

41. 3 November 1645, Paris, NRS GD18/2455, fo. 17v.

42. F. Roberts, and I. MacPhail, *Dumbarton Common Good Accounts, 1614–1660* (Dumbarton: Lennox Herald, 1972), appendix B. The author thanks Claire McLoughlin (University of St Andrews) for permission to use her tabulations of this data.

43. J. Anderson, *The Burgesses and Guild Brethren of Glasgow, 1573–1750*, Scottish Record Society (Edinburgh: J. Skinner, 1925). Data compiled from this source by Smout, 'The Glasgow Merchant Community in the Seventeenth Century', p. 59.

44. E. Furgol, 'Scotland Turned Sweden: the Scottish Covenanters and the Military Revolution, 1638–1651', in J. Morrill (ed.), *The Scottish National Covenant in its British Context, 1638–51* (Edinburgh: Edinburgh University Press, 1990), pp. 134–54, on p. 136.

45. W. Welwood, *An Abridgement of All Sea-Lawes* (London: Humfrey Lownes for Thomas Man, 1613), pp. 48–9.

46. John Dougall to John Clerk, 14 May 1642, Dieppe, NRS GD18/2416.

47. 1 April 1643, repayment of debt acknowledged by James Murray, 22 March 1644, NRS GD29/1309.
48. Montereul to Cardinal Mazarin, 2 April 1647, Edinburgh, Fotheringham (ed. and trans.), *Diplomatic Correspondence*, vol. 2, pp. 66, 70.
49. James Bruce to Lord Lothian, 5 April 1651, La Rochelle, NRS GD40/2/5/13/6.
50. John Dougall to John Clerk, 21 January and 10 April 1636, Rouen, NRS GD18/2380/1/1–2; John Dougall to John Clerk, 7 November and 2 December 1643, Le Havre, NRS GD18/2380/4/42, p. 48.
51. William Erskine to John Clerk, various correspondence, February 1644–October 1645, NRS GD18/2457.
52. Discharge, Alexander Dick to Robert Angus, 1 November 1639, NRS GD172/1765.
53. Discharge, Andrew Beaton and Michel Mel, Dieppe, 18 June 1643, NRS GD7/2/38.
54. Account, Lord Ross and Monsieur [Daldeguie], 23 August 1643, NRS GD3/13/2/1/9.
55. 1 September 1647, NLS Culloden Papers, Ch.1657.
56. Courthope, *Journal of Thomas Cuningham*, pp. 242–3.
57. Closed account between John Clerk and Henry Hope, 26 July 1644, NRS GD18/2437.
58. John Clerk to Lady Pittendrum, 15 April 1645, Paris, NRS GD18/2455, fo. 13v.
59. John Clerk to Lady Pittendrum, 20 May 1645, Paris, NRS GD18/2455, fo. 14r.
60. John Clerk to Lady Pittendrum, 20 September 1645, 3 November 1645, Paris, NRS GD18/2455, fos. 17r–17v.
61. James Mowat to John Clerk, 1647, Paris, NRS GD18/2484.
62. Sir Charles Erskine to Mary Hope, 2–12 September 1643, NLS ms.5089, fos. 11–12, 15.
63. Instructions for George Morisone to the conventione of burrowes to be holden at Brunt Iland, 7 April 1646, *ACL*, vol. 3, p. 44.
64. For examples of these individuals/families trading in France see: Letters and accounts, John Clerk and Robert Inglis, 1636–76, NRS GD18/2379/1–8; Bill of exchange drawn on Alexander Burnet, 29 December 1677, GD237/11/157/4–5; Gilbert Pape, procurator for William Gray vs. M. Mel, 1647–8, GD18/2486; Correspondence, Gilbert Pape and William Robertson to John Clerk, 1645, GD18/2466.
65. Enthoven, 'Thomas Cunningham', pp. 55, 57.
66. Montereul to Mazarin, 7 October 1645, Fotheringham (ed. and trans.), *Diplomatic Correspondence*, vol. 1, p. 8.
67. Bellièvre to Brienne, 24 June 1647, London, Fotheringham (ed. and trans.), *Diplomatic Correspondence*, vol. 2, p. 165.
68. Howat, *Stuart and Cromwellian Foreign Policy*, p. 48.
69. Balfour (ed.), *The Scots Peerage*, vol. 1, p. 565.
70. Secretary Coke to Secretary Windebank, 9 May 1639, *CSPD*, vol. 13, p. 143.
71. Robert Baillie to William Spang, 28 September 1639, in D. Laing (ed.) *The Letters and Journals of Robert Baillie, Principal of the University of Glasgow 1637–1662*, 3 vols (Edinburgh: Alex Lawrie & Co., 1841), vol. 1, p. 191.
72. Montereul to Mazarin, 7 October 1645, Fotheringham (ed. and trans.), *Diplomatic Correspondence*, vol. 1, p. 8.
73. 24 August 1644, *CSPD*, vol. 30, p. 448
74. Prince Rupert to Sir Thomas Allin, 8 January 1649, R. Anderson (ed.), *The Journals of Sir Thomas Allin, 1660–1678*, 2 vols (London: Navy Records Society, 1890), II, pp. 212–13.
75. Bellièvre to Brienne, 24 September 1646, London, Fotheringham (ed. and trans.), *Diplomatic Correspondence*, vol. 1, p. 269.

76. Montereul to Mazarin, 20 January 1647, Newcastle, Fotheringham (ed. and trans.), *Diplomatic Correspondence*, vol. 2, p. 401.
77. Montereul to Mazarin, 20 January 1647, Newcastle, Fotheringham (ed. and trans.), *Diplomatic Correspondence*, vol. 2, p. 404.
78. Montereul to Mazarin, 20 January 1647, Newcastle, Fotheringham (ed. and trans.), *Diplomatic Correspondence*, vol. 2, pp. 404–5.
79. Bellièvre to Brienne, 4 April 1647, London, Fotheringham (ed. and trans.), *Diplomatic Correspondence*, vol. 2, pp. 86–7.
80. Bellièvre to Brienne, 11 April 1647, London, see also Bellièvre to Brienne, 15 April 1647, London, Fotheringham (ed. and trans.), *Diplomatic Correspondence*, vol. 2, pp. 98–9, 106, 109–11.
81. Bellièvre to Brienne, 18 April 1647, London, Fotheringham (ed. and trans.), *Diplomatic Correspondence*, vol. 1, p. 109.
82. *Scottish Dove*, 5–12 August 1646, cited in Fotheringham (ed. and trans.), *Diplomatic Correspondence*, vol. 2, Appendix P, pp. 588, 593–4.
83. Montereul to Cardinal Mazarin, 28 September 1645, London, Fotheringham (ed. and trans.), *Diplomatic Correspondence*, vol. 1, pp. 11–17.
84. Montereul to Mazarin, 28 September 1645, Fotheringham (ed. and trans.), *Diplomatic Correspondence*, vol. 1, p. 15.
85. Montereul to Mazarin, 9 April 1647, Edinburgh, Fotheringham (ed. and trans.), *Diplomatic Correspondence*, vol. 2, p. 83.
86. Howat, *Stuart and Cromwellian Foreign Policy*, pp. 48–9.
87. Richelieu to Bellièvre, 6 October 1638, Paris; 13 November 1638, Avenel (ed.), *Richelieu*, vol. 6, pp. 211–13, 238–40.
88. Mazarin to the Comte de Harcourt, 1 January 1644, Chéruel (ed.), *Lettres du Cardinal Mazarin*, vol. 1, p. 354.
89. Montereul to Mazarin, 7 June 1646, Newcastle, Fotheringham (ed. and trans.), *Diplomatic Correspondence*, vol. 1, p. 208.
90. Bellièvre to Brienne, 14 March 1647, London, Fotheringham (ed. and trans.), *Diplomatic Correspondence*, vol. 2, pp. 43, 74.
91. Mazarin to Bellièvre, 12 January 1647, Paris, Chéruel (ed.), *Mazarin*, vol. 2, pp. 356–7.
92. 'The Earl of Loudoun's Narrative of the Union of England and Scotland', September 1653, in C. Firth (ed.), *Scotland and the Commonwealth: Letters and Papers Relating to the Military Government of Scotland, from August 1651 to December 1653* (Edinburgh: Scottish History Society, 1895), pp. 208–13.
93. J. Jones, *The Anglo-Dutch Wars of the Seventeenth Century* (London: Longman, 1996), p. 84.
94. Providing more balanced views of the political relationship are J. Casada, 'The Scottish Representation in Richard Cromwell's Parliament', *Scottish Historical Review*, 51:152 (1972), pp. 124–47; P. Pinckney, 'The Scottish Representation in the Cromwellian Parliament of 1656', *Scottish Historical Review*, 46:142 (1967), pp. 95–114.
95. Cromwell to Frederick III, 12 May 1657, Westminster, DRA Tyske Kancellis Udenrigske Afdeling, England A1. Thanks to Steve Murdoch (University of St Andrews) for providing me with an image of this document.
96. Graham, *A Maritime History of Scotland*, p. 330.
97. Smout, *Scottish Trade on the Eve of Union*, p. 195; Keith, 'The Economic Condition of Scotland', p. 284.
98. Bund (ed.), *Tabellr Overskibsfart*.

99. Roberts and MacPhail, *Dumbarton Common Good Accounts*, p. 264.

100. Devine, 'The Cromwellian Union', pp. 6, 12.

101. Andrew Hay to Archibald Hay, 10 April 1649, Holyrood, NRS GD504/9/88.

102. Benjamin Fletcher to Alexander Hayes, February 1642, Rouen, NRS GD34/843/1/20.

103. Benjamin Fletcher was connected to the commercial network of John Clerk of Penicuik as well as to the Hays: A. Hay to Benjamin Fletcher, NRS GD34/843/2/15.

104. Devine, 'The Cromwellian Union', pp. 6, 12.

105. Roberts and MacPhail, *Dumbarton Common Good Accounts*, appendix B; *ASWA, passim*.

106. Records of the *Juridiction Consulaire* of Dieppe, October 1653–April 1656, ADSM, 200 BP 35 (unpaginated); Records for the Admiralty of Havre, 10 February 1655–17 March 1664, ADSM, 216 BP 122.

107. January and March 1654, January 1655, January 1656, ADSM, 200 BP 35 (unpaginated).

108. ADCM, series B: Admiralty of La Rochelle, Consular jurisdiction of La Rochelle, records from the mid-sixteenth to eighteenth centuries.

109. Howat, *Stuart and Cromwellian Foreign Policy*, p. 2.

110. Murdoch, *Britain, Denmark-Norway and the House of Stuart*, pp. 173–80.

111. A. Macinnes, *The British Revolution, 1629–1660* (Basingstoke, Hampshire: Palgrave Macmillan, 2005), p. 208.

112. 9 September 1652, Firth and Rait (eds), *Acts and Ordinances*, vol. 2, pp. 612–4. See also *The Acts Done and Past in the Second, Third, Fourth and Fifth Sessions of the First Triennial Parliament of our Soveraigne Lord Charles*, p. 43.

113. Talbott, '"If it Please God, I Come Home": Scottish Return Migration from France in the Long Seventeenth Century', pp. 58–60; S. Talbott, 'An Alliance Ended?: Franco-Scottish Commercial Relations, 1560–1713' (PhD thesis, University of St Andrews, 2010), pp. 84–5, 105–6.

114. James Mowat to John Clerk, 17 January 1650, Paris NRS GD18/2593/3; see also same to same, 19 January 1650, Paris, NRS GD18/2595/4.

115. Account between Lothian and Clerk, 8 March 1650–5 June 1652, NRS GD18/2445.

116. James Mowat to John Clerk, 17 January 1650, Paris, NRS GD18/2505/4.

117. James Mowat to John Clerk, 22 January 1650, Paris, NRS GD18/2505/6.

118. 13 January 1652, Aberdeen, ACA Propinquity Book I, fo. 42v.

119. 24 February–27 March 1651, NLS Culloden Papers, Ch.1673–5.

120. 4 March 1662, ADCM, B309.

121. Annabella Lothian to William, Earl of Lothian, 4 March 1651, La Rochelle, NRS GD40/2/5/13/1.

122. John Inglis to George Maine, 8 April 1659, London, NRS RH9/2/133.

123. Alexander Charteris to John Clerk, 8 April 1654, Paris, NRS GD18/2528/3.

124. 30 January 1662, NRS GD72/139.

125. Additional instructions to Baillie Cullen, September 1652, Aberdeen, *ACL*, vol. 3, p. 214.

126. Andrew Hay to Archibald Hay, 10 April 1649, Holyrood, NRS GD504/9/88.

127. 28 August 1649, Firth and Rait (eds), *Acts and Ordinances*, vol. 2, pp. 239–40.

128. HL 434906, Battie, *The Merchants Remonstrance*, p. 2.

5 'In Pursuit of His Majesty's Enemies': Franco-Stuart Conflict, 1627–1667

1. T. Cogswell, 'Foreign Policy and Parliament: The Case of La Rochelle, 1625–26', *English Historical Review*, 99:391 (1984), pp. 241–67, on pp. 247–65; Murdoch, *The Terror of the Seas?*, pp. 157, 163–4, 170–1; R. Lockyer, 'George Villiers', *ODNB*.
2. G. Rommelse, *The Second Anglo-Dutch War (1665–1667): Raison d'état, Mercantilism and Maritime Strife* (Hilversum: Verloren, 2006), p. 14; Jones, *The Anglo-Dutch Wars*, p. 166; Voltaire, *The Age of Louis XIV*, p. 75.
3. Jones, *The Anglo-Dutch Wars*, pp. 166–7.
4. Ibid., pp. 167–8; A. Bryant (ed.), *The Letters of King Charles II* (New York: Longmans, 1968), p. 274, speech of Charles II to both Houses, 7 January 1674; also pp. 222, 243–5; Howat, *Stuart and Cromwellian Foreign Policy*, Appendix 3, pp. 166–71.
5. Downing to Bennett, 12 December 1664, The Hague, TNA SP84/173/65.
6. J. Jones, *Britain and Europe in the Seventeenth Century* (London: Edward Arnold Ltd, 1966), p. 68.
7. Donaldson, *Scotland, James V–James VII*, p. 387.
8. Lythe, *The Economy of Scotland*, pp. 211, 172. Ian Whyte supports this assessment: Whyte, *Scotland before the Industrial Revolution*, p. 272.
9. 'Enregistrement des exportations du Havre pour d'autres ports (de France ou de l'étranger)', 9 July 1627–11 April 1629, ADSM 216 BP 145, fos. 15r–59r.
10. NRS E72/9/3.
11. It is essential to differentiate between piracy and privateering. For discussion of this in the Scottish context see Murdoch, *The Terror of the Seas?*, pp. 2–9. It is still all too common that the two notions are conflated, and it is still being said that the 'difference between piracy and privateering [was] negligible'. Charters, Rosenhaft and Smith (eds), Introduction to *Civilians and War*, p. 9.
12. Graham, 'Scottish Maritime Interest', pp. 88–109; Graham, *A Maritime History of Scotland*, pp. 151–5.
13. ADCM B5607.
14. Murdoch, *The Terror of the Seas?*, pp. 320–1. See Chapter 6, pp. 118, 123.
15. Murdoch, *The Terror of the Seas?*, p. 174.
16. 2 September, Leith, 2 September 1628, NRS AC7/1, p. 190.
17. 3 February 1629, Edinburgh, NRS AC7/1, p. 246. This may be the same case as the *Green Dragon*, reported in the Privy Council 5 March 1629, *RPCS*, 2nd series, vol. 3, p. 86. See Murdoch, *The Terror of the Seas?*, pp. 175, 395, 397.
18. 5 March 1629, *RPCS*, 2nd series, vol. 3, p. 86; Murdoch, *The Terror of the Seas?*, p. 175.
19. 30 January 1630, 23 February 1630, 18 March 1630, Edinburgh, NRS AC7/1, pp. 259, 269, 272.
20. 1 February 1667, London, NRS RH9/17/32/11.
21. Downing to Bennett, 16 December 1664, The Hague, TNA SP84/173/69.
22. De Bacquoy to Bennett, 14 February 1665, Leeuwarden, TNA SP84/174/84; Alvise Saguedo, Venetian Ambassador in France to the Doge and Senate, 9 January 1665, *CSPV*, vol. 34, pp. 74–5.
23. Graham, 'The Scottish Marine during the Dutch Wars', p. 69.
24. Sunderland Report, *London Gazette*, 1 July 1667, issue 170.
25. Rommelse, *The Second Anglo-Dutch War*, pp. 132–3.
26. Roberts and MacPhail, *Dumbarton Common Good Accounts*, p. 264.
27. 31 December 1628, Edinburgh, NRS AC7/2, p. 117.

28. 31 December 1628, Edinburgh, NRS AC7/2, p. 117.
29. Murdoch, *The Terror of the Seas?*, pp. 27–8, 262.
30. P. Crowhurst, *The Defence of British Trade, 1689–1815* (Folkestone, Kent: Dawson & Sons, 1977), p. 16.
31. Murdoch, *The Terror of the Seas?*, pp. 279, 328. For an idea of the numbers of Scottish privateers who paid the sum of £2,000 between 1665 and 1667 see Appendix VI:1, pp. 386–95.
32. G. Rommelse, 'English Privateering against the Dutch Republic during the Second Anglo-Dutch War (1664–7)', *Tijdschrift voor overdruk zeegeschiedenis*, 22 (2003), pp. 17–31, on p. 21.
33. 7 December 1627, *APCE*, vol. 43, p. 167, cited in Murdoch, *The Terror of the Seas?*, p. 171.
34. 29 December 1629, Edinburgh, NRS AC7/2, pp. 231, 241.
35. 8 January 1630, 22 March 1630, 12 June 1630, Edinburgh, NRS AC7/2, pp. 251, 260, 291; 2 April, 6 June 1630, *RPCS*, 2nd series, vol. 3, pp. 521–3, 589; Murdoch, *The Terror of the Seas?*, p. 178.
36. 17 February 1631, *RPCS*, 2nd series, vol. 4, p. 148.
37. Murdoch, *The Terror of the Seas?*, pp. 174–5; see also J. Bruijn, 'Dutch Privateering during the Second and Third Anglo-Dutch wars', *Low Countries History Yearbook: Acta Historicae Neerlandicae*, 11 (1978), pp. 79–93, on p. 92.
38. SAUL, ms38352, p. 52.
39. A. Little, 'A Comparative Survey of Scottish Service in the English and Dutch Maritime Communities c. 1650–1707', in Grosjean and Murdoch (eds), *Scottish Communities Abroad in the Early Modern Period*, pp. 332–62, on p. 336; for the later Stuart wars see pp. 339–45.
40. 17 July 1626, ACA, Aberdeen Council Minutes, LI, pp. 275, 276.
41. 25 July 1626, *RPCS*, 2nd series, vol. 1, p. 669.
42. 10 August 1626, Edinburgh, *ACL*, vol. 1, pp. 249–50.
43. Balfour, *Annales*, vol. 2, pp. 146–7, cited in *RPCS*, 2nd series, vol. 1, pp. 430, 432 n., lxvi.
44. 28 September 1626, Edinburgh, *RPCS*, 2nd series, vol. 1, p. 431.
45. 21 November 1626, *RPCS*, 2nd series, vol. 1, p. 445.
46. October 1626, ACA, Aberdeen Council Minutes, LI, p. 299.
47. Smout, *Scottish Trade on the Eve of Union*, p. 64; 15 March 1665, J. Stuart (ed.), *Extracts from the Council Register of the Burgh of Aberdeen*, 2 vols (Edinburgh: Spalding Club, 1871–2), vol. 2, p. 215; Little, 'A. Comparative Survey', p. 340, n. 26.
48. 5 May 1627, NRS GD7/2/33. See Chapter 4, p. 83.
49. Welwood, *An Abridgement of All Sea-Lawes*, pp. 48–9.
50. 10 December 1629, Edinburgh, NRS AC7/2, p. 219.
51. 29 April 1628, NRS AC7/2, p. 77.
52. 24 October 1667, NRS GD172/1919.
53. 30 November 1633, NRS GD172/2400.
54. McNeill and MacQueen, *Atlas of Scotland*, p. 270. No distinction is made between the Dutch Republic and the Spanish Netherlands.
55. Graham, *A Maritime History of Scotland*, p. 144. Data compiled by Graham from the books of shore dues (1638), privilege (1660–3) and censors records (1667) of Leith, NRS E71–2. Graham does not specify whether the 'Low Countries' includes the Dutch Republic, the Spanish Netherlands, or both.

56. Graham, *A Maritime History of Scotland*, p. 144.
57. [1667], SRA Anglica VII, DXLII (unfoliated).
58. 10 April 1667, SRA Anglica VII, DXLII (unfoliated). Thanks to Steve Murdoch (University of St Andrews) for providing images of both of these documents.
59. Rommelse, 'English Privateering', p. 21.
60. 26 September 1667, SRA Anglica VII, DXLII, 1660–70 (unfoliated).
61. See Murdoch, *The Terror of the Seas?*, Appendix VI:2, 'Neutral Prizes Taken in the Second Anglo-Dutch War, 1665–8', pp. 396–7.
62. 5 May 1627, Paris, NRS GD7/2/33.
63. Bond, Earl of Montrose to Andrew Bethune [Beaton], Paris, in the name of William Dick, 11 September 1634, Edinburgh, NRS GD220/6/638; Beaton dealt with the Earls of Mar and Erskine, 22 September 1637, 2 November 1638, GD124/2/54. Beaton had ties James Mel: J Smyth to Andrew Beaton, 14 March 1634, Edinburgh, NRS GD7/2/34.
64. 18 February 1666, ADCM, B5667.
65. 20 June 1666, 28 August 1666, NRS E72/9/1.
66. 16 September 1664–8 December 1666, NLS Adv.mss.31.3.2, fos. 38r–46v.
67. 1 February 1665, NLS Adv.mss.31.3.2, fo. 40v.
68. M. Lee, *The Road to Revolution, Scotland under Charles I, 1625–37* (Illinois: University of Illinois Press, 1985), p. 82; 6 January 1627, *RPCS*, 2nd series, vol. 1, pp. 488–9.
69. 5 February 1628, Holyrood, *RPCS*, 2nd series, vol. 1, pp. 567–8; *RPCS*, 2nd series, vol. 1, p. lxxiii.
70. 26 February 1628, Holyrood, *RPCS*, 2nd series, vol. 2, pp. xxxii, 243, see also 11 March 1628, pp. 265–6; 25 March 1628, pp. 284–5.
71. 26 March 1628, *RPCS*, 2nd series, vol. 2, pp. xxxiii–xxxiv, 305–7.
72. 7 April 1628, Holyrood, NRS AC7/1, p. 152.
73. 26 April 1628, NRS AC7/1, p. 153.
74. 28 April 1628, NRS AC7/1, p. 154.
75. 27 January–February 1629, NRS AC7/1, pp. 232–9.
76. 29 January 1629, Holyrood, *RPCS*, 2nd series, vol. 3, pp. 24–5.
77. 12 February 1629, Holyrood, *RPCS*, 2nd series, vol. 3, pp. xxii–xxxiii, 44. Maurice Lee suggests that this was prompted by the fall of La Rochelle in 1628, as Charles 'cut his losses', made peace and 'promptly' reopened the wine trade: Lee, *The Road to Revolution*, pp. 82–3.
78. 30 January 1627, Holyrood, *RPCS*, 2nd series, vol. 1, pp. 506–7.
79. 1 February 1627, Holyrood, *RPCS*, 2nd series, vol. 1, pp. 527–8.
80. 16 April 1628, NRS AC7/2, p. 63.
81. 28 January 1629, Edinburgh, NRS AC7/2, p. 132.
82. 24 June 1628, Holyrood, *RPCS*, 2nd series, vol. 2, p. 340. Prohibition: 5 February 1628, Holyrood, *RPCS*, 2nd series, vol. 2, pp. 567–8.
83. Murdoch, *The Terror of the Seas?*, p. 175.
84. 21 July 1625, Edinburgh, *RPCS*, 2nd series, vol. 1, pp. 88–9.
85. 19 July 1627, Holyrood, *RPCS*, 2nd series, vol. 2, pp. 20–1.
86. 9 January 1627, Holyrood, *RPCS*, 2nd series, vol. 1, pp. lxxiii, 486–7. See Chapter 1, p. 29.
87. 28 May 1627, Holyrood, *RPCS*, 2nd series, vol. 1, p. 613.
88. Rommelse, *The Second Anglo-Dutch War*, p. 151.

89. D. Bell, *The First Total War: Napoleon's Europe and the Birth of Modern War* (London: Bloomsbury, 2007); D. Bell, 'The Limits of Conflict in Napoleonic Europe – and their Transgression', in Charters, Rosenhaft and Smith (eds), *Civilians and War in Europe*, pp. 201–8.

90. Lythe, *The Economy of Scotland*, p. 211.

91. Lee, *The Road to Revolution*, p. 82.

92. Downing to Bennett, 12 December 1664, The Hague, TNA SP84/173/65.

93. William Coventry to Secretary Bennett, 19 November 1664, *CSPD*, 1664–5, p. 79; Little, 'A Comparative Survey', p. 339.

94. Little, 'A Comparative Survey', pp. 333–74.

95. Robert Meine to Williamson, 7 August 1666, *CSPD*, 1666–7, p. 15.

96. Murdoch, *The Terror of the Seas?*, pp. 173–4.

97. Ibid., p. 238. For the older view that England dictated Britain's foreign policy see Smout, *Scottish Trade on the Eve of Union*, pp. 18, 185.

98. Courthope, *The Journal of Thomas Cuningham*, pp. 245–6.

99. *RPCS*, 2nd series, vol. 1, pp. lxxii, 479–80, n.

6 'For the Security and Encouragement of the Free Trade of Scotland': The Nine Years' War and the War of the Spanish Succession, 1688–1713

1. J. Miller, 'Crown, Parliament and People', in J. Jones (ed.), *Liberty Secured? Britain Before and After the Glorious Revolution* (Stanford, CA: Stanford University Press, 1992), pp. 53–87, on p. 60.

2. Howat, *Stuart and Cromwellian Foreign Policy*, p. 5.

3. T. Claydon, *William III and the Godly Revolution* (Cambridge: Cambridge University Press, 2002), pp. 11–12.

4. Brewer, *The Sinews of Power*, cited in J. Jones, 'The Revolution in Context', in Jones (ed.), *Liberty Secured?*, pp. 25–52, on p. 37.

5. Smout, 'The Road to Union', p. 187.

6. B. Lenman, 'The Scottish Episcopal Clergy and the Ideology of Jacobitism', in E. Cruickshanks (ed.), *Ideology and Conspiracy: Aspects of Jacobitism, 1689–1759* (Edinburgh: John Donald, 1982), pp. 36–48, on p. 43.

7. Graham, 'In Defence of the Scottish Maritime Interest', p. 90.

8. Smout, 'The Road to Union', p. 184.

9. Smout, *Scottish Trade on the Eve of Union*, p. 245.

10. *RPCS*, 3rd series, vol. 16, 1691, p. 277; see also *CSPD*, 1689–90, pp. 310, 371.

11. 6 August 1689, Edinburgh, *RPCS*, 3rd series, vol. 14, p. 18. This was later reiterated. 22 April 1693, *APS*, vol. 9, Appendix, p. 72; 23 May 1693, p. 82; 1 July 1695, p. 111; 2 July 1695, p. 118.

12. Historical Manuscripts Commission, *Fourteenth Report, The Manuscripts of the House of Lords, 1692–1693* (London: H. M. S. O., 1894), pp. 384ff.

13. 4 May 1691, *RPCS*, 3rd series, vol. 16, p. 274; Historical Manuscripts Commission, *Calendar of Stuart Papers belonging to His Majesty the King, preserved at Windsor Castle*, 7 vols (London: H. M. S. O., 1902–23), vol. 1, p. 67.

14. 31 October 1689, *CSPD*, 1689–90, p. 310.

15. 24 and 27 December 1700, 31 January 1701, *APS*, vol. 10, pp. 232, 233, 278; 31 January 1701, NRS PA7/17/1/90/i–vi.
16. Murdoch, *The Terror of the Seas?*, p. 296.
17. Keith, *Commercial Relations of England and Scotland*, p. 150.
18. Schaeper, *The French Council of Commerce*, p. 112.
19. *Flying Post or the Post Master*, 1102 (2 June 1702); Schaeper, *The French Council of Commerce*, p. 112.
20. Schaeper, *The French Council of Commerce*, p. 112.
21. TNA SP34/33/65, fo. 190.
22. *Flying Post or the Post Master*, 3390 (18 June 1713). A copy of the treaty suspending arms between France and England in 1713 can be found at ADLA C 690.
23. 22 April 1689, *APS*, vol. 9, p. 58.
24. 12 March 1696, GCA T–PM/109/79.
25. 1 September 1698, *RPS*, 1698/7/161.
26. Whyte, *Scotland before the Industrial Revolution*, p. 124.
27. J. Jones, *War and Economy in the Age of William III and Marlborough* (Oxford: Basil Blackwell, 1988), p. 17.
28. Ibid., p. 161.
29. [?] to [Sir Charles] Hedges, 14 April 1705, La Rochelle, TNA SP78/154/18.
30. Charles Lord Yester to his father [John, second Marquess of Tweedale], Dagaty, 23 September 1701, W. Fraser (ed.), *The Earls of Cromertie, their Kindred, Country and Correspondence*, 2 vols (Edinburgh, 1876), vol. 1, p. 148.
31. 19 September 1689, *RPCS*, 3rd series, vol. 14, pp. 306–7.
32. 11 October 1689, *RPCS*, 3rd series, vol. 14, p. 405.
33. Smout, *Scottish Trade on the Eve of Union*, p. 69; Keith, *Commercial Relations of England and Scotland*, p. 155.
34. 12 July 1709, Edinburgh, *CRB*, vol. 4, p. 489.
35. 4 September 1706, ACA Propinquity Book II (unfoliated).
36. ACA Propinquity Book I, fos. 169, 170, 172; Murdoch, *The Terror of the Seas?*, p. 301
37. Murdoch, *The Terror of the Seas?*, pp. 404–6.
38. Ibid., pp. 310–6; Smout, *Scottish Trade on the Eve of Union*, pp. 65, 69.
39. *Daily Courant*, London, 5–6 June 1707, issue 1661.
40. Murdoch, *The Terror of the Seas?*, pp. 320–1. For the older view see Graham, 'In Defence of the Scottish Maritime Interest', pp. 88–109; Graham, *A Maritime History of Scotland*, pp. 151–5.
41. J. Bromley, 'The Jacobite Privateers in the Nine Years' War', in A.Whiteman, J. Bromley and P. Dickson (eds), *Statesman, Scholars and Merchants: Essays in Eighteenth-Century History Presented to Dame Lucy Sutherland* (Oxford: Clarendon, 1973), pp. 17–43, on p. 21.
42. 1689–91, ADLA B 4887.
43. 1692–7, ADSM 216 BP 316.
44. D. Defoe, *Reasons Against a War with France or an Argument Shewing that the French King's Owning the Prince of Wales as King of England, Scotland and Ireland; is No Sufficient Ground of a War* (London, 1701), TNA SP9/248, pp. 12–13.
45. *Review of the Affairs of France*, London, 19 December 1704, issue 83.
46. 1704–10, ADSM 216 BP 317.
47. 1702–5, ADSM 214 BP 12–15.
48. 1702, ADCM B62/118.

49. TNA SP32/4/101, cited in Keith, *Commercial Relations of England and Scotland*, pp. 151–3.

50. 22 May 1693, *RPCS*, cited in Keith, *Commercial Relations of England and Scotland*, p. 153.

51. Keith, 'The Economic Causes for the Scottish Union', pp. 47, 54.

52. n.d., *c.* 1702–7; NRS, PA7/21, fo. 196; Murdoch, *The Terror of the Seas?*, p. 322, n.199.

53. I. Grant, *Social and Economic Development in Scotland before 1603* (London: Oliver & Boyd, 1930), p. 344.

54. Pagan, *The Convention of the Royal Burghs*, p. 159; Keith, 'The Economic Causes for the Scottish Union', p. 51.

55. 13 January 1694, Stockholm, NRS RH15/106/772; Murdoch, *The Terror of the Seas?*, p. 312.

56. *London Gazette*, 13 May 1695, issue 3079.

57. Captain Masterton, Account of illegal trade between France and Ireland, with suggested solutions, 5 July 1704, TNA SP34/4/55.

58. Information of Daniel Collett, 29 November 1704, Liverpool, TNA SP34/5/2A, fos. 3–4.

59. Thomas Collier to the Earl of Dartmouth, 21 March 1712, Jersey, TNA SP34/18/16, fos. 40–1; see also Collier to Dartmouth, 4 February 1712, Jersey, TNA SP47/3/96.

60. Robert Leslie to John Taylor, Esq., [?1702], *Calendar of Treasury Papers*, 6 vols (London, 1868–89), vol. 3, p. 90. See also 17 April 1706, ADG C 4260.

61. 23 January 1703, *Calendar of Treasury Papers*, vol. 3, pp. 105–6.

62. Francis, *The Wine Trade*, p. 125.

63. Scoville, 'The French Economy', p. 233.

64. Data taken from 'Accompt of Wines Exported overland to England', November 1669–November 1670, NRS E73/23. Total French wine = 20 tuns, 1 hogshead, 28 gallons, 1 tearce; Spanish = 12 butts, 10 gallons (converts to 6 tuns, 10 gallons).

65. Data compiled from the second series of customs books (wine) for Leith, NRS E72/15. Records are not extant for 1681–2, 1686–8. Spanish wine is measured in butts; French in tuns. Conversion rate: 1 tun = 2 butts.

66. T. Barclay and E. Graham, *The Early Transatlantic Trade of Ayr, 1640–1730* (Ayr: Ayrshire Archaeological and Natural History Society, 2005); D. Dobson, *Scottish Trade with Colonial Charleston, 1683–1783* (Glasgow: Humming Earth, 2009).

67. Entry books of wine, Leith, NRS E72/15/22; E72/15/29; E72/15/33, from data available for 1680–1, 1683–4 and 1684–5. The only year for which separate figures are included for the custom as well as the excise – 1683–4 – this is equal, being £60 per tun French or £30 per butt/£60 per tun Spanish. Years run November–November.

68. Schaeper, *The French Council of Commerce*, p. 131.

69. Scoville, 'The French Economy', pp. 233, 238.

70. For example, see *Mercator*, 30 January 1713–2 February 1713, issue 109; and 9–11 March 1713, issue 125.

71. *Mercator*, 18–20 February 1713, issue 117.

72. *Tatler*, 10–13 March 1710, issue 301.

73. 30 March 1689, *Calendar of Treasury Papers*, vol. 1, p. 34.

74. Whatley, *The Scottish Salt Industry*, p. 43.

75. *Collection for Improvement of Husbandry and Trade*, London, 5 July 1695, issue 153.

76. 23 April 1689, *RPS*, 1689/3/153; 4 May 1691, *RPCS*, 3rd series, vol. 16, pp. 276–8.

77. Leith entry book: Imports (wines), 1688–89, NRS E72/15/42; Accounts of collectors of HM Customs and Foreign Excise at Leith, 1 November 1688–1 November 1689, NRS E73/66, folders 1 and 2. See also 'Account of collectors of HM Customs and Foreign Excise at Leith', 1 November 1689–1 November 1690, E73/88/6–7.
78. 4 May 1691, *RPCS*, 3rd series, vol. 16, pp. 276–8.
79. NRS E72/15/51, p. 1.
80. *Post-Man and the Historical Account*, London, 20 January 1705, issue 1366.
81. J.K. to Hedges, 1 April 1705, La Rochelle, TNA SP78/154.
82. *Post-Man and the Historical Account*, London, 26 October 1705, issue 1548, Paris.
83. 15 February 1706, Edinburgh, NRS AC13/1, pp. 40, 259.
84. 5 February 1706, AN Marine B^7 504/213; 1 March 1706, ADSM, 214 BP 4, fo. 160v.
85. 1712, Rouen, NRS GD237/11/108/29.
86. *British Mercury*, London, 21 January 1713, issue 393: Gravesend, 18 January, report of the *Susanna* arriving from Bordeaux.
87. Robert Arbuthnot to [?James Menzies of Pitfoddells], 16 May 1713, Rouen, NRS GD237/11/108/29.
88. 1701–1704, NRS CS96/1145–1150/3.
89. Smout, *Scottish Trade on the Eve of Union*, p. 66; this has been refuted by Murdoch, 'The French Connection', *passim*; Murdoch, *The Terror of the Seas?*, pp. 310–6. See 17 December 1707, NRS CS96/3074; 27 February 1723, NRS RH15/32/21; Historical Manuscripts Commission, *Calendar of Stuart Papers*, vol. 3, p. 305.
90. 13 January 1692, Historical Manuscripts Commission, *Calendar of Stuart Papers*, vol. 1, p. 67.
91. 23 May 1693, *RPS*, 1693/4/54.
92. 2 November 1691, ADCM B5688/51.
93. 28 May 1692, ADCM B5688/85.
94. 1692, ADCM B5688/113–14, 177, 179–80, 195, 207.
95. 15 January–3 December 1695, ADCM B5691/57–90.
96. ADG 6 B 73–7, 79, 82 226, 229, 3 E art. 1812–13, 1801, supplemented by the *Archives Canada France database* at http://bd.archivescanadafrance.org/sdx-222-acf-pleade-2/acf/home.shtm [accessed 17 March 2009].
97. ADG 6 B 75–7.
98. 23 April 1689, *RPS*, 1689/3/153; 4 May 1691, *RPCS*, 3rd series, vol. 16, pp. 276–8.
99. Letter from James Ogilvy, first earl of Seafield, 26 August 1705, Edinburgh, Hume-Brown (ed.), *James Ogilvy, First Earl of Seafield and Others: Letters relating to Scotland in the reign of Queen Anne*, p. 77.
100. 14 September 1705, *RPS*, 1705/6/120.
101. 1690, ADCM B5630.
102. Schaeper, *The French Council of Commerce*, p. 113.
103. C. Whatley, *The Scots and the Union* (Edinburgh: Edinburgh University Press, 2006), p. 200; Murdoch, 'The French Connection', p. 37; Graham, 'In Defence of the Scottish Maritime Interest', p. 103.
104. 11 May 1708, TNA HCA 26/13; Murdoch, *The Terror of the Seas?*, p. 307; *London Gazette*, 10 May 1708, 7 September 1710, issue 4741.
105. 1711, NRS RH9/1/200.
106. Historical Manuscripts Commission, *Report on the Manuscripts of Lord Polwarth*, 3 vols (London: H. M. S. O., 1911–31), vol. 1, pp. 9–10.
107. *RPCS*, 3rd series, vol. 13, p. 529.

108. 30 May 1689, Edinburgh, *RPCS*, 3rd series, vol. 13, pp. 395–6.

109. 11 February 1690, *RPCS*, 3rd series, vol. 15, pp. 74–5.

110. 11 February 1690, *RPCS*, 3rd series, vol. 15, pp. 77–8.

111. Lenman, 'The Scottish Episcopal Clergy', p. 43.

112. 28 February 1693, *CSPD*, 1693, p. 47; Little, 'A Comparative Survey', p. 343.

113. 12 May 1702, *CSPD*, 1700–2, p. 457; Murdoch, 'The French Connection', p. 36.

114. Sée and Cormack, 'Commercial Relations between France and Scotland', p. 276.

115. J.G. to Caspar Frederick Henning in London, 5 May 1702, Paris, TNA SP78/153/72.

116. Lenman and Gibson (eds), *The Jacobite Threat*, pp. 85–6.

117. Schaeper, *The French Council of Commerce*, p. 114. The French offered a similar favour to the Dutch: Sée and Cormack, 'Commercial Relations between France and Scotland', p. 275.

118. Kay and Maclean, *Knee Deep in Claret*, pp. 85–6.

119. *Review of the State of the British Nation*, 1 May 1707, issue 35. This issue was discussed at length in subsequent issues; see 17 May 1707, issue 42.

120. Petition of several merchants of Scotland to Queen Anne, 21 July 1707, TNA PC1/14/15. A copy of this petition is held at NRS GD220/6/1769/4.

121. Report of the court of the exchequer, 1707, London, TNA PC1/14/15.

122. Lord Treasurer's report on the Scots Merchants' Petition, 28 July 1707, TNA PC1/14/15.

123. Declaration of officers of the customhouse, London, 26 July 1707, TNA PC1/14/15.

124. Whatley, *The Scots and the Union*, p. 199.

125. 20 January 1709, *Calendar of Treasury Papers*, vol. 4, pp. 90–1.

126. Schaeper, *The French Council of Commerce*, pp. 110–11, 113; Murdoch, 'The French Connection', pp. 36–7.

127. 5 February 1706, AN Marine B⁷ 504/213.

128. Sée and Cormack, 'Commercial Relations between France and Scotland', pp. 276–7.

129. De Bruyn Kops, *A Spirited Exchange*, p. 7.

130. *RPCS*, 3rd series, vol. 15, p. 125; Murdoch, 'The French Connection', p. 35.

131. Moses Corbett, 1691, *CSPD*, 1690–1, p. 479.

132. Smout, *Scottish Trade on the Eve of Union*, p. 168.

7 Beyond 1707: Franco-'British' Relations?

1. James Mowat to John Clerk, 22 January 1650, Paris, NRS GD18/2505/6.

2. Lythe, *The Economy of Scotland*, p. 230.

3. *Procès-verbal relatif au Henri, de Hull en Angleterre*, AMN GG774, 1713.

4. Including: Murdoch, *Network North*; Grosjean, *An Unofficial Alliance*; Zickermann, *Across the German Sea*.

5. 1690, ADCM B5630.

6. See Chapter 2, p. 40; Smout, *Scottish Trade on the Eve of Union*, p. 98.

7. *Repertoir des conges par l'éstranger*, Nantes, ADLA B4725.

8. Captain Masterton, 'Account of illegal trade between France and Ireland, with suggested solutions', 5 July 1704, TNA SP34/4/55.

9. É. Ó Ciosáin, 'Regrouping in Exile: Irish Communities in Western France in the Seventeenth Century', in R. Armstrong and T. Ó hAnnracháin (eds), *Community in Early Modern Ireland* (Dublin: Four Courts Press, 2006), pp. 133–53, on p. 144.

10. M. Villar Garcia, 'Irish Migration and Exiles in Spain: Refugees, Soldiers, Traders and Statesmen', in O'Connor and Lyons, (eds), *Irish Communities in Early Modern Europe*, pp. 172–99, on pp. 192–5; O. Recio Morales, 'Identity and Loyalty: Irish Traders in Seventeenth-century Iberia', in Dickson, Parmentier and Ohlmeyer (eds), *Irish and Scottish Mercantile Networks in Europe*, pp. 197–210, on pp. 197, 201; S. Fannin, 'The Irish Community in Eighteenth-Century Cadiz', in T. O'Connor and M. Lyons (eds), *Irish Migrants in Europe after Kinsale, 1602–1820* (Dublin: Four Courts Press, 2003), pp. 135–48, on p. 135.

11. Lythe, *The Economy of Scotland*, p. 171.

12. J. Bosher, 'The Gaigneur Clan in the Seventeenth-Century Canadian Trade', in O. Janzen (ed.), *Merchant Organization and Maritime Trade, 1660–1815* (St Johns, Newfoundland: International Maritime Economic History Association, 1998), pp. 15–51, on pp. 23–4.

13. E. Cruickshanks, *The Glorious Revolution* (Basingstoke, Hampshire: Palgrave Macmillan, 2000), p. 59.

14. M. Lyons, 'The Emergence of an Irish Community in Saint-Malo, 1550–1710', in O'Connor and Lyons (eds), *The Irish in Europe*, pp. 107–26, on p. 125; Ó Ciosáin, 'Regrouping in Exile', p. 144; Ó Ciosáin, 'Hidden by 1688 and After', p. 134.

15. O'Connor, 'Irish Clerics and Jacobites in Early Eighteenth-Century Paris', pp. 175–6.

16. In particular, see AMN: parish St-Clément, GG26, 1692; Church of Saint-Léonard, GG161, January 1700; parish Saint-Nicolas, GG223, May 1693; parish Saint-Nicolas GG233, 1722; GG239, November 1735; GG496, October 1701. There are numerous examples throughout AMN GG240–437.

17. Ó Ciosáin, 'Regrouping in Exile', p. 144; Ó Ciosáin, 'Hidden by 1688 and After', p. 134.

18. 30 December 1688, ADCM B222.

19. R. d'Ambrières and É. Ó Ciosáin, 'Irish Bishops and Clergy in Exile in Mid-seventeenth-century France', *Irish Historical Studies*, 24:141 (2008), pp. 16–37; É. Ó Ciosáin and A. de Forville, 'Irish Nuns in Nantes, 1650–1659', *Archivium Hibernicum*, 58 (2004), pp. 167–73.

20. d'Ambrières and Ó Ciosáin, 'Irish Bishops and Clergy in Exile', p. 16.

21. Lyons, 'The Emergence of an Irish Community in Saint-Malo', p. 125; Ó Ciosáin, 'Regrouping in Exile', p. 144; Ó Ciosáin, 'Hidden by 1688 and After', p. 134.

22. Murdoch, 'The French Connection', p. 39.

23. Bromley, 'The Jacobite Privateers', p. 21.

24. R. Hayes, *Old Irish Links with France: Some Echoes of Exiled Ireland* (Dublin: M. H. Gill & Son, 1940), pp. 63–4.

25. AN B⁷ 496/225, 5 February 1691.

26. Bromley, 'The Jacobite Privateers', p. 40; Privy Council minutes, Kensington, 29 March 1696, Historical Manuscripts Commission, *Report on the Manuscripts of the Duke of Buccleuch and Queensberry*, vol. 2, i, p. 319.

27. Lord Moreton to [?Newcastle], 8 August 1745, TNA SP36/66, fo. 368.

28. Bellièvre to Brienne, 14 March 1647, London, Fotheringham (ed. and trans.), *Diplomatic Correspondence*, vol. 2, p. 43.

29. 22 May–17 October 1690, Nantes, AMN GG495.

30. January 1691, Beinecke Library, Yale, OSB MSS 60, Folder 2.

31. 4 July 1714, TNA SP 34/23/41, fos. 82–3.

32. Dickson, 'Introduction', p. 3.

33. For examples of such scholarship and an alternative analysis, see Haggerty, "'You Promise Well and Perform as Badly": The Failure of the "Implicit Contract of Family" in the Scottish Atlantic', p. 268, n. 6.

34. Murdoch, *Network North*, p. 91.

35. 14 September, October 1686, Edinburgh, *RPCS*, 3rd series, vol. 12, pp. 450–1, 478.

36. I. Steele, 'Introduction' to Janzen (ed.), *Merchant Organization and Maritime Trade in the North Atlantic*, pp. 1–13, on p. 3; Bosher, 'The Gaigneur Clan', pp. 15–16, 20.

37. S. Talbott, "'My Heart is a Scotch Heart": Scottish Calvinist Exiles in France in their Continental Context, 1605–1638', in Worthington (ed.), *British and Irish Emigrants and Exiles in Europe*, pp. 197–214. See Chapter 1, pp. 25–7.

38. De Bruyn Kops, *A Spirited Exchange*, pp. 70, 105.

39. 1680–5, ADLA I 10; 1676–82, ADLA I 12.

40. Privy Council Minutes, 29 March 1696, Kensington, Historical Manuscripts Commission, *Duke of Buccleuch and Queensberry*, vol. 2, i, p. 319.

41. P. Croft, 'Trading with the Enemy, 1585–1604', *Historical Journal*, 32:2 (1989), pp. 281–302, on pp. 297–9, 301.

42. L. Cullen, 'The Smuggling Trade in Ireland in the Eighteenth Century', *Proceedings of the Royal Irish Academy*, 67 (1969), pp. 149–75, on p. 151.

43. Recio Morales, 'Identity and Loyalty', p. 201.

44. S. Murdoch, 'Irish Entrepreneurs and Sweden in the First Half of the Eighteenth Century', in O'Connor and Lyons (eds), *Irish Communities in Early Modern Europe*, pp. 348–66, on pp. 358–64.

45. Murdoch, *Network North*, p. 91; S. Talbott, 'Jacobites, Anti-Jacobites and the Ambivalent: Scottish Identities in France, 1680–1720', in B. Sellin, P. Carboni and A. Thiec (eds), *Écosse: l'identité nationale en question* (Nantes: University of Nantes, 2009), pp. 73–87, on pp. 82–3.

46. Captain Masterton, 'Account of Illegal Trade between France and Ireland, with Suggested Solutions', 5 July 1704, TNA SP34/4/55.

47. D. Dickson, 'The Cork Merchant Community in the Eighteenth Century: A Regional Perspective', in L. Cullen and P. Butel (eds), *Négoce et industrie en France et en Irlande aux XVIIIe et XIXe siècles* (Paris: Éditions du Centre national de la recherche scientifique, 1980), pp. 45–50, on p. 46.

48. D. Dickson, *New Foundations: Ireland, 1600–1800* (Dublin: Helicon, 1987), p. 120.

49. [n.d. ?1707-8], AN Marine B⁷ 505/351.

50. Murdoch, *Network North*, pp. 120–2.

51. Ó Ciosáin, 'Regrouping in Exile', p. 149.

52. P. Monod, 'Dangerous Merchandise: Smuggling, Jacobitism, and Commercial Culture in Southeast England, 1690–1760', *Journal of British Studies*, 30:2 (1991), pp. 150–82, on p. 169.

53. C. Nordmann, 'Les Jacobites Ecossais en France au XVIIIe Siècle', in M. Plaisant (ed.), *Regards sur l'Ecosse au XVIIIe Siècle* (Lille: Villeneuve d'Asq, University of Lille, 1977), pp. 80–108, on p. 82.

54. F. McLynn, *The Jacobites* (London: Routledge & Kegan Paul, 1985), pp. 136–41; Talbott, 'Jacobites, Anti-Jacobites and the Ambivalent', pp. 73–88.

55. Campbell to Mar, 12 November 1717, Historical Manuscripts Commission, *Calendar of Stuart Papers*, vol. 5, p. 194, discusses the 'virulent Whigs' present in Bordeaux; Talbott, 'Jacobites, Anti-Jacobites and the Ambivalent', *passim*.
56. Monod, 'Dangerous Merchandise', p. 170.
57. Murdoch, 'Irish Entrepreneurs and Sweden', p. 358.
58. C. Ehrenstein, 'Erskine, John, 22nd or 6th earl of Mar and Jacobite duke of Mar', *ODNB*.
59. Duke of Mar to Robert Arbuthnot, 15 March 1716, Paris, Historical Manuscripts Commission, *Calendar of Stuart Papers*, vol. 2, p. 17.
60. A. Ross, 'Arbuthnot [Arbuthnott], John', *ODNB*.
61. *CSPD*, 1690–1, p. 479.
62. 14 June 1700, Historical Manuscripts Commission, *Calendar of Stuart Papers*, vol. 1, p. 149.
63. NRS RH15/106; Murdoch, *Network North*, p. 145.
64. Talbott, 'Jacobites, Anti-Jacobites and the Ambivalent', pp. 73–88.
65. Ibid., pp. 81–2; Nordmann, 'Les Jacobites Ecossais', p. 83; Murdoch, 'The French Connection', pp. 21–3, 40.
66. L. Cullen, 'Apotheosis and Crisis: the Irish Diaspora in the Age of Choiseul', in O'Connor and Lyons (eds), *Irish Communities in Early Modern Europe*, pp. 6–31, on p. 13; D. Dickson, *Old World Colony: Cork and South Munster, 1630–1830* (Madison, WI: University of Wisconsin Press, 2005), p. 143; J. Agnew, *Belfast Merchant Families in the Seventeenth Century* (Dublin: Four Courts Press, 1996), pp. 109, 116, 188–9.
67. Bromley, 'The Jacobite Privateers', p. 22.
68. Ó Ciosáin, 'Hidden by 1688 and After', pp. 126, 137–8.
69. Matthew Prior to Bolingbroke, 13 March 1714, Versailles, TNA SP78/158, fo. 73.
70. Dickson, *Old World Colony*, p. 167.
71. L. Cullen, *The Brandy Trade under the Ancien Régime: Regional Specialization in the Charente* (Cambridge: Cambridge University Press, 1998), p. 35; L. Cullen, 'The Irish Merchant Communities of Bordeaux, La Rochelle and Cognac in the Eighteenth Century', in Butel and Cullen (eds), *Négoce et industrie en France et en Irlande*, pp. 51–63; Hayes, *Old Irish links*, pp. 83, 133, 164–5.
72. See Introduction, pp. 3–4; de Bruyn Kops, *A Spirited Exchange*; Haggerty, *The British-Atlantic Trading Community*; Haggerty, 'Merely for Money'?; Lamikiz, *Trade and Trust*.
73. Murdoch, 'Community, Commodity and Commerce', pp. 31–66; Grosjean and Murdoch, 'The Scottish Community in Seventeenth-Century Gothenburg', p. 191. See Chapter 2, p. 39.
74. M. Mollat, *Le commerce maritime normand à la fin du Moyen Age: étude d'histoire économique et sociale* (Paris: Librairie Pion, 1952), p. 508.
75. Monsieur Poncet to Clerk, enclosing a letter and account for Mr Hope, 22 February 1655, Paris, NRS GD18/2542.
76. Alexander Charteris to John Clerk 8 April 1654, Paris, NRS GD18/2528/3.
77. De Bruyn Kops, *A Spirited Exchange*, p. 56.
78. 30 May 1603, Bordeaux, NRS RH9/5/5.
79. 19 January 1665, Edinburgh, *RPCS*, 3rd series, vol. 2, p. 5.
80. See, for example, Henry Lavie to John Anderson, Petter Gemmull, John Walkinshaw, John Cauldwell, Hugh Nisbet, & Alexander Knox, 26 October 1674, Bourdeaux, NLS Acc.8100/143; Murdoch, 'The French Connection', p. 30.
81. 9 June 1676, AMB GG 855/34.
82. ADG 6 B 22, fos. 8v–9r.

83. 25 February 1758, AMB GG 863/22; 14 July 1783, AMB GG 868/867. Talbott, 'Scottish Return Migration from France', pp. 55–8.
84. 27 October 1717, ADG 6 B 59.
85. 19 [July] 1718, ADG 6 B 59.
86. 4 May 1718, ADG 6 B 59.
87. Ó Ciosáin, 'Regrouping in Exile', p. 150.
88. AMN EE 267.
89. *Rôles d'équipage*, ADSM 216 BP 345.
90. Thomas Collier to the Earl of Dartmouth, 21 March 1712, Jersey, TNA SP34/18/16, fos. 40–1.
91. Ó Ciosáin, 'Hidden by 1688 and After', pp. 133–4.
92. ADLA B71, cited in Ó Ciosáin, 'Regrouping in Exile', p. 137.
93. Sahlins, *Unnaturally French*, pp. 159, 172. The Scots' naturalization privileges were reconfirmed by Louis XIV in September 1646: Moncrieff (ed.), *Memoirs concerning the Ancient Alliance*, p. 32.
94. ADC Affaires Étrangères, Mémoires et Documents (Angleterre) 7, fos. 120v–123r: 'Extrait des registres du Conseil d'estat' [1739]. I am grateful to Professor Daniel Szechi (University of Manchester) for providing me with images of this document. See Chapter 1, p. 29.
95. Ó Ciosáin, 'Hidden by 1688 and After', p. 136.
96. F. Bayard, 'Naturalisation in Lyon during the Ancien Régime', *French History*, 4:3 (1990), pp. 277–316, on pp. 296–7
97. ADLA B 84; G. Saupin, 'Les Réseaux Commerciaux des Irlandais de Nantes sous le Règne de Louis XIV', in Dickson, Parmentier, and Ohlmeyer (eds), *Irish and Scottish Mercantile Networks in Europe*, pp. 115–46.
98. Huntington Library, Black Family Papers, HM49125–227.
99. Talbott, 'British Commercial Interests', pp. 408–9.
100. 4 March 1662, ADCM, B309.
101. Ó Ciosáin, 'Hidden by 1688 and After', p. 135.
102. Charters, Rosenhaft and Smith (eds), 'Introduction', to *Civilians and War in Europe*, p. 8.
103. Lyons, 'The emergence of an Irish community in Saint-Malo', p. 125.
104. Bosher, 'The Gaigneur Clan', p. 36.
105. Croft, 'Trading with the Enemy', pp. 282, 295.

Conclusion

1. Subrahmanyam, 'Introduction' to Subrahmanyam (ed.), *Merchant Networks in the Early Modern World*, pp. iii–xiv.
2. De Bruyn Kops, *A Spirited Exchange*, p. 340.
3. Ohlmeyer, 'Seventeenth-Century Ireland and Scotland and their Wider Worlds', p. 459.
4. Supplication by the lord provost and magistrates of Edinburgh, 19 August 1684, Edinburgh, *RPCS*, 3rd series, vol. 9, pp. 115–6.
5. 23–9 January 1707, Macray (ed.), *Correspondence of Colonel Hooke*, vol. 2, p. 109–11.
6. Devine, *Scotland's Empire*, p. 3.
7. Ibid.; Lythe, *The Economy of Scotland*, p. 230.
8. L. Colley, *Britons: Forging the Nation, 1707–1837* (Yale, CT: Yale University Press, 1992), p. 5.
9. Lythe, *The Economy of Scotland*, p. 211.

10. Smout, 'The Road to Union', pp. 184, 187.
11. 23 January 1703, *Calendar of Treasury Papers*, vol. 3, pp. 105–6.
12. De Bruyn Kops, *A Spirited Exchange*, p. 340.
13. *Universal Dictionary of Trade and Commerce* (1762).
14. Brewer, *The Sinews of Power*, p. 170.
15. T. O'Connor and M. Lyons, 'Introduction' to O'Connor and Lyons (eds), *Irish Communities in Early Modern Europe*, pp. 1–5, on p. 3.
16. De Bruyn Kops, *A Spirited Exchange*, p. 340.
17. Ibid., p. 245.
18. Subrahmanyam, 'Introduction' to Subrahmanyam, *Merchant Networks in the Early Modern World*, pp. iii–xiv.
19. Captain Masterton to Thomas Knox, 29 June 1704, TNA SP34/4/53A, fo. 90.
20. James Axton, weaver at Paris, *CSPD*, 1690–1, p. 479; Caryll, 14 June 1700, *Stuart Papers*, I, p. 149.
21. J. Parmentier, 'The Ray Dynasty: Irish Mercantile Empire Builders in Ostend, 1690–1790', in O'Connor and Lyons (eds), *Irish Communities in Early Modern Europe*, pp. 367–82, on pp. 369–90.
22. Agnew, *Belfast Merchant Families*, p. 116.
23. T. M. Truxes, 'New York City's Irish Merchants and Trade with the Enemy during the Seven Years' War', in D. Dickson, and C. Ó Gráda (eds), *Reconfiguring Ireland, Essays in Honour of L. M. Cullen* (Dublin: Four Courts Press, 2003), pp. 147–64, on p. 149.
24. *Flying-Post; or, The Post-Master*, 4–6 June 1713, issue 3384, p. 2.
25. Barclay and Talbott, 'New Perspectives', pp. 128–9; results can be seen in the work of de Bruyn Kops, *A Spirited Exchange*; Haggerty, *'Merely for Money'?*; Lamikiz, *Trade and Trust*. See Introduction, pp. 3–4.
26. HL 434906, Battie, *The Merchants Remonstrance*, p. 2.

WORKS CITED

Manuscript Sources

SCOTLAND

Aberdeen City Archives

Aberdeen Council Minutes.

Aberdeen Propinquity Books, vols I and II.

SRO 25/3/2 Acts of Convention, 4 July 1610 to July 1636.

Aberdeen University Special Collections

ms213 *Memoires touchant l'ancienne alliance* (copy at NLS mss.88).

ms934 Tax Agreement, Aberdeenshire.

ms3175/Z/156 Letter-book of Robert Gerard, Merchant of Aberdeen.

Glasgow City Archives, The Mitchell Library

TD589/972 Petition – Weavers, Spinners and other Labourers.

T-PM/109 Maxwell of Pollock: Proclamation Concerning Jacobites.

T-PM/113 Maxwell of Pollock: Correspondence, Sixteenth and Seventeenth Centuries.

National Records of Scotland, Edinburgh

AC7 Admiralty Court Registers of Decreets.

AC13 Admiralty Court Commissions and Deputations.

CS96 Productions in Processes.

E71 Exchequer Records: Customs Books (First Series).

E72 Exchequer Records: Customs Books (Second Series).

E73 Exchequer Records: Customs Accounts.

E74	Exchequer Records: Bullion Accounts.
GD3	Papers of the Montgomerie Family, Earls of Eglinton.
GD7	Papers of the Bethune Family of Blebo, Fife.
GD18	Papers of the Clerk Family of Penicuik.
GD29	Papers of the Bruce Family of Kinross (Kinross House Papers).
GD34	Papers of the Hay Family of Haystoun, Peeblesshire.
GD40	Papers of the Kerr Family, Marquises of Lothian (Lothian Muniments).
GD72	Papers of the Hay Family of Park.
GD124	Papers of the Erskine Family, Earls of Mar and Kellie.
GD150	Papers of the Earls of Morton.
GD172	Papers of the Henderson Family of Fordell.
GD220	Papers of the Graham Family, Dukes of Montrose (Montrose Muniments).
GD237	Records of Messrs Tods Murray and Jamieson WS, Lawyers, Edinburgh.
GD253	Papers of Messrs D. and J. H. Campbell, WS, Solicitors, Edinburgh.
GD406	Papers of the Douglas Hamilton Family, Dukes of Hamilton and Brandon.
GD504	Papers of the Sprot Family of Haystoun, Peeblesshire.
JC62	Correspondence and Papers addressed to Robert Galbraith, merchant burgess in Edinburgh.
PA7	Supplementary Warrants and Parliamentary Papers.
RH9/2	Miscellaneous Letters and Autographs.
RH9/5	Foreign Papers.
RH9/17/32	Papers relative to Shipping.
RH15/32	Arthur Clephane, Seed Merchant in Edinburgh.
RH15/59	John Charteris, Merchant in Edinburgh.
RH15/106	Papers of Andrew Russell.

National Library of Scotland, Edinburgh

Acc.8100 (143)	Gray of Carntyre and Anstruther Gray of Kilmany.
Adv.mss.23.3.26	Eaglescarnie Papers.
Adv.mss.31.3.2	Account Book of Archibald Hamilton, Merchant in Edinburgh.
Ch.1657	Culloden Papers: Miscellaneous Affairs.
Ch.1673–5	Culloden Papers: Miscellaneous Affairs.
ms.5070–138	Erskine Murray Papers.
mss.88	*Memoires touchant l'ancienne alliance* (copy at AUSC ms213).
mss.98 (xiii)	Miscellaneous Letters and Documents.

University of St Andrews Special Collections

ms38352   Log-book of Alexander Gillespie.

ms38527   Watson Papers.

ENGLAND

National Archives at Kew, London

C47   Chancery Miscellanea.

E30   Exchequer: Treasury of Receipt: Diplomatic Documents.

HCA   Records of the High Court of Admiralty and Colonial Vice-Admiralty Courts.

PC   Records of the Privy Council.

SP9   State Papers: Williamson Collection, Pamphlets, Miscellaneous.

SP34   State Papers Domestic, Anne.

SP36   State Papers Domestic, George II.

SP47   State Papers Channel Islands.

SP54   State Papers Scotland, series II.

SP78   State Papers Foreign, France.

SP84   State Papers Foreign, Holland.

SP104   State Papers Foreign, Entry Books.

SP117   State Papers: Gazettes and Pamphlets, France.

FRANCE

Archives départementales de la Charente-Maritime, La Rochelle

Series B   Amirauté de marennes ou de saintonge.

Series B   Amirauté de la Rochelle.

Series B   Juridiction Consulaire de la Rochelle.

Archives départementales de la Gironde, Bordeaux

Series C   Chambre de Commerce.

Series 6 B   Amirauté de Guyenne.

Series 7 B   Fonds des Négociants.

Series 3 E   Notarial Registers.

Archives départementales de la Loire-Atlantique, Nantes

Series B   Chambre des comptes.

Series B   Amirauté de Nantes.
Series C   Administrations provinciales.
Series I   Etat civil protestant.

Archives départementales de Seine-Maritime, Rouen

200 BP   Juridiction consulaire de Dieppe.
214 BP   Amirauté de Dieppe.
216 BP   Amirauté du Havre.

Archives diplomatiques de la Corneuve, Paris

Affaires Étrangères, Mémoires et Documents (Angleterre) 7.

Archives municipales de Bordeaux

GG 854–77   Les registres paroissiaux de la ville de Bordeaux.

Archives municipales de Nantes

Series EE   Affaires Militaires: Marine.
Series GG   Aumônerie.
Series HH   Agriculture; Industrie; Commere.

Archives nationales, Paris

Series B[7]   Archives de la Marine: Pays étrangers, commerce et consulats.
Series J   Trésor des chartes.

DENMARK

Rigsarkivet (Danish Central State Archives), Copenhagen

Tyske Kancellis Udenrigske Afdeling, England.

SWEDEN

Riksarkivet (Swedish National Archives), Stockholm

Anglica VII, DXLII.

United States of America

Huntington Library, San Marino, California

HL89284   Ridpath, G., *Scotland's Grievances, relating to Darien, &c. Humbly Offered to the Consideration of the Parliament* ([Edinburgh], 1700).

HL434906   Battie, J., *The Merchants Remonstrance* (London, 1648).

HM49125–227 Black Family Papers.

Beinecke Library, Yale

OSB MSS 60   London Newsletters.

Printed Primary Sources

Acts of the Parliament of Scotland, 1124–1707, 12 vols (Edinburgh, 1814–44).

Anon., *The Tariff Settled by the French King and Council, September 18, 1664: Shewing the Duties Agreed to be Paid upon the Several Sorts of Merchandizes, Goods, Wares etc, being the Growth, Product and Manufactures of Great Britain, which should be Imported from England unto France* (London, 1713).

The Acts Done and Past in the Second, Third, Fourth and Fifth Sessions of the First Triennial Parliament of our Soveraigne Lord Charles, by the Grace of God, King of Scotland, England, France and Ireland, Defender of the Faith. Holden at Edinburgh, Stirling, Pearth, and S. Andrews Respective (Edinburgh, 1646).

Anderson, R. (ed.), *The Journals of Sir Thomas Allin, 1660–1678*, 2 vols (London: Navy Records Society, 1890).

Archives Canada France database at http://bd.archivescanadafrance.org/sdx-222-acf-pleade-2/acf/home.shtm [accessed 17 March 2009].

Articles Concluded at Paris the xxiiij of February 1605, stylo Angliae, by Commissioners of the High and Mightie Kings, James by the Grace of God King of Great Britaine, France, and Ireland, Defender of the Faith, &c. and Henrie the Fourth Most Christian French King, and King of Navar, for the More Commodious Entercourse in Traffique Betweene their Subjects (London, 1606).

Avenel, M. (ed.), *Lettres, instructions diplomatiques et papiers d'état du Cardinal de Richelieu*, 8 vols (Paris: Imprimerie impériale, 1853–77).

Bain, J. (ed.), *The Hamilton Papers*, 2 vols (Edinburgh: H. M. General Register House, 1890–2).

Balfour, P. J. (ed.), *The Scots Peerage: Founded on Wood's Edition of Sir Robert Douglas's Peerage of Scotland: Containing an Historical and Genealogical Account of the Nobility of that Kingdom*, 9 vols (Edinburgh: David Douglas, 1904–14).

British Mercury (newspaper), accessed via the *Burney Collection: 17th and 18th Century Newspapers* database.

Bryant, A. (ed.), *The Letters of King Charles II* (New York: Longmans, 1968).

Bund, N. (ed.), *Tabellr Overskibsfart Og Varetranspot Gennem Øresund, 1497–1660* (Copenhagen, 1906).

Calendar of Letters, Dispatches and State Papers relating to the Negotiations between England and Spain: Preserved in the Archives at Simancas and Elsewhere, 13 vols (London: H. M. S. O., 1862–1954).

Calendar of State Papers, Domestic Series (London: H. M. S. O., 1856–1927).

Calendar of Treasury Papers, 6 vols (London: Longman, 1868–89).

Calderwood, D., *The History of the Kirk of Scotland*, 8 vols (Edinburgh: Wodrow Society, 1842–9).

Cameron, A. (ed.), *The Warrender Papers*, 2 vols (Edinburgh: Edinburgh University Press, 1932).

Chéruel, A. (ed.), *Lettres du Cardinal Mazarin pendant son ministère*, 9 vols (Paris: Imprimerie nationale, 1872–1906).

Collection for Improvement of Husbandry and Trade (periodical), accessed via the *Burney Collection: 17th and 18th Century Newspapers* database.

Courthope, E. (ed.), *The Journal of Thomas Cuningham of Campvere, 1640–1654: With his Thrissels-banner and Explication Thereof* (Edinburgh: Scottish History Society, 1928).

Cramond, W. (ed.), *The Annals of Banff*, 2 vols (Aberdeen: Spalding Club, 1891–3).

Daily Courant (newspaper), accessed via the *Burney Collection: 17th and 18th Century Newspapers* database.

Defoe, D., *Essays upon Projects* (1697).

—, *Reasons Against a War with France or an Argument Shewing that the French King's Owning the Prince of Wales as King of England, Scotland and Ireland; is No Sufficient Ground of a War* (London, 1701).

—, *The Trade with France, Italy, Spain and Portugal Considered, with Some Observations on the Treaty of Commerce between Great Britain and France* (London, 1713).

Dickenson, W., and G. Donaldson (eds), *A Source Book of Scottish History*, 3 vols (Edinburgh: Nelson, 1958).

Firth, C. (ed.), *Scotland and the Commonwealth: Letters and Papers relating to the Military Government of Scotland, from August 1651 to December 1653* (Edinburgh: Scottish History Society, 1895).

Firth, C., and R. Rait (eds), *Acts and Ordinances of the Interregnum: 1642–1660*, 3 vols (London: H. M. S. O., 1911).

Flying-Post; or, The Post-Master (newspaper), accessed via the *Burney Collection: 17th and 18th Century Newspapers* database.

Fotheringham, J. (ed. and trans.), *The Diplomatic Correspondence of Jean de Montereul and the Brothers de Bellièvre: French Ambassadors in England and Scotland, 1645–48*, 2 vols (Edinburgh: Scottish History Society, 1898–9).

Fraser, W. (ed.), *The Earls of Cromertie, their Kindred, Country and Correspondence*, 2 vols (Edinburgh, 1876).

Gardiner, S. (ed.), *The Constitutional Documents of the Puritan Revolution, 1625–1660* (Oxford: Clarendon Press, 1899).

Historical Manuscripts Commission, *Fourteenth Report, The Manuscripts of the House of Lords, 1692–1693* (London: H. M. S. O., 1894).

—, *Report on the Manuscripts of the Duke of Buccleuch and Queensberry*, 2 vols (London: H. M. S. O., 1899–1926).

—, *Calendar of Stuart Papers belonging to His Majesty the King, preserved at Windsor Castle*, 7 vols (London: H. M. S. O., 1902–23).

—, *Report on the manuscripts of Lord Polwarth*, 3 vols (London: H. M. S. O., 1911–31).

Hume-Brown, P. (ed.), *James Ogilvy, First Earl of Seafield and Others: Letters relating to Scotland in the Reign of Queen Anne* (Edinburgh: Scottish History Society, 1915).

Laing, D. (ed.), *The Letters and Journals of Robert Baillie, Principal of the University of Glasgow 1637–1662*, 3 vols (Edinburgh: Alex Lawrie & Co., 1841).

Lenman, B., and J. Gibson (eds), *The Jacobite Threat, England, Scotland, Ireland, France: A Source Book* (Edinburgh: Scottish Academic Press, 1990).

London Gazette (newspaper), accessed via the *Burney Collection: 17th and 18th Century Newspapers* database.

Lyle, J. (ed.), *Acts of the Privy Council of England: New Series*, 45 vols (London: H. M. S. O., 1890–1964).

MacDonald, A. (ed.), *Papers relative to the Royal Guard of Scottish Archers in France* (Edinburgh: Maitland, 1835).

Mackie, J. (ed.), *Calendar of State Papers relating to Scotland and Mary Queen of Scots, 1547–1603*, 9 vols (Edinburgh: H. M. S. O., 1898–1969).

Macray, W. (ed.), *Correspondence of Colonel Hooke*, 2 vols (London: J. B. Nichols and Sons, 1870–1).

Marwick, J. (ed.), *Records of the Convention of the Royal Burghs of Scotland: with Extracts from other Records relating to the Affairs of the Burghs of Scotland, 1295–1711*, 5 vols (Edinburgh: William Paterson, 1866–80).

Mercator (newspaper), accessed via the *Burney Collection: 17th and 18th Century Newspapers* database.

Millar, A. (ed.), *The Compt Buik of David Wedderburne, Merchant of Dundee, 1587–1630* (Edinburgh: Scottish History Society, 1989).

Moncrieff, T. (ed.), *Memoirs concerning the Ancient Alliance between the French and the Scots and the Privileges of the Scots in France* (Edinburgh: W. Cheyne, 1751).

Post-Man and the Historical Account (newspaper), accessed via the *Burney Collection: 17th and 18th Century Newspapers* database.

Records of the Parliaments of Scotland to 1707, online at http://www.rps.ac.uk/ [accessed 30 September 2013].

Register of the Privy Council of Scotland, 38 vols (Edinburgh: Oliver & Boyd, 1877–1970).

Review of the State of the British Nation (periodical), accessed via the *Burney Collection: 17th and 18th Century Newspapers* database.

Roberts, F., and I. MacPhail (eds), *Dumbarton Common Good Accounts, 1614–1660* (Dumbarton: Lennox Herald, 1972).

Review of the Affairs of France (periodical), accessed via the *Burney Collection: 17ᵗʰ and 18ᵗʰ Century Newspapers* database.

Spalding, J., *Memorialls of the Trubles in Scotland and England, AD 1624–AD 1645*, ed. J. Stuart, 2 vols (Aberdeen: Spalding Club, 1850–1).

Spottiswoode, J., *The History of the Church of Scotland* (Menston, Yorkshire: Scolar Press, 1972).

Stuart, J. (ed.), *Extracts from the Council Register of the Burgh of Aberdeen*, 2 vols (Edinburgh: Spalding Club, 1871–2).

Tatler (periodical), accessed via the *Burney Collection: 17ᵗʰ and 18ᵗʰ Century Newspapers* online database.

Taylor, L. (ed.), *Aberdeen Council Letters*, 6 vols (Oxford: Oxford University Press, 1942–61).

— (ed.), *Aberdeen Shore Work Accounts, 1596–1670* (Aberdeen: Aberdeen University Press, 1972).

Teulet, A. (ed.), *Relations Politiques de la France et de l'Espagne avec l'Écosse au XVIe Siècle (1515–1561) / State Papers relating to France and Scotland in the 16th Century (1513–1561)*, 5 vols (Paris: Renouard, 1862).

Thompson, T. (ed.), *Memoirs of his Own Life by Sir James Melville of Halhill* (Edinburgh: Bannatyne Club, 1827).

Welwood, W., *An Abridgement of All Sea-Lawes; Gathered Forth of All Writings and Monuments, which are to be Found Among Any People or Nation, upon the Coasts of the Great Ocean and Mediterranean Sea: And Specially Ordered and Disposed for the Use and Benefit of All Benevolent Sea-Farers, Within his Majesties Dominions of Great Britanne, Ireland, and the Adjacent Isles Therof* (London: Humfrey Lownes for Thomas Man, 1613).

Secondary Sources

Agnew, J., *Belfast Merchant Families in the Seventeenth Century* (Dublin: Four Courts Press, 1996).

Allan, D., 'The Enlightenment and the Book' (review), *Library*, 8:4 (2007), pp. 456–8.

d'Ambrières, R., and E. Ó Ciosáin, 'Irish Bishops and Clergy in Exile in Mid-Seventeenth-Century France', *Irish Historical Studies*, 24:141 (2008), pp. 16–37.

Anderson, J., *The Burgesses and Guild Brethren of Glasgow, 1573–1750* (Edinburgh: J. Skinner, 1925).

Aston, T. (ed.), *Crisis in Europe 1560–1660: Essays from Past and Present* (London: Routledge, 1965).

Ball, J., *Merchants and Merchandise: The Expansion of Trade in Europe, 1500–1630* (London: Croon Helm, 1977).

Bamford, P., 'French Shipping in Northern European Trade, 1660–1789', *Journal of Modern History*, 26:3 (1954), pp. 207–19.

Barbour, V., 'Dutch and English Merchant Shipping in the Seventeenth Century', in P. Emmer and F. Gaastra (eds), *The Organization of Interoceanic Trade in European Expansion, 1450–1800* (Aldershot: Variorum, 1996), pp. 103–32.

Barclay, K., and S. Talbott, 'New Perspectives on Seventeenth- and Eighteenth-Century Scotland', *Journal of Scottish Historical Studies*, 31:1 (2011), pp. 119–33.

Barclay, T., and E. Graham, *The Early Transatlantic Trade of Ayr, 1640–1730* (Ayr: Ayrshire Archaeological and Natural History Society, 2005).

Bayard, F., 'Naturalization in Lyon during the Ancien Régime', *French History*, 4:3 (1990), pp. 277–316.

Bell, D., *The First Total War: Napoleon's Europe and the Birth of Modern War* (London: Bloomsbury, 2007).

—, 'The Limits of Conflict in Napoleonic Europe – and their Transgression', in E. Charters, E. Rosenhaft and H. Smith (eds), *Civilians and War in Europe, 1618–1815* (Liverpool: Liverpool University Press, 2012), pp. 201–8.

Ben-Porath, Y., 'The F-Connection: Families, Friends, and Firms and the Organisation of Exchange', *Population and Development Review*, 6:1 (1980), pp. 1–30.

Benedict, P., *Rouen during the Wars of Religion* (Cambridge: Cambridge University Press, 1981).

Black, J., 'Was there a Military Revolution in Early Modern Europe?', *History Today*, 58:7 (2008), pp. 34–41.

Bonner, E., 'Continuing the "Auld Alliance" in the Sixteenth Century: Scots in France and French in Scotland', in G. Simpson (ed.), *The Scottish Soldier Abroad, 1247–1967* (Edinburgh: John Donald, 1992), pp. 31–46.

—, 'French Naturalization of the Scots in the Fifteenth and Sixteenth Centuries', *Historical Journal*, 40:4 (1997), pp. 1085–115.

—, 'Scotland's "Auld Alliance" with France', *History*, 84:273 (1999), pp. 5–30.

Bonney, R., *The King's Debts: Finance and Politics in France, 1589–1661* (Oxford: Clarendon Press, 1981).

Bosher, J., 'The Gaigneur Clan in the Seventeenth-Century Canadian Trade', in O. Janzen (ed.), *Merchant Organization and Maritime Trade in the North Atlantic, 1660–1815* (St Johns, Newfoundland: International Maritime Economic History Association, 1998), pp. 15–51.

Bossenga, G., 'Society', in W. Doyle (ed.), *Old Regime France* (Oxford: Oxford University Press, 2001), pp. 43–72.

Boulle, P., 'French Mercantilism, Commercial Companies and Colonial Profitability', in P. Emmer and F. Gaastra, *The Organization of Interoceanic Trade in European Expansion, 1450–1800* (Aldershot: Variorum, 1996), pp. 233–54.

Brennan, T., *Burgundy to Champagne: the Wine Trade in Early Modern France* (Baltimore, MD: Johns Hopkins University Press, 1997).

Brewer, J., *The Sinews of Power: War, Money and the English State, 1688–1783* (London: Unwin Hyman, 1989).

Broadie, A., *Agreeable Connexions: Scottish Enlightenment Links with France* (Edinburgh: John Donald, 2013).

Bromley, J., 'The Jacobite Privateers in the Nine Years' War', in A. Whiteman, J. Bromley and P. Dickson (eds), *Statesman, Scholars and Merchants: Essays in Eighteenth-Century History Presented to Dame Lucy Sutherland* (Oxford: Clarendon, 1973), pp. 17–43.

Bruijn, J., 'Dutch Privateering during the Second and Third Anglo-Dutch Wars', *Low Countries History Yearbook: Acta Historicae Neerlandicae*, 11 (1978), pp. 79–93.

de Bruyn Kops, H., *A Spirited Exchange: the Wine and Brandy Trade between France and the Dutch Republic in its Atlantic Framework, 1600–1650* (Leiden: Brill, 2007).

Cameron, A., 'Scottish Students at Paris University 1466–1492', *Juridical Review*, 48 (1936), pp. 228–55.

Canny, N., 'Writing Early Modern History: Ireland, Britain and the Wider World', *Historical Journal*, 46:3 (2003), pp. 723–47.

Casada, J., 'The Scottish Representation in Richard Cromwell's Parliament', *Scottish Historical Review*, 51:152 (1972), pp. 124–47.

Catterall, D., *Community Without Borders: Scots Migrants and the Changing Face of Power in the Dutch Republic, c. 1600–1700* (Leiden: Brill, 2002).

Charters, E., E. Rosenhaft and H. Smith (eds), 'Introduction', to *Civilians and War in Europe, 1618–1815* (Liverpool: Liverpool University Press, 2012), pp. 1–21.

Claydon, T., *William III and the Godly Revolution* (Cambridge: Cambridge University Press, 1996).

Cogswell, T., 'Foreign Policy and Parliament: The Case of La Rochelle, 1625–26', *English Historical Review*, 99:391 (1984), pp. 241–67.

Cole, C., *Colbert and a Century of French Mercantilism*, 2 vols (London: Frank Cass, 1964).

Colley, L., *Britons: Forging the Nation, 1707–1837* (Yale, CT: Yale University Press, 1992).

Condliffe, J., *The Commerce of Nations* (London: George Allen & Unwin, 1951).

Contamine, P., 'Scottish Soldiers in France in the Second Half of the Fifteenth Century: Mercenaries, Immigrants or Frenchmen in the Making?', in G. Simpson (ed.), *The Scottish Soldier Abroad, 1247–1967* (Edinburgh: John Donald, 1992), pp. 16–30.

Cornette, J., *Chronique de Règne de Louis XIV: de la fin de la Fronde à l'aube des Lumières* (Paris: Sedes, 1997).

Corp, E., 'The Jacobite Presence in Toulouse during the Eighteenth Century', *Diasporas, Histoire et Sociétés*, 5 (2004), pp. 124–45.

Croft, P., 'Trading with the Enemy, 1585–1604', *Historical Journal*, 32:2 (1989), pp. 281–302.

Crowhurst, P., *The Defence of British Trade, 1689–1815* (Folkestone, Kent: Dawson & Sons, 1977).

Cruickshanks, E., *The Glorious Revolution* (Basingstoke, Hampshire: Palgrave Macmillan, 2000).

Cullen, L., 'The Smuggling Trade in Ireland in the Eighteenth Century', *Proceedings of the Royal Irish Academy*, 67 (1969), pp. 149–75.

—, 'The Irish Merchant Communities of Bordeaux, La Rochelle and Cognac in the Eighteenth Century', in P. Butel and L. Cullen (eds), *Négoce et industrie en France et en Irlande aux XVIII et XIX siecles* (Paris: Éditions du Centre national de la recherche scientifique, 1980), pp. 51–63.

—, *The Brandy Trade under the Ancien Régime: Regional Specialization in the Charente* (Cambridge: Cambridge University Press, 1998).

—, 'Apotheosis and Crisis: The Irish Diaspora in the Age of Choiseul', in T. O'Connor, and M. Lyons (eds), *Irish Communities in Early Modern Europe* (Dublin: Four Courts Press, 2006), pp. 6–31.

Cummings, A., 'Scotland's Links with Europe, 1600–1800', *History Today*, 35 (1985), pp. 45–9.

Davidson, J., and A. Gray, *The Scottish Staple at Veere: A Study in the Economic History of Scotland* (London: Longmans, 1905).

Dawson, D., and P. Morère (eds), *Scotland and France in the Enlightenment* (Lewisburg: Bucknell University Press, 2004).

Devine, T., 'The Cromwellian Union and the Scottish Burghs', in J. Butt and J. Ward (eds), *Scottish Themes: Essays in Honour of Professor S. G. E. Lythe* (Edinburgh: Scottish Academic Press, 1976), pp. 1–16.

—, *Scotland's Empire, 1600–1815* (London: Allen Lane, 2003).

—, 'The Spoils of Empire', in T. Devine (ed.), *Scotland and the Union, 1707–2007* (Edinburgh: Edinburgh University Press, 2008), pp. 91–108.

Dickson, D., *New Foundations: Ireland, 1600–1800* (Dublin: Helicon, 1987).

—, 'The Cork Merchant Community in the Eighteenth Century: A Regional Perspective', in L. Cullen and P. Butel (eds), *Négoce et industrie en France et en Irlande aux XVIIIe et XIXe siècles* (Paris: Éditions du Centre national de la recherche scientifique, 1980), pp. 45–50.

—, *Old World Colony: Cork and South Munster, 1630–1830* (Madison, WI: University of Wisconsin Press, 2005).

—, 'Introduction', to D. Dickson, J. Parmentier and J. Ohlmeyer (eds), *Irish and Scottish Mercantile Networks in Europe and Overseas in the Seventeenth and Eighteenth Centuries* (Gent: Academia Press, 2007), pp. 1–4.

Dietz, B., 'England's Overseas Trade in the Reign of James I', in A. Smith (ed.), *The Reign of James VI and I* (New York: St Martin's Press, 1973), pp. 106–23.

Ditchburn, D., *Scotland and Europe: the Medieval Kingdom and its Contacts with Christendom, 1215–1545, Volume I: 'Religion, Culture and Commerce'* (East Linton: Tuckwell Press, 2001).

Ditchburn, D., and A. MacDonald, 'Medieval Scotland, 1100–1560', in R. Houston and W. Knox (eds), *The New Penguin History of Scotland: From the Earliest Times to the Present Day* (London: Penguin, 2001), pp. 96–181.

Dobson, D., *Scottish Trade with Colonial Charleston, 1683–1783* (Glasgow: Humming Earth, 2009).

Donagan, B., 'War, Property and the Bonds of Society: England's "Unnatural" Civil Wars', in E. Charters, E. Rosenhaft and H. Smith (eds), *Civilians and War in Europe, 1618–1815* (Liverpool: Liverpool University Press, 2012), pp. 52–67.

Donaldson, G., *Scotland, James V–James VII* (Edinburgh: Oliver & Boyd, 1965).

Dow, J., 'A Comparative Note on the Sound Toll Registers, Stockholm Customs Accounts, and Dundee Shipping Lists, 1589, 1613–1622', *Scandinavian Economic History Review*, 12:1 (1964), pp. 79–85.

Drummond, A., *The Kirk and the Continent* (Edinburgh: Saint Andrew Press, 1956).

Durkan, J., 'The French Connection in the Sixteenth and Early Seventeenth Centuries', in T. C. Smout (ed.), *Scotland and Europe 1200–1850* (Edinburgh: John Donald, 1986), pp. 19–44.

Enthoven, V., 'Thomas Cunningham (1604–1669): Conservator of the Scottish Court at Veere', in D. Dickson, J. Parmentier and J. Ohlmeyer (eds), *Irish and Scottish Mercantile Networks in Europe and Overseas in the Seventeenth and Eighteenth Centuries* (Gent: Academia Press, 2007), pp. 39–66.

Enthoven, V., S. Murdoch and E. Williamson (eds), *The Navigator: The Log of John Anderson, VOC Pilot-Major, 1640–1643* (Leiden: Brill, 2010).

Fannin, S., 'The Irish Community in Eighteenth-century Cadiz', in T. O'Connor and M. Lyons (eds), *Irish Migrants in Europe after Kinsale, 1602–1820* (Dublin: Four Courts Press, 2003), pp. 135–48.

Félix, J., 'The Economy', trans. D. Bell, in W. Doyle (ed.), *Old Regime France* (Oxford: Oxford University Press, 2001), pp. 7–41.

Fenwick, H., *The Auld Alliance* (Kineton: Roundwood Press, 1971).

Fleming, J. A., *The Medieval Scots Scholar in France* (Glasgow: W. Maclellan, 1952).

Fontaine, L., 'Antonio and Shylock: Credit and Trust in France, c. 1680–c. 1780', *Economic History Review*, 54:1 (2001), pp. 39–57.

Forbes-Leith, W., *The Scots Men-at-Arms and Life-Guards in France* (Edinburgh: W. Paterson, 1882).

Forte, A., 'Marine Insurance and Risk Distribution in Scotland before 1800', *Law and History Review*, 5:2 (1987), pp. 393–412.

Francis, A., *The Wine Trade* (London: A&C Black, 1972).

Furgol, E., 'Scotland Turned Sweden: The Scottish Covenanters and the Military Revolution, 1638–1651', in J. Morrill (ed.), *The Scottish National Covenant in its British Context, 1638–51* (Edinburgh: Edinburgh University Press, 1990), pp. 134–54.

Gardner, G., *The Scottish Exile Community in the Netherlands, 1660–1690* (East Linton: Tuckwell Press, 2004).

Glozier, M., 'Scots in the French and Dutch Armies during the Thirty Years' War', in S. Murdoch (ed.), *Scotland and the Thirty Years' War* (Leiden: Brill, 2001), pp. 117–142.

—, *Scottish Soldiers in France in the Reign of the Sun King* (Leiden: Brill, 2004).

Graham, E., 'The Scottish Marine during the Dutch Wars', *Scottish Historical Review*, 61 (1982), pp. 67–74.

—, 'In Defence of the Scottish Maritime Interest, 1681–1713', *Scottish Historical Review*, 81 (1992), pp. 88–109.

—, *A Maritime History of Scotland, 1650–1790* (East Linton: Tuckwell Press, 2002).

Grant, I., *Social and Economic Development in Scotland before 1603* (London: Oliver & Boyd, 1930).

—, *The Economic History of Scotland* (London: Longmans Green, 1934).

Grassby, R., 'Social Status and Commercial Enterprise under Louis IV', in R. Kierstead (ed.), *State and Society in Seventeenth-Century France* (New York: New Viewpoints, 1975), pp. 200–32.

Grosjean, A., *An Unofficial Alliance: Scotland and Sweden, 1569–1654* (Leiden: Brill, 2003).

Grosjean, A., and S. Murdoch, 'The Scottish Community in Seventeenth-Century Gothenburg', in A. Grosjean and S. Murdoch (eds), *Scottish Communities Abroad in the Early Modern Period* (Leiden: Brill, 2005), pp. 191–223.

Guthrie, W., *A General History of Scotland from the Earliest Accounts to the Present Time*, 10 vols (London: Robinson & Roberts, 1768).

Guy, I., 'The Scottish Export Trade, 1460–1599', in T. C. Smout (ed.), *Scotland and Europe, 1200–1850* (Edinburgh: John Donald, 1986), pp. 62–81.

Haggerty, S., *The British-Atlantic Trading Community, 1760–1810: Men, Women and the Distribution of Goods* (Leiden: Brill, 2006).

—, '"You Promise Well and Perform as Badly": The Failure of the "Implicit Contract of Family" in the Scottish Atlantic', *International Journal of Maritime History*, 33:2 (2011), pp. 267–82.

—, *'Merely for Money'?: Business Culture in the British Atlantic, 1750–1815* (Liverpool: Liverpool University Press, 2013).

Hamilton, H., *An Economic History of Scotland in the Eighteenth Century* (Oxford: Clarendon Press, 1963).

Hancock, D., 'Combining Success and Failure: Scottish Networks in the Atlantic Wine Trade', in D. Dickson, J. Parmentier and J. Ohlmeyer (eds), *Irish and Scottish Mercantile Networks in Europe and Overseas in the Seventeenth and Eighteenth Centuries* (Gent: Academia Press, 2007), pp. 5–38.

Hauser, H., *La Pensée et l'action économiques du Cardinal de Richelieu* (Paris: Presses Universitaires de France, 1944).

Hayes, R., *Old Irish Links with France: Some Echoes of Exiled Ireland* (Dublin: M. H. Gill & Son, 1940).

Hobsbawm, E., 'The General Crisis of the Seventeenth Century', *Past & Present*, 6 (1954), pp. 44–65.

Hoffman, P., 'Rural, Urban and Global Economies', in M. Holt (ed.), *Renaissance and Reformation France, 1500–1648* (Oxford: Oxford University Press, 2002), pp. 62–98.

Holmes, G., 'Introduction', to G. Holmes (ed.), *Britain After the Glorious Revolution* (London: Macmillan, 1969), pp. 1–38.

Holt, M., *The French Wars of Religion, 1562–1629* (Cambridge: Cambridge University Press, 1995).

Hopper, A., *The World of John Secker (1716–95), Quaker Mariner* (Norfolk: Norfolk Record Society, 2011).

Houston, R., 'The Scots Kirk, Rotterdam, 1643–1795: A Dutch or Scottish Church?', in J. Roding and L. van Voss (eds), *The North Sea and Culture, 1550–1800* (Hilversum: Verloren, 1996), pp. 266–84.

Howat, G., *Stuart and Cromwellian Foreign Policy* (London: A&C Black, 1974).

Jones, J., *Britain and Europe in the Seventeenth Century* (London: Edward Arnold Ltd, 1966).

—, *War and Economy in the Age of William III and Marlborough* (Oxford: Basil Blackwell, 1988).

— (ed.), *Liberty Secured? Britain Before and After the Glorious Revolution* (Stanford, CA: Stanford University Press, 1992).

—, 'The Revolution in Context', in Jones (ed.), *Liberty Secured? Britain Before and After the Glorious Revolution*, pp. 25–52.

—, *The Anglo-Dutch Wars of the Seventeenth Century* (London: Longman, 1996).

Kay, B., *The Scottish World: A Journey into the Scottish Diaspora* (Edinburgh: Mainstream Publishing, 2006).

Kay, B., and C. Maclean, *Knee Deep in Claret: A Celebration of Wine and Scotland* (Isle of Skye: Auld Alliance Publishing, 1994).

Keith, T., 'The Economic Condition of Scotland under the Commonwealth and Protectorate', *Scottish Historical Review*, 5:19 (1908), pp. 273–84.

—, 'The Economic Causes for the Scottish Union', *English Historical Review*, 24:93 (1909), pp. 44–60.

—, *Commercial Relations of England and Scotland, 1603–1707* (Cambridge: Cambridge University Press, 1910).

Knecht, R., *Richelieu* (Essex: Longman, 1991).

Laidlaw, J. (ed.), *The Auld Alliance; France and Scotland over 700 Years* (Edinburgh: Edinburgh University Press, 2011).

Lamikiz, X., *Trade and Trust in the Eighteenth-century Atlantic World: Spanish Merchants and their Overseas Networks* (Suffolk: Boydell & Brewer, 2010).

Lee, M., *The Road to Revolution, Scotland under Charles I, 1625–37* (Illinois: University of Illinois Press, 1985).

Lenman, B., 'The Scottish Episcopal Clergy and the Ideology of Jacobitism', in E. Cruickshanks (ed.), *Ideology and Conspiracy: Aspects of Jacobitism, 1689–1759* (Edinburgh: John Donald, 1982), pp. 36–48.

Levasseur, E., *Histoire du Commerce de la France*, 2 vols (Paris: Rousseau, 1911).

Little, A., 'A Comparative Survey of Scottish Service in the English and Dutch Maritime Communities c. 1650–1707', in A. Grosjean and S. Murdoch (eds), *Scottish Communities Abroad in the Early Modern Period* (Leiden: Brill, 2005), pp. 332–62.

Lynch, M., *Scotland, A New History* (London: Pimlico, 1992).

Lyons, M., 'The Emergence of an Irish Community in Saint-Malo, 1550–1710', in T. O'Connor and M. Lyons (eds), *The Irish in Europe, 1580–1815* (Dublin: Four Courts Press, 2001), pp. 107–26.

Lythe, S. G. E., *The Economy of Scotland in its European Setting, 1550–1625* (London: Oliver & Boyd, 1960).

Lythe, S. G. E., and J. Butt, *An Economic History of Scotland, 1100–1939* (Glasgow: Blackie, 1975).

MacDonald, A., *The Burghs and Parliament in Scotland, c. 1550–1651* (Aldershot: Ashgate, 2007).

MacDougall, N., *An Antidote to the English: The Auld Alliance, 1295–1560* (East Linton: Tuckwell Press, 1988).

Mackie, J., 'Henry VIII and Scotland', *Transactions of the Royal Historical Society*, 29 (1947), pp. 93–114.

Mackillop, A., 'A Union for Empire? Scotland, the English East India Company and the British Union', in S. Brown and C. Whatley (eds), *Union of 1707: New Dimensions, Scottish Historical Review*, supplementary issue (Edinburgh: Edinburgh University Press, 2008), pp. 116–34.

Macinnes, A., *The British Revolution, 1629–1660* (Basingstoke, Hampshire: Palgrave Macmillan, 2005).

—, *Union and Empire: The Making of the United Kingdom in 1707* (Cambridge: Cambridge University Press, 2007).

Mackenney, R., *Tradesmen and Trades: The World of the Guilds in Venice and Europe, c. 1250– c. 1650* (London: Croon Helm, 1987).

Macpherson, J., 'Auld Alliance', *Scottish Field*, 114 (1967), p. 41.

Mathias, P., 'Risk, Credit and Kinship in Early Modern Enterprise', in J. McCusker and K. Morgan (eds), *The Early Modern Atlantic Economy* (Cambridge: Cambridge University Press, 2000), pp. 15–35.

Mauro, F., 'Merchant Communities, 1350–1750', in J. Tracy (ed.), *The Rise of Merchant Empires: Long Distance Trade in the Early Modern World, 1350–1750* (Cambridge: Cambridge University Press, 1990), pp. 255–86.

McLynn, F., *The Jacobites* (London: Routledge & Kegan Paul, 1985).

McNeill, P., and H. MacQueen (eds), *Atlas of Scottish History to 1707* (Edinburgh: Edinburgh University Press, 1996).

Mijers, E., *'News from the Republick of Letters': Scottish Students, Charles Mackie and the United Provinces, 1650–1750* (Leiden: Brill, 2012).

Miller, J., 'Crown, Parliament and People', in J. Jones (ed.), *Liberty Secured? Britain Before and After the Glorious Revolution* (Stanford, CA: Stanford University Press, 1992), pp. 53–87.

Mollat, M., *Le commerce maritime normand à la fin du Moyen Age: étude d'histoire économique et sociale* (Paris: Librairie Pion, 1952).

Monod, P., 'Dangerous Merchandise: Smuggling, Jacobitism, and Commercial Culture in Southeast England, 1690–1760', *Journal of British Studies*, 30:2 (1991), pp. 150–82.

Montagu, V., 'The Scottish College in Paris', *Scottish Historical Review*, 4:16 (1907), pp. 399–416.

Mousnier, R., J. Elliott, L. Stone, H. Trevor-Roper, E. Kossman, E. Hobsbawm and J. Hexter, 'Discussion of H. R. Trevor-Roper, "The General Crisis of the Seventeenth Century"', *Past & Present*, 18 (1960), pp. 8–42.

Mowat, S., *The Port of Leith: Its History and its People* (Edinburgh: Forth Ports & John Donald, 1994).

Murdoch, S., 'Introduction', to S. Murdoch (ed.), *Scotland and the Thirty Years' War* (Leiden: Brill, 2001), pp. 1–23.

—, *Britain, Denmark-Norway and the House of Stuart, 1603–1660: A Diplomatic and Military Analysis* (East Linton: Tuckwell Press, 2003).

—, *Network North: Scottish Kin, Commercial and Covert Association in Northern Europe, 1603–1746* (Leiden: Brill, 2006).

—, 'Irish Entrepreneurs and Sweden in the First Half of the Eighteenth Century', in T. O'Connor and M. Lyons (eds), *Irish Communities in Early Modern Europe* (Dublin: Four Courts Press, 2006), pp. 348–66.

—, 'Fabricating Nobility?: Genealogy and Social Mobility among Franco-Scottish Families in the Early Modern Period', *Ranam: Recherches Anglaise et Américaines*, 40 (2007), pp. 37–52.

—, 'Scotland and Europe', in B. Harris and A. MacDonald (eds), *Scotland: The Making and Unmaking of the Nation, c. 1100–1707* (Dundee: Dundee University Press, 2007), pp. 126–44.

—, 'The French Connection: Bordeaux's "Scottish" Networks in Context, c. 1670–1720', in G. Leydier, *Scotland and Europe, Scotland in Europe* (Newcastle: Cambridge Scholars Publishing, 2007), pp. 26–55.

—, 'Community, Commodity and Commerce: The Stockholm–Scots in the Seventeenth Century', in D. Worthington (ed.), *British and Irish Emigrants and Exiles in Europe, 1603–1688* (Leiden: Brill, 2010), pp. 31–66.

—, *The Terror of the Seas? Scottish Maritime Warfare, 1513–1713* (Leiden: Brill, 2010).

—, 'The Repatriation of Capital to Scotland: A Case Study of Dutch Testaments and Notarial Instruments 1560–1707', in M. Varricchio (ed.), *Back to Caledonia: Scottish Return Migration from the Seventeenth Century to the Present* (Edinburgh: John Donald, 2012), pp. 34–53.

Murphy, E., '"No Affair Before us of Greater Concern": The War at Sea in Ireland, 1641–1645' (unpublished PhD thesis, Trinity College Dublin, 2008).

Nash, R. C., 'The Economy', in J. Bergin (ed.), *The Seventeenth Century* (Oxford: Oxford University Press, 2001), pp. 11–49.

Nordmann, C., 'Les Jacobites Ecossais en France au XVIIIe Siècle', in M. Plaisant (ed.), *Regards sur l'Ecosse au XVIIIe siècle* (Lille: Villeneuve d'Asq, University of Lille, 1977), pp. 80–108.

Ó Ciosáin, É., 'Regrouping in Exile: Irish Communities in Western France in the Seventeenth Century', in R. Armstrong and T. Ó hAnnracháin (eds), *Community in Early Modern Ireland* (Dublin: Four Courts Press, 2006), pp. 133–53.

—, 'Hidden by 1688 and After: Irish Catholic Migration to France, 1590–1685', in D. Worthington (ed.), *British and Irish Emigrants and Exiles in Europe, 1603–1688* (Leiden: Brill, 2010), pp. 125–38.

Ó Ciosáin, É., and A. L. de Forville, 'Irish Nuns in Nantes, 1650–1659', *Archivium Hibernicum*, 58 (2004), pp. 167–73.

O'Connor, P., 'Irish Clerics and Jacobites in Early Eighteenth-Century Paris, 1700–30', in T. O'Connor and M. Lyons (eds), *The Irish in Europe 1580–1815* (Dublin: Four Courts Press, 2001), pp. 175–90.

Ogilvie, S., 'Germany and the Seventeenth-Century Crisis', *Historical Journal*, 35:2 (1992), pp. 417–41.

Ohlmeyer, J., 'Irish Privateers during the Civil War, 1642–50', *Mariner's Mirror*, 76 (1990), pp. 119–33.

—, 'Seventeenth-Century Ireland and Scotland and their Wider Worlds', in T. O'Connor, and M. Lyons (eds), *Irish Communities in Early Modern Europe* (Dublin: Four Courts Press, 2006), pp. 457–83.

Pagan, T., *The Convention of the Royal Burghs of Scotland* (Glasgow: Glasgow University Press, 1926).

Palm, F., 'The Siege and Capture of La Rochelle in 1628: Its Economic Significance', *Journal of Political Economy*, 31:1 (1923), pp. 114–27.

—, 'Mercantilism as a Factor in Richelieu's Policy of National Interests', *Political Science Quarterly*, 39:4 (1924), pp. 650–64.

Parker, D., *La Rochelle and the French Monarchy: Conflict and Order in Seventeenth Century France* (London: Royal Historical Society, 1980).

Parker, G., and L. Smith (eds), *The General Crisis of the Seventeenth Century* (London: Routledge, 1978).

Parker, G. (ed.), *The Thirty Years' War* (London: Routledge and Kegan Paul, 1984).

—, *The Military Revolution, 1500–1800* (Cambridge: Cambridge University Press, 1996).

Parmentier, J., 'The Ray Dynasty: Irish Mercantile Empire Builders in Ostend, 1690–1790', in T. O'Connor and M. Lyons (eds), *Irish Communities in Early Modern Europe* (Dublin: Four Courts Press, 2006), pp. 367–82.

Pinckney, P., 'The Scottish Representation in the Cromwellian Parliament of 1656', *Scottish Historical Review*, 46:142 (1967), pp. 95–114.

Pocock, J. G. A., 'British History: A Plea for a New Subject', *Journal of Modern History*, 47:4 (1975), pp. 601–21.

—, 'The Limits and Divisions of British History: In Search of an Unknown Subject', *American Historical Review*, 87:2 (1982), pp. 311–36.

Recio Morales, O., 'Identity and Loyalty: Irish Traders in Seventeenth-Century Iberia', in D. Dickson, J. Parmentier and J. Ohlmeyer (eds), *Irish and Scottish Mercantile Networks in Europe and Overseas in the Seventeenth and Eighteenth Centuries* (Gent: Academia Press, 2007), pp. 197–210.

Riddell, J., *Remarks upon Scotch Peerage Law* (Edinburgh: T. Clark, 1833).

de Ridder-Symoens, H. (ed.), *A History of the University in Europe, Volume II: Universities in Early Modern Europe, 1500–1800* (Cambridge: Cambridge University Press, 2003).

Roberts, J., *The Military Revolution* (Belfast: M. Boyd, 1956).

Rommelse, G., 'English Privateering against the Dutch Republic during the Second Anglo-Dutch War (1664–7)', *Tijdschrift voor overdruk zeegeschiedenis*, 22 (2003), pp. 17–31.

—, *The Second Anglo-Dutch War (1665–1667): Raison d'état, Mercantilism and Maritime Strife* (Hilversum: Verloren, 2006).

Rooseboom, M., *The Scottish Staple in the Netherlands* (The Hague: M. Nijhoff, 1910).

Roseveare, H., 'Merchant Organization and Maritime Trade in the North Atlantic, 1660–1815: Some Reflections', in O. Janzen (ed.), *Merchant Organization and Maritime Trade in the North Atlantic, 1660–1815* (St Johns, Newfoundland: International Maritime Economic History Association, 1998), pp. 259–67.

Rössner, P., *Scottish Trade in the Wake of Union (1700–1760)* (Stuttgart: Franz Steiner Verlag, 2008).

Rowlands, G., *The Dynastic State and the Army under Louis XIV: Royal Service and Private Interest, 1661–1701* (Cambridge: Cambridge University Press, 2002).

—, 'France 1709: Le Crunch', *History Today*, 59:2 (2009), pp. 42–7.

Saupin, G., 'Les Réseaux Commerciaux des Irlandais de Nantes sous le Règne de Louis XIV', in D. Dickson, J. Parmentier and J. Ohlmeyer (eds), *Irish and Scottish Mercantile Networks in Europe and Overseas in the Seventeenth and Eighteenth Centuries* (Gent: Academia Press, 2007), pp. 115–46.

Savary, J., *Le Parfait Négociant*, 2 vols (Paris: Chez les frères Estienne, 1777 edition).

Sahlins, P., *Unnaturally French: Foreign Citizens in the Old Regime and After* (London: Cornell University Press, 2004).

Schaeper, T., *The French Council of Commerce, 1700–1715: A Study of Mercantilism after Colbert* (Columbus, OH: Ohio State University Press, 1983).

Scoville, W., 'The French Economy in 1700–1701: An Appraisal by the Deputies of Trade', *Journal of Economic History*, 22:2 (1962), pp. 231–52.

—, *Persecution of Huguenots and French Economic Development 1680–1720* (Whitefish, Montana: Kessinger Publishing, 2006 edition).

Sée, H., and A. Cormack, 'Commercial Relations between France and Scotland in 1707', *Scottish Historical Review*, 23 (1926), pp. 275–9.

Smith, A., *An Inquiry into the Nature and Causes of the Wealth of Nations*, 8 vols (Edinburgh: A&C Black, 1863).

Smith, A., *The Reign of James VI and I* (London: St Martin's Press, 1973).

—, *Creating a World Economy: Merchant Capital, Colonialism and World Trade, 1400–1825* (Boulder, CO: Westview Press, 1991).

Smith, H., *Shetland Life and Trade, 1550–1914* (Edinburgh: John Donald, 1984).

Smout, T. C., *Scottish Trade on the Eve of Union, 1660–1707* (London: Oliver & Boyd, 1963).

—, 'The Glasgow Merchant Community in the Seventeenth Century', *Scottish Historical Review*, 47:143 (1968), pp. 53–71.

—, 'The Road to Union', in G. Holmes (ed.), *Britain After the Glorious Revolution* (London: Macmillan, 1969), pp. 176–96.

Steele, I., 'Introduction', to O. Janzen (ed.), *Merchant Organization and Maritime Trade in the North Atlantic, 1660–1815* (St Johns, Newfoundland: International Maritime Economic History Association, 1998), pp. 1–13.

Subrahmanyam, S. (ed.), *Merchant Networks in the Early Modern World* (Aldershot: Variorum, 1996).

Takeda, J., *Between Crown and Commerce: Marseille and the early modern Mediterranean* (Baltimore, MD: Johns Hopkins University Press, 2011).

Talbott, S., 'Jacobites, Anti-Jacobites and the Ambivalent: Scottish Identities in France, 1680–1720', in B. Sellin, P. Carboni and A. Thiec (eds), *Écosse: l'identité nationale en question* (Nantes: University of Nantes, 2009), pp. 73–88.

—, '"My Heart is a Scotch Heart": Scottish Calvinist Exiles in France in their Continental Context, 1605–1638', in D. Worthington (ed.), *British and Irish Emigrants and Exiles in Europe, 1603–1688* (Leiden: Brill, 2010), pp. 197–214.

—, 'An Alliance Ended? Franco-Scottish Commercial Relations, 1560–1713' (PhD thesis, University of St Andrews, 2010).

—, 'Communities on the Continent: Franco-Scottish network building in a comparative European context, 1560–1685', in M. Landi (ed.), *L'Écosse et ses doubles: ancien monde, nouveau monde* (Paris: L'Harmattan, 2010), pp. 21–41.

—, 'Beyond "The Antiseptic Realm of Theoretical Economic Models": New Perspectives on Franco-Scottish Commerce and the Auld Alliance in the Long Seventeenth Century', *Journal of Scottish Historical Studies*, 31:2 (2011), pp. 149–68.

—, 'British Commercial Interests on the French Atlantic Coast, c. 1560–1713', *Historical Research*, 85:229 (2012), pp. 395–409.

—, '"If it Please God, I Come Home": Scottish Return Migration from France in the Long Seventeenth Century', in M. Varricchio (ed.), *Back to Caledonia: Scottish Return Migration from the Seventeenth Century to the Present* (Edinburgh: John Donald, 2012), pp. 54–72.

—, 'The Auld Alliance: "Still in Vigour"?', *History Scotland* (January/February 2012), pp. 6–7.

—, 'Commerce and the Jacobite Court: Scottish Migrants in France, 1688–1718', in K. German, L. Graham and A. Macinnes (eds), *Living with Jacobitism* (London: Pickering & Chatto, forthcoming 2014).

—, 'The Letter-Book of John Clerk, 1644–45', *Scottish History Society Miscellany*, 15 (forthcomng, 2014).

Trevor-Roper, H., 'The General Crisis of the Seventeenth Century', *Past and Present*, 16 (1959), pp. 31–64.

—, *The Crisis of the Seventeenth Century* (Indianapolis: Liberty Fund, 2001).

Truxes, T. M., 'New York City's Irish Merchants and Trade with the Enemy during the Seven Years' War', in D. Dickson and C. Ó Gráda (eds), *Reconfiguring Ireland, Essays in Honour of L. M. Cullen* (Dublin: Four Courts Press, 2003), pp. 147–64.

Tucker, M., *Maîtres et étudiants ecossais à la Faculté de Droit de l'Université de Bourges 1480–1703* (Paris: Champion, 2001).

—, 'Scottish Students and Masters at the Faculty of Law of the University of Bourges in the Sixteenth and Seventeenth Centuries', in T. van Heijnsbergen and N. Royan (eds), *Literature, Letters and the Canonical in Early Modern Scotland* (East Linton: Tuckwell Press, 2002), pp. 111–20.

Usher, A., 'Colbert and Governmental Control of Industry in Seventeenth-Century France', *Review of Economics and Statistics*, 16:11 (1934), pp. 237–40.

Villar Garcia, M., 'Irish Migration and Exiles in Spain: Refugees, Soldiers, Traders and States-men', in T. O'Connor and M. Lyons (eds), *Irish Communities in Early Modern Europe* (Dublin: Four Courts Press, 2006), pp. 172–99.

Voltaire, *The Age of Louis XIV*, trans. M. Pollock (London: J. M. Dent, 1958).

Whatley, C., *The Scottish Salt Industry, 1570–1850* (Aberdeen: Aberdeen University Press, 1987).

—, *The Scots and the Union* (Edinburgh: Edinburgh University Press, 2006).

Whyte, I., *Scotland before the Industrial Revolution: An Economic and Social History* (London: Longman, 1995).

—, *Scotland's Society and Economy in Transition, c. 1500–c. 1760* (London: Palgrave Macmil-lan, 1997).

Wilson, P., 'Was the Thirty Years' War a "Total War"?', in E. Charters, E. Rosenhaft and H. Smith (eds), *Civilians and War in Europe, 1618–1815* (Liverpool: Liverpool University Press, 2012), pp. 21–35.

Woodward, D., 'Anglo-Scottish Trade and English Commercial Policy during the 1660s', *Scottish Historical Review*, 56:162 (1977), pp. 153–74.

Worthington, D., *Scots in Habsburg Service, 1618–1648* (Leiden: Brill, 2004).

Wrightson, K., *Earthly Necessities: Economic Lives in Early Modern Britain* (London: Yale University Press, 2000).

Zahedieh, N., 'Credit, Risk and Reputation in Late Seventeenth-Century Colonial Trade', in O. Janzen (ed.), *Merchant Organization and Maritime Trade in the North Atlantic, 1660–1815* (St Johns, Newfoundland: International Maritime Economic History Asso-ciation, 1998), pp. 53–74.

Zickermann, K., *Across the German Sea: Early Modern Scottish Connections with the Wider Elbe-Weser Region* (Leiden: Brill, 2013).

INDEX

For Product Safety Concerns and Information please contact our EU
representative GPSR@taylorandfrancis.com
Taylor & Francis Verlag GmbH, Kaufingerstraße 24, 80331 München, Germany

www.ingramcontent.com/pod-product-compliance
Ingram Content Group UK Ltd.
Pitfield, Milton Keynes, MK11 3LW, UK
UKHW021615240425
457818UK00018B/576